For Mom and Dad

**Close to Home** is distributed internationally by Universal Press Syndicate.

***When Bad Things Happen to Stupid People*** © 2005 by John McPherson. All rights reserved. Printed in the United States of America. No part of this book may be used or reproduced in any manner whatsoever without written permission except in the case of reprints in the context of reviews. For information, write Andrews McMeel Publishing, an Andrews McMeel Universal company, 4520 Main Street, Kansas City, Missouri 64111.

05 06 07 08 09  BBG  10 9 8 7 6 5 4 3 2 1

ISBN-13: 978-0-7407-5365-7
ISBN-10: 0-7407-5365-7

Library of Congress Catalog Control Number: 2005929086

**Close to Home** may be viewed on the Internet at www.uComics.com.

Visit the **Close to Home** Web store at www.closetohome.com.

www.andrewsmcmeel.com

──── **ATTENTION: SCHOOLS AND BUSINESSES** ────

Andrews McMeel books are available at quantity discounts with bulk purchase for educational, business, or sales promotional use. For information, write to: Special Sales Department, Andrews McMeel Publishing, 4520 Main Street, Kansas City, Missouri 64111.

# When Bad Things Happen to Stupid People

A Close to Home Collection by John McPherson

**Andrews McMeel
Publishing**

Kansas City

**Other *Close to Home* Books
By John McPherson**

*Close to Home*
*One Step Closer to Home*
*Dangerously Close to Home*
*Home: The Final Frontier*
*The Honeymoon Is Over*
*The Silence of the Lamberts*
*Striking Close to Home*
*The Close to Home Survival Guide*
*Close to Home Uncut*
*The Scourge of the Vinyl Car Seats*
*Close to Home Exposed*
*Ferociously Close to Home*

**Treasury Collections**
*Close to Home Revisited*
*Close to Home Unplugged*

**Also from John McPherson**
*High School Isn't Pretty*
*Close to Home: A Book of Postcards*
*The Barber of Bingo*
*The Get Well Book*
*Give Mommy the Superglue and Other Tips on Surviving Parenthood*
*Get Well, Doctor's Orders! A Close to Home Get Well Box*

# Contents

# Introduction

Most cartoonists I have met knew that they wanted to be cartoonists when they were seven or eight years old. (Some even knew they would become cartoonists when they were still in the womb.) This was not the case for me. I drew a lot as a kid, but not any more than any other kid I knew.

The idea of being a cartoonist didn't hit me until I was about twenty-one, sitting in dull engineering classes. For some reason, those were fertile moments for my mind to wander, and I started jotting down what I thought were funny cartoon ideas. I had no art background whatsoever, so I thought about sending my ideas to some cartoonist to see if he or she would draw them up. Of course, I didn't know any cartoonists, so the ideas sat in my notebooks for a few years, until one day, I decided to just draw one up. It took me about seven hours to put in on paper, but when I was done, it looked vaguely like a cave drawing. Nonetheless, I was hooked and kept drawing more and more cartoons.

After several months, with about twenty cartoons under my belt, I sent them to a small semi-monthly paper and, unbelievably, the editor liked them and agreed to run one per issue. I was paid a whopping $5 a cartoon.

All this time I worked as an engineer by day and drew cartoons at night. Sometimes, when things were slow at my job or my boss was away, I drew cartoons by day.

I wanted to try to eclipse my hefty $10 a month income from my panel (which at that time was called *Incognito*). So I started submitting cartoons to magazines. I would put together eight or ten cartoons and send them off in a self-addressed stamped envelope to various magazines. I received various rejection letters. I sent out over 160 batches that next year, and got 160 rejections. But, honestly, I was having so much fun drawing the cartoons that getting them published would have just been icing on the cake.

So in June 1986 I was pretty psyched when *Campus Life* magazine bought two of my cartoons for $50 a piece. I splurged and used the money to get a muffler for my car. From that point on, I found it much easier to break into other magazines and eventually got my way into the *Saturday Evening Post*. I moonlighted my way into about forty magazines by 1989 and was starting to make as much from cartooning as I was from engineering.

In 1990, Zondervan Publishing House approached me about publishing two collections of my cartoons. So with some book contracts under my belt and steady freelance work, I walked in and told my boss that I was quitting to become a cartoonist. Now *that* was a fun day. That night, I remember lying wide awake wondering what I had just done, but I got over those early jitters and never looked back.

I worked feverishly freelancing and then in 1992 got offers from both Creators Syndicate and Universal Press Syndicate to syndicate a panel. I went with UPS, and *Close to Home* began in about fifty-five papers on November 29, 1992.

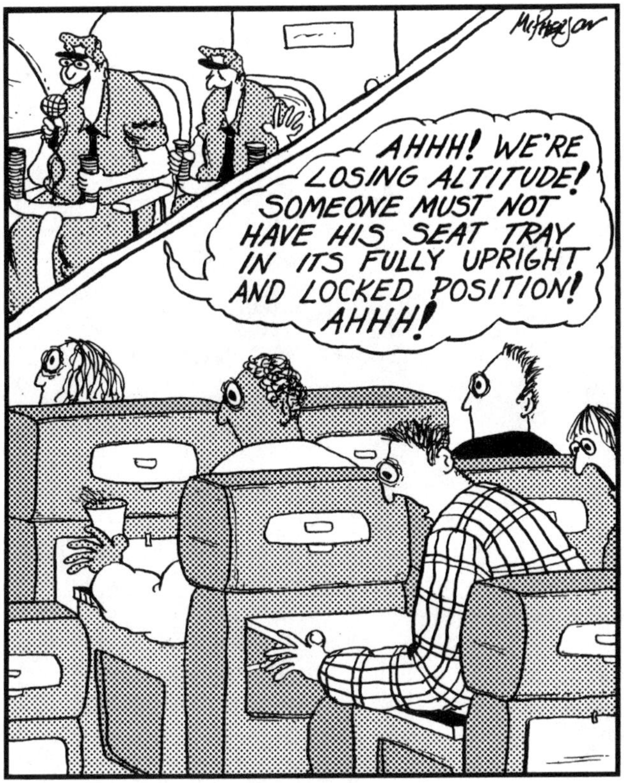
McPHERSON
AHHH! WE'RE LOSING ALTITUDE! SOMEONE MUST NOT HAVE HIS SEAT TRAY IN ITS FULLY UPRIGHT AND LOCKED POSITION! AHHH!

**Pilot humor**

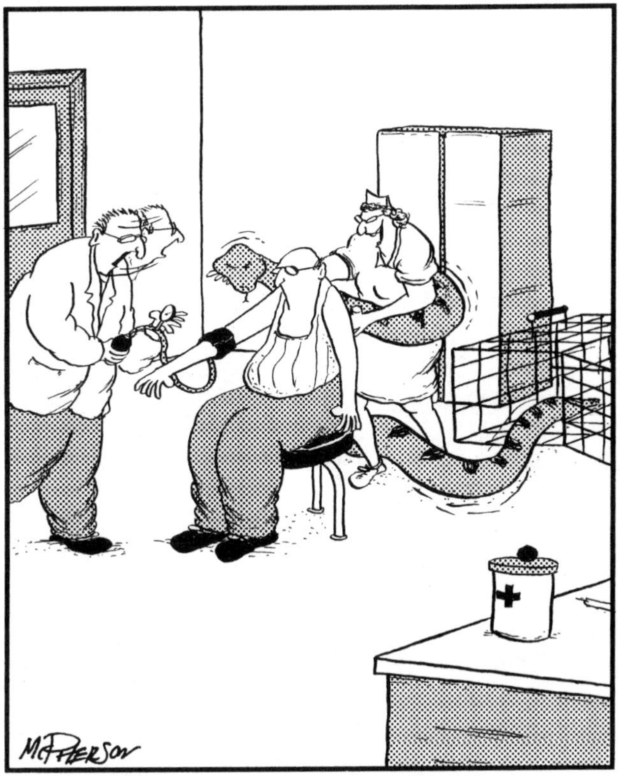
McPHERSON

**"Okay, last time your blood pressure was a bit on the high side. Let's see how it is. . . . *Knock it off*, Mrs. Halstead!"**

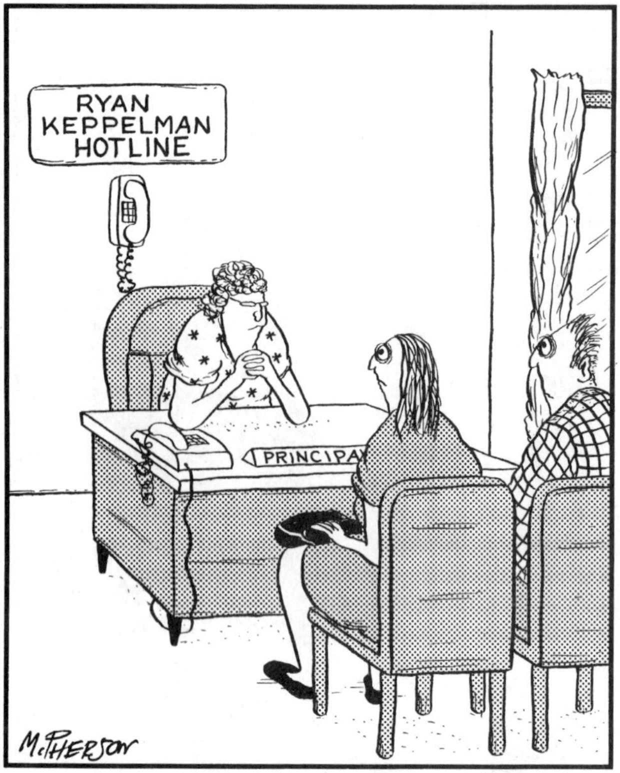
RYAN
KEPPELMAN
HOTLINE
PRINCIPA
McPHERSON

It was not until they entered the principal's office that the Keppelmans realized the severity of Ryan's discipline problem.

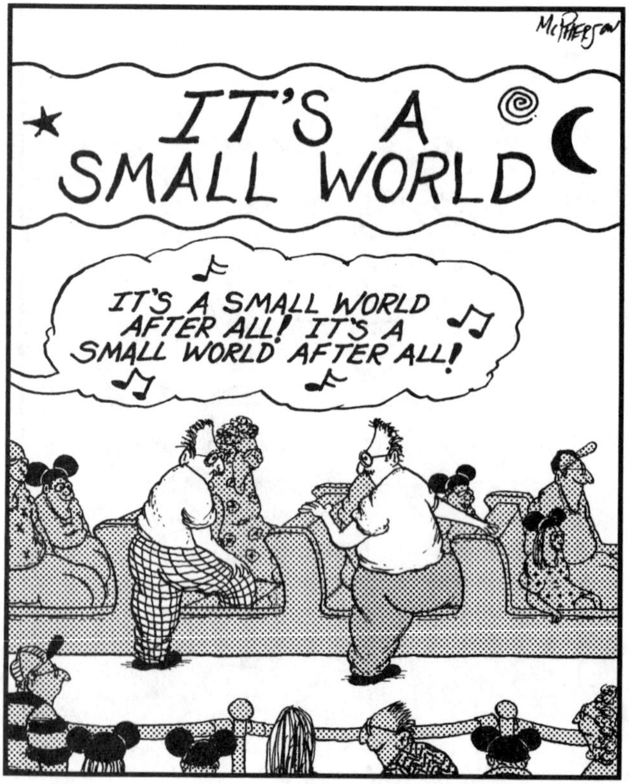
McPHERSON
IT'S A
SMALL WORLD
IT'S A SMALL WORLD
AFTER ALL! IT'S A
SMALL WORLD AFTER ALL!

Separated at birth, the Fenlo twins are reunited in the most ironic of settings.

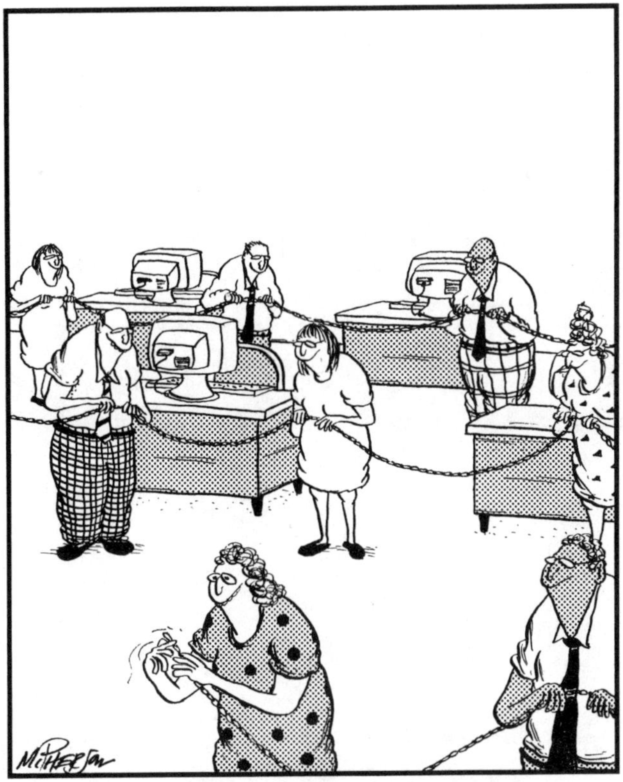

With the computer network down throughout the office, employees worked diligently to break the Guinness record for longest chain of paper clips.

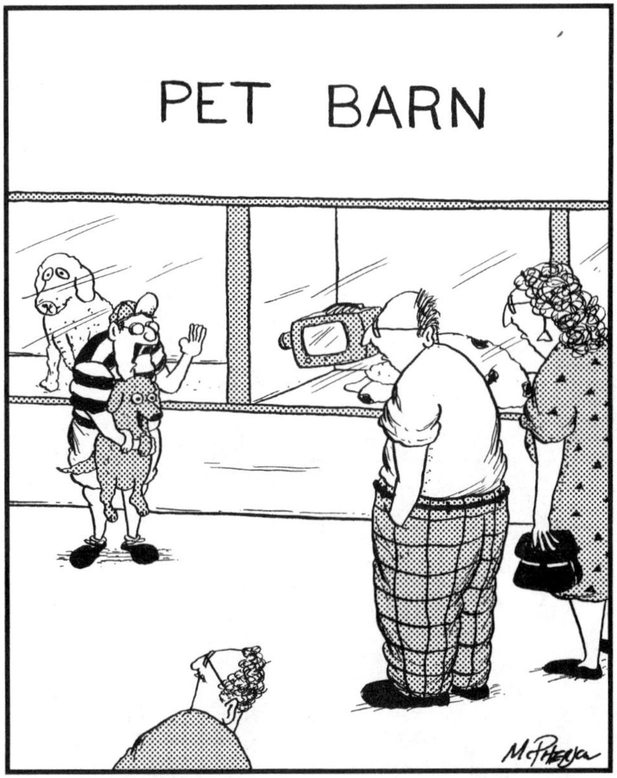
PET BARN

"I, Jimmy Delmonte, do solemnly swear that the feeding, walking, and overall care of Sparkles shall be my responsibility and mine alone. . . ."

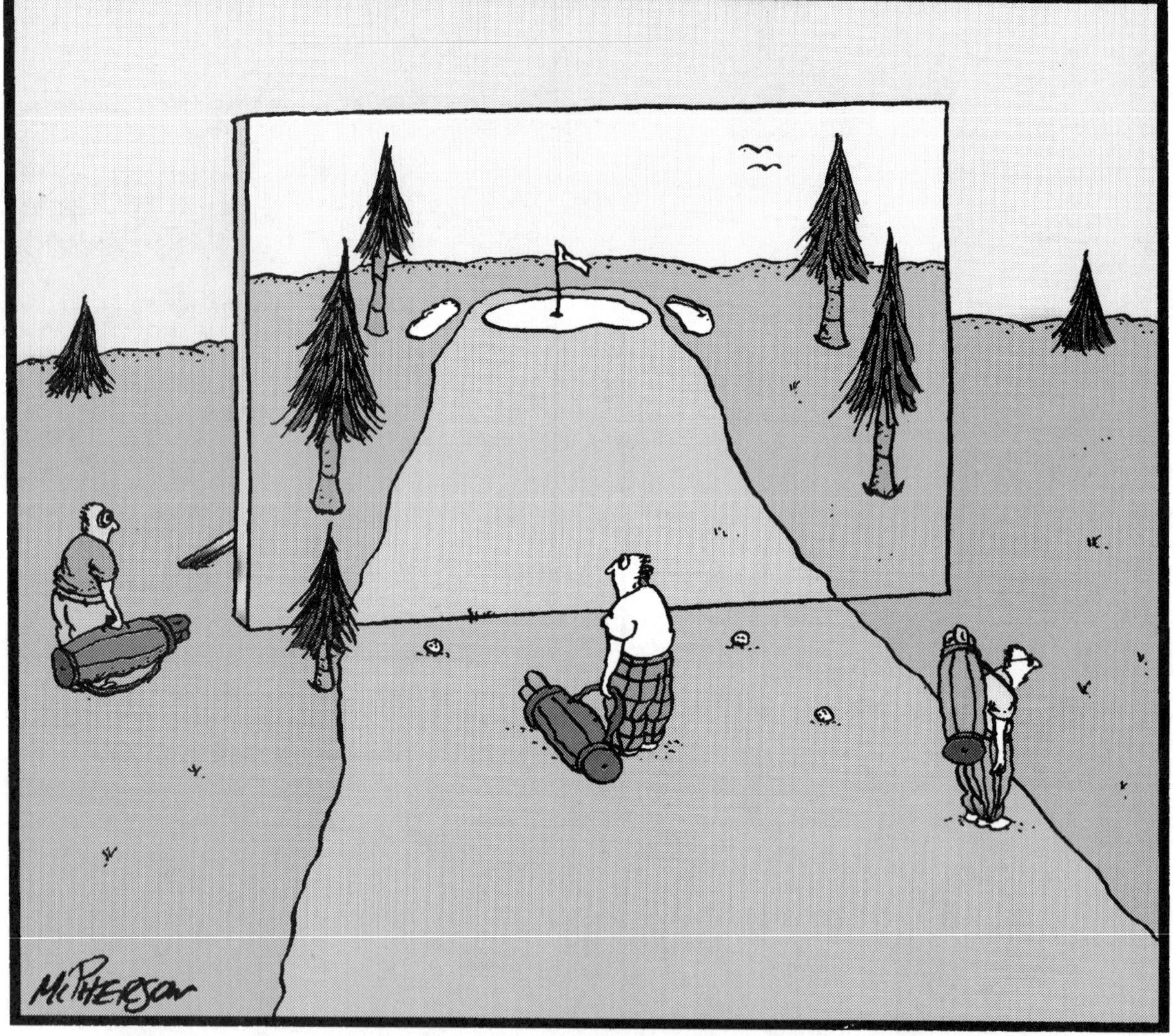

"Well, we can forget about getting our $50 greens fees back. Those two dirtbags in the pro shop just climbed into a Camaro and are flooring it out of here."

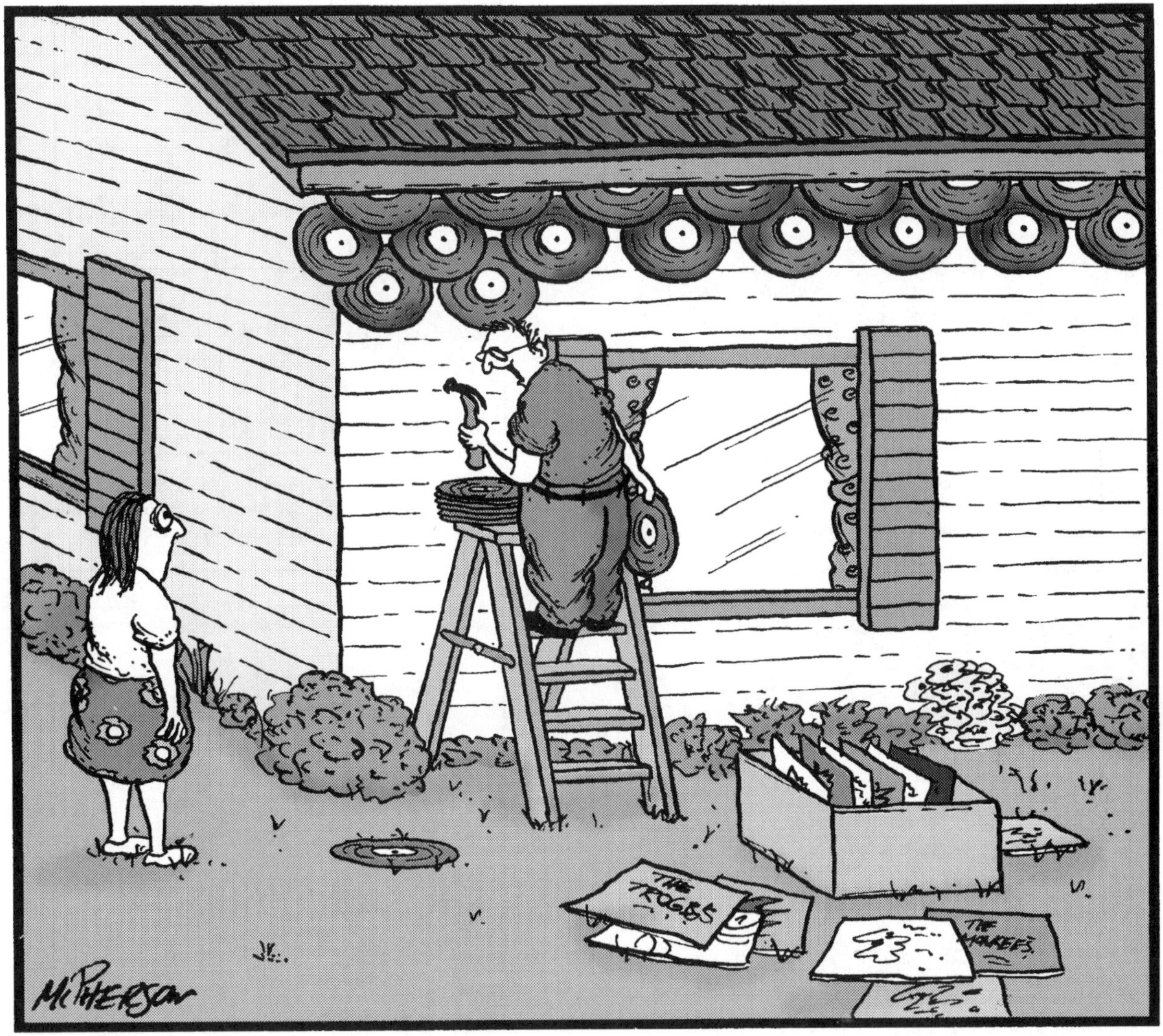
THE TROGGS
THE MONKEES
McPHERSON

**"Okay, two questions: 1. When was the last time we listened to anything other than a CD? And 2. Do we have $4,500 for vinyl siding?"**

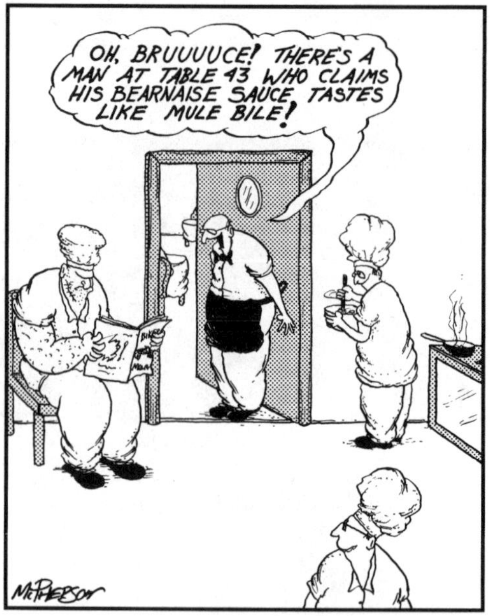
OH, BRUUUUCE! THERE'S A MAN AT TABLE 43 WHO CLAIMS HIS BEARNAISE SAUCE TASTES LIKE MULE BILE!
McPHERSON

To spare their chefs from having to deal with irate diners, many restaurants employ former pro wrestlers as stand-ins.

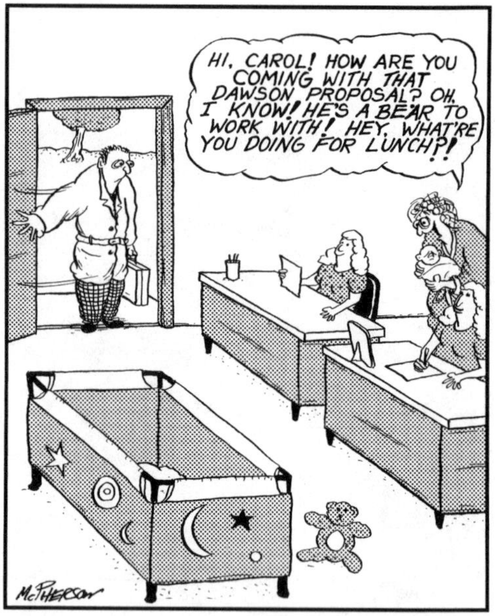
HI, CAROL! HOW ARE YOU COMING WITH THAT DAWSON PROPOSAL? OH, I KNOW! HE'S A BEAR TO WORK WITH! HEY, WHAT'RE YOU DOING FOR LUNCH?!
McPHERSON

After Denise created the second wax figure of one of her coworkers, Paul began to see the toll that her days home alone with the baby were taking on her.

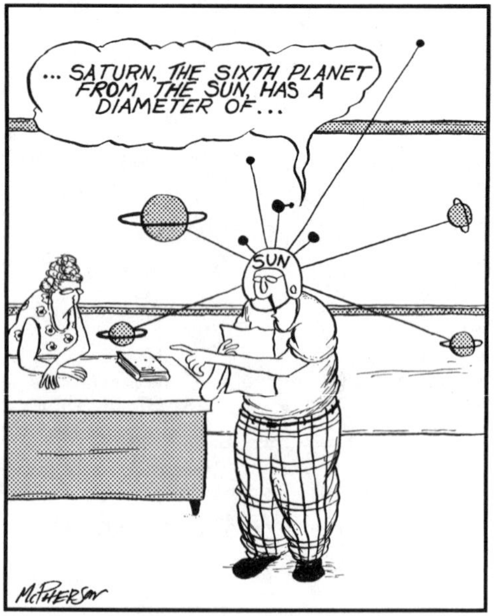
... SATURN, THE SIXTH PLANET FROM THE SUN, HAS A DIAMETER OF...
SUN
McPHERSON

Wes Lunker uses a visual aid to enhance his report on the solar system.

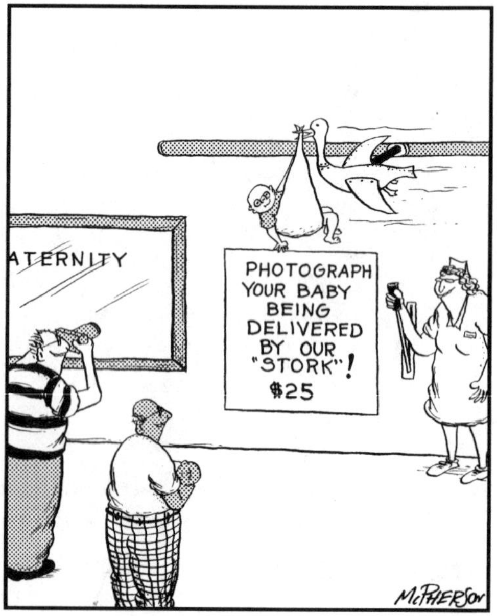
ATERNITY
PHOTOGRAPH YOUR BABY BEING DELIVERED BY OUR "STORK"! $25
McPHERSON

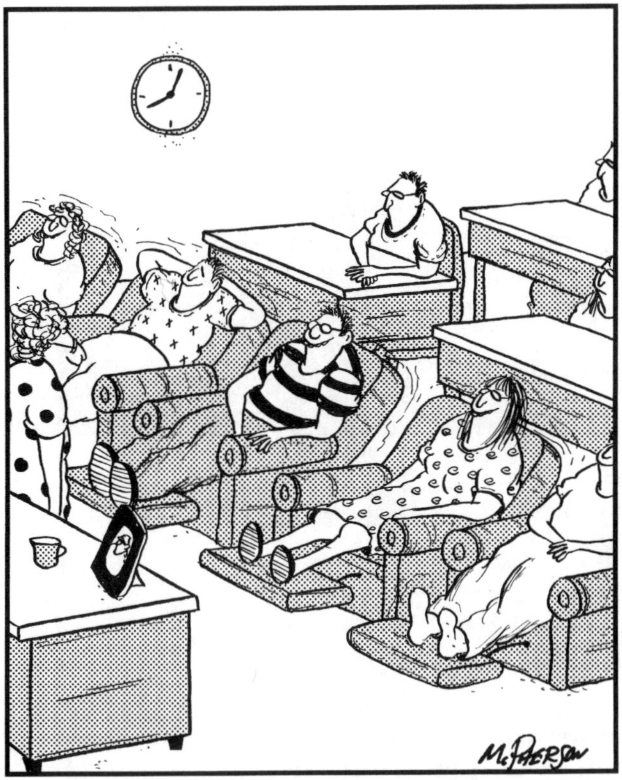
McPHERSON

To encourage students to sit in the front row, Varsteen High equipped all of its classrooms with electronic massage recliners.

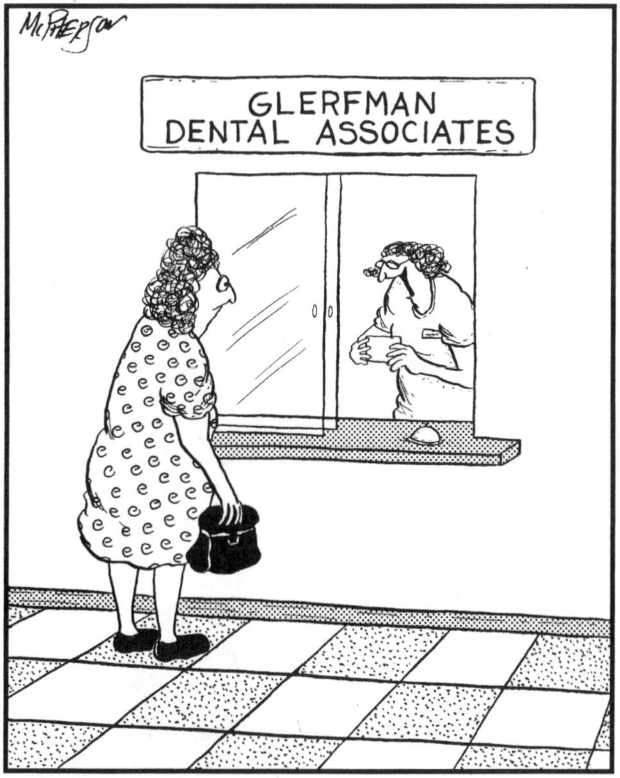
McPHERSON
GLERFMAN
DENTAL ASSOCIATES

"Can I interest you in one of our new dental credit cards? Three percent of all your purchases can be applied toward the cost of a root canal, extraction, or gum surgery."

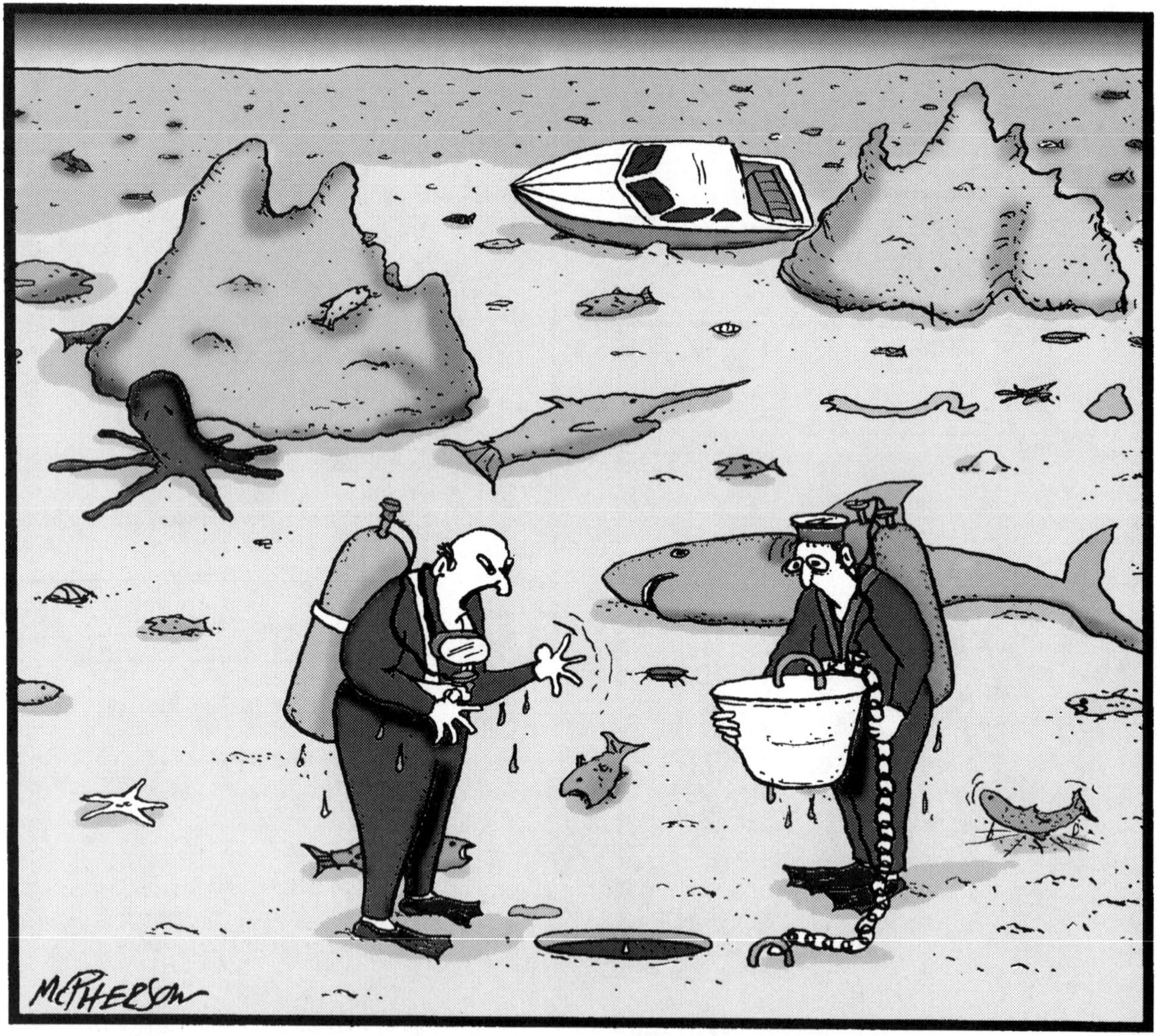
McPHERSON

"Are you *satisfied*?! Yes, it was what you thought it was!"

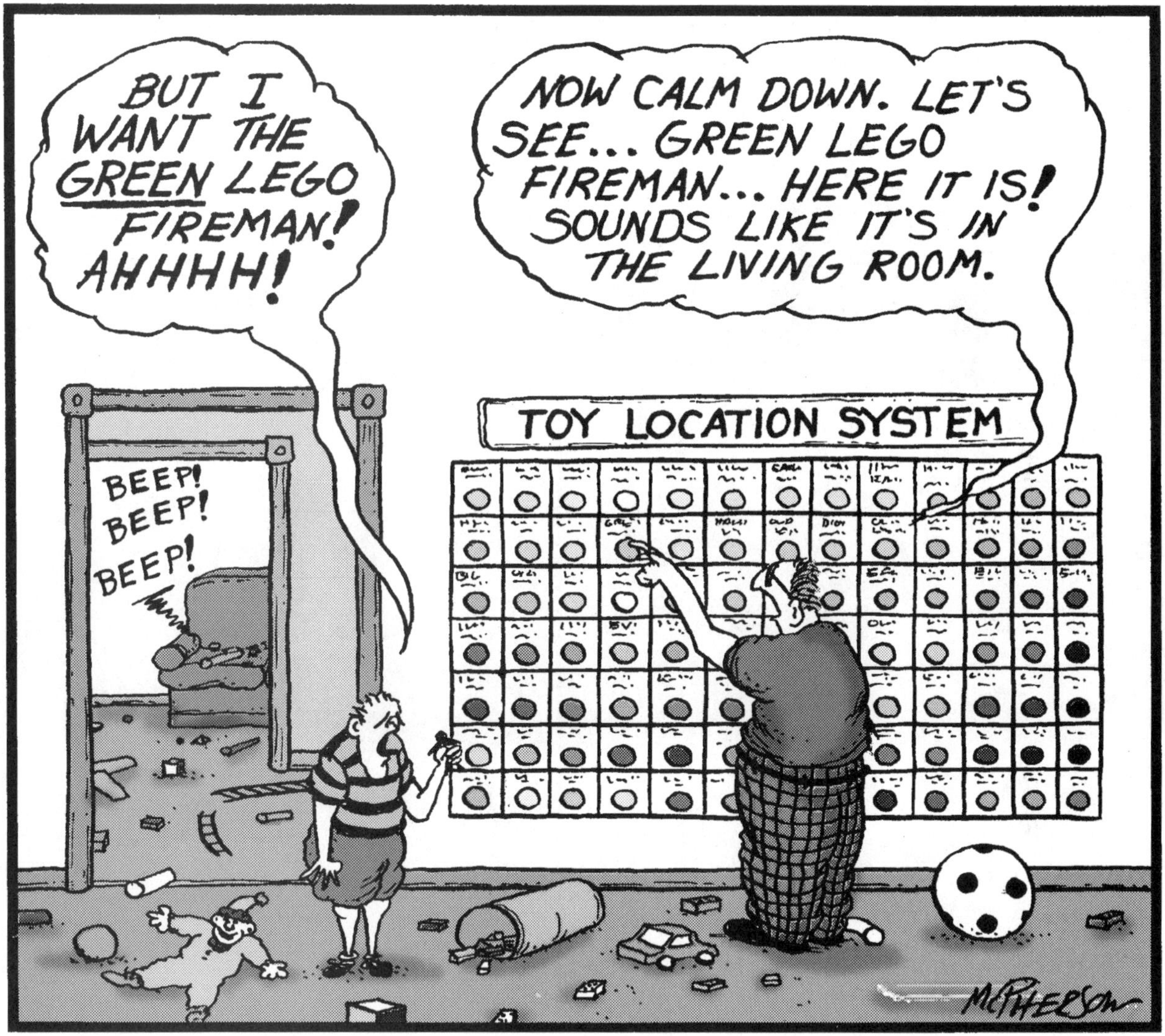
BUT I WANT THE GREEN LEGO FIREMAN! AHHHH!
NOW CALM DOWN. LET'S SEE... GREEN LEGO FIREMAN... HERE IT IS! SOUNDS LIKE IT'S IN THE LIVING ROOM.
TOY LOCATION SYSTEM
BEEP! BEEP! BEEP!
MCPHERSON

"There now. Do you see what happens
when we don't learn to share?"

With his long-distance footsie device firmly
in place, Dan proceeded to liven up
an otherwise dull meeting.

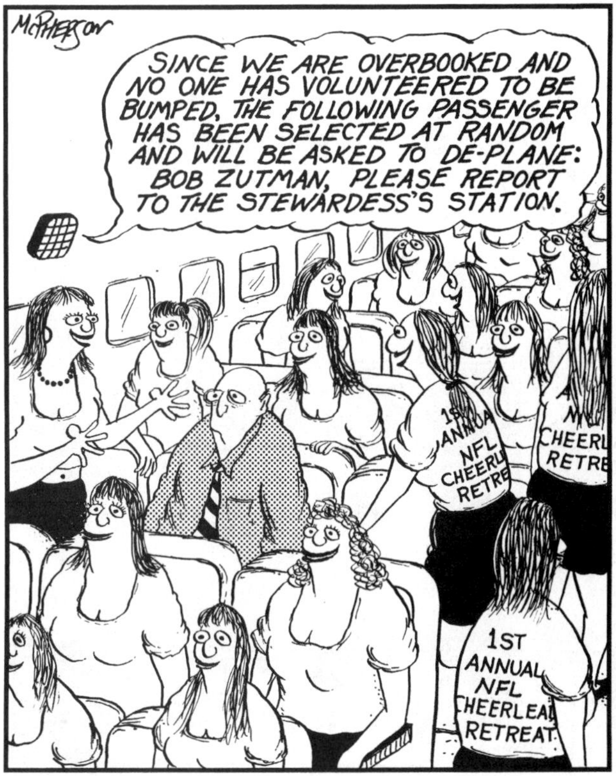
SINCE WE ARE OVERBOOKED AND NO ONE HAS VOLUNTEERED TO BE BUMPED, THE FOLLOWING PASSENGER HAS BEEN SELECTED AT RANDOM AND WILL BE ASKED TO DE-PLANE: BOB ZUTMAN, PLEASE REPORT TO THE STEWARDESS'S STATION.

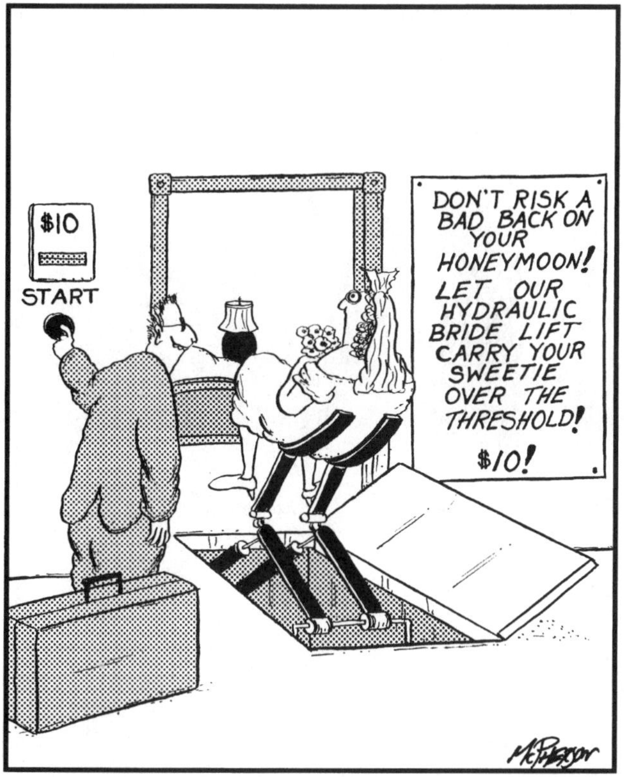
$10
START
DON'T RISK A BAD BACK ON YOUR HONEYMOON! LET OUR HYDRAULIC BRIDE LIFT CARRY YOUR SWEETIE OVER THE THRESHOLD! $10!

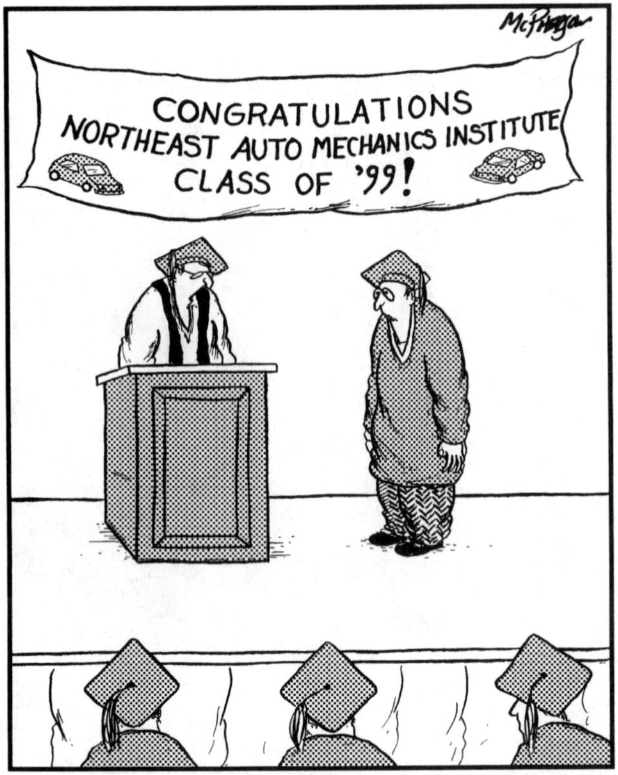
McPherson
CONGRATULATIONS
NORTHEAST AUTO MECHANICS INSTITUTE
CLASS OF '99!

**"Your diploma's not going to be ready for another two weeks, plus it turns out your tuition is going to be about $1,200 more than we originally estimated."**

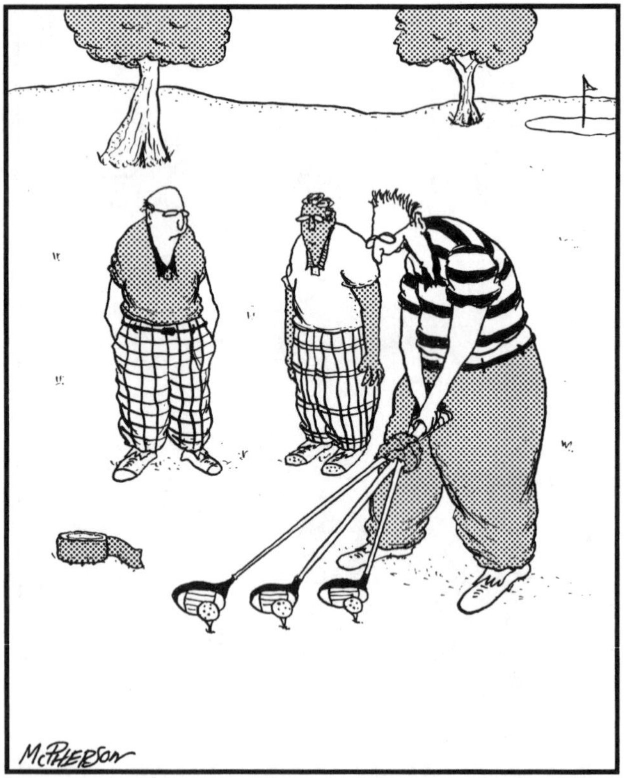
McPherson

**"Okay, boys! Let's find out once and for all which brand of golf ball really does go the farthest!"**

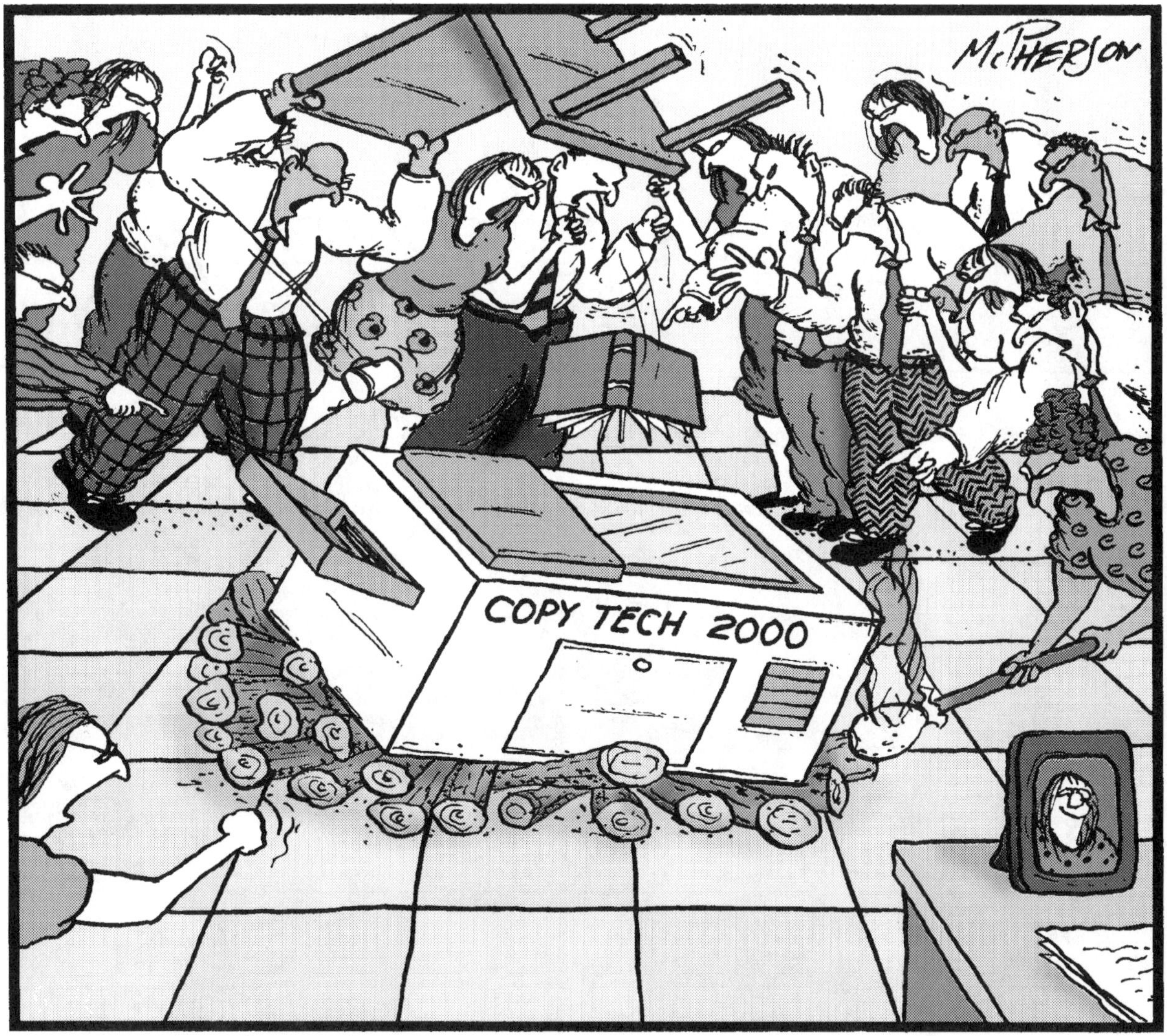
McPHERSON
COPY TECH 2000

**Mob rule sweeps through the office after the copier breaks down for the eleventh time in three hours.**

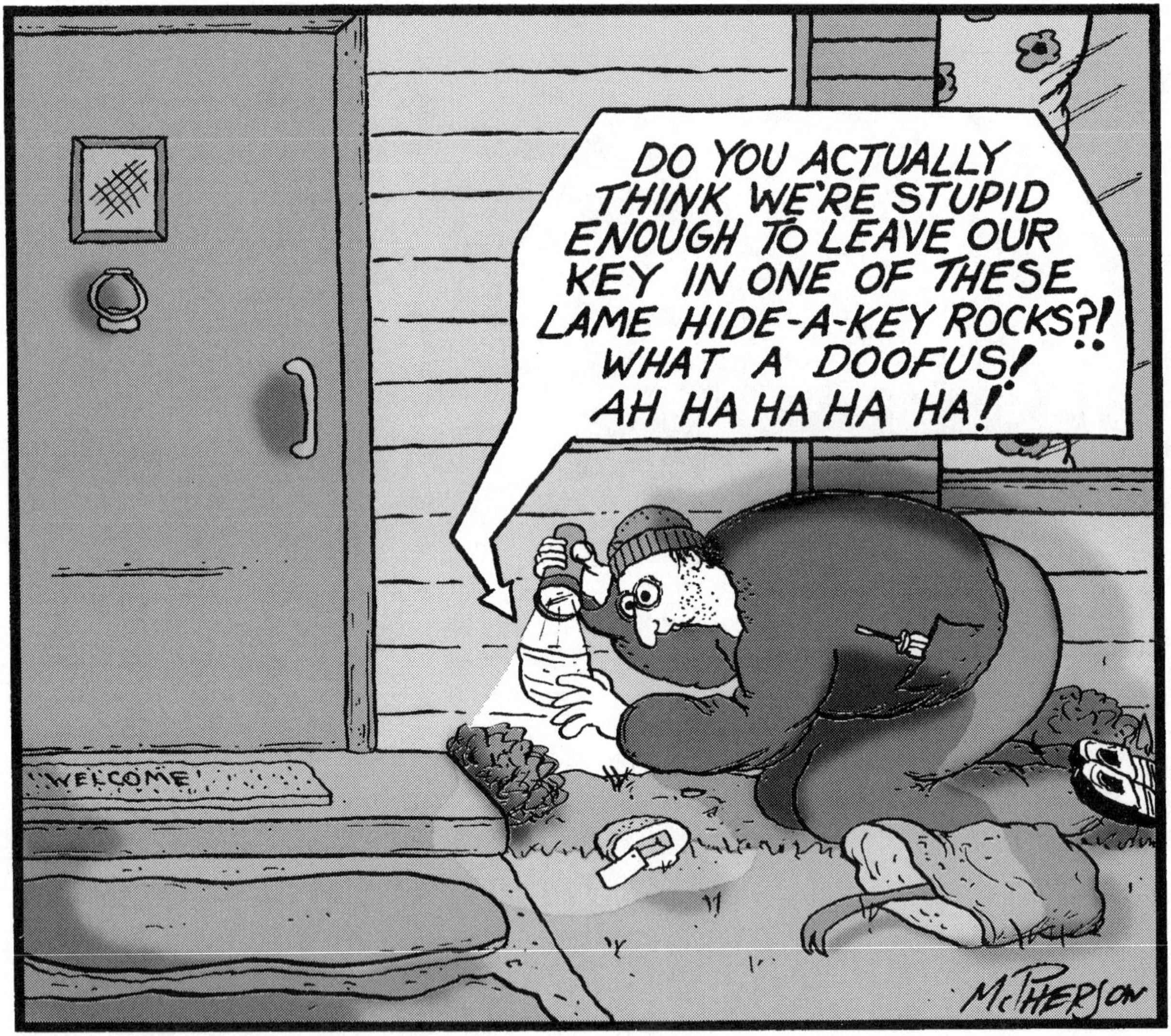
DO YOU ACTUALLY THINK WE'RE STUPID ENOUGH TO LEAVE OUR KEY IN ONE OF THESE LAME HIDE-A-KEY ROCKS?! WHAT A DOOFUS! AH HA HA HA HA!
WELCOME
McPHERSON

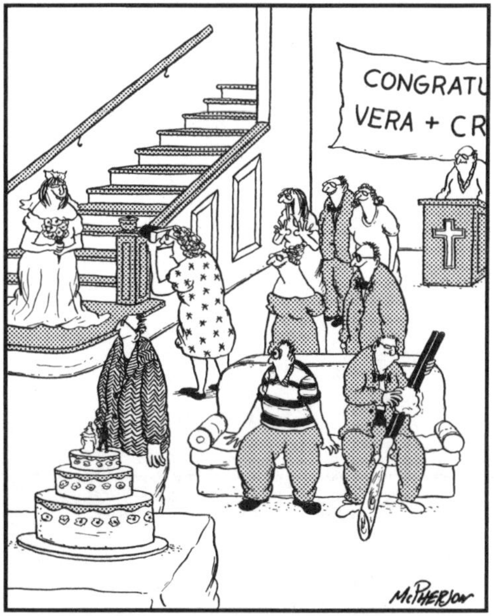
CONGRATU
VERA + CR

As his blind date reached the bottom of the stairs, Craig's feelings of apprehension quickly turned to sheer panic.

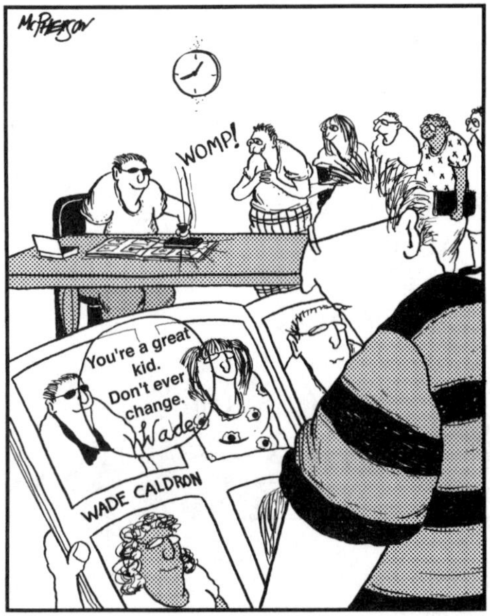
WOMP!
You're a great kid. Don't ever change. Wade
WADE CALDRON

To save time when signing yearbooks, the more popular students at Wagmont High relied on rubber stamps.

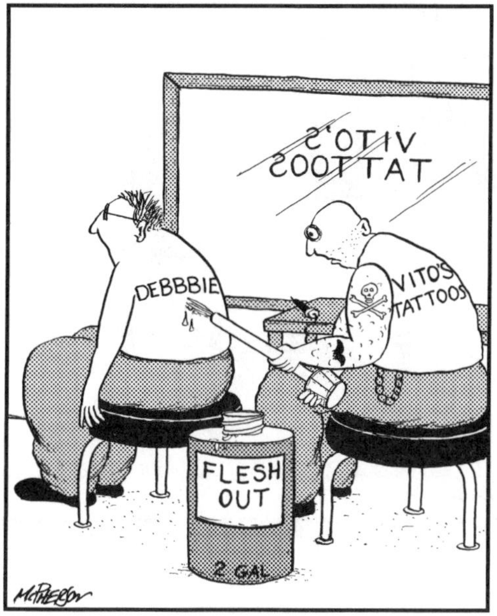
VITO'S TATTOOS
DEBBBIE
VITO'S TATTOOS
FLESH OUT
2 GAL

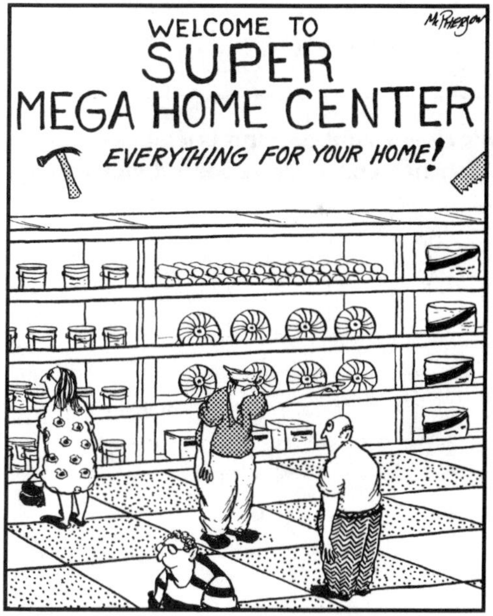
WELCOME TO
SUPER
MEGA HOME CENTER
EVERYTHING FOR YOUR HOME!

"Nails? Hmmm . . . let me think. . . . Okay, you need to catch the green tram to sector I-48. Pick up the brown tram there at 1:15 and take it to the end of the line. Head west . . ."

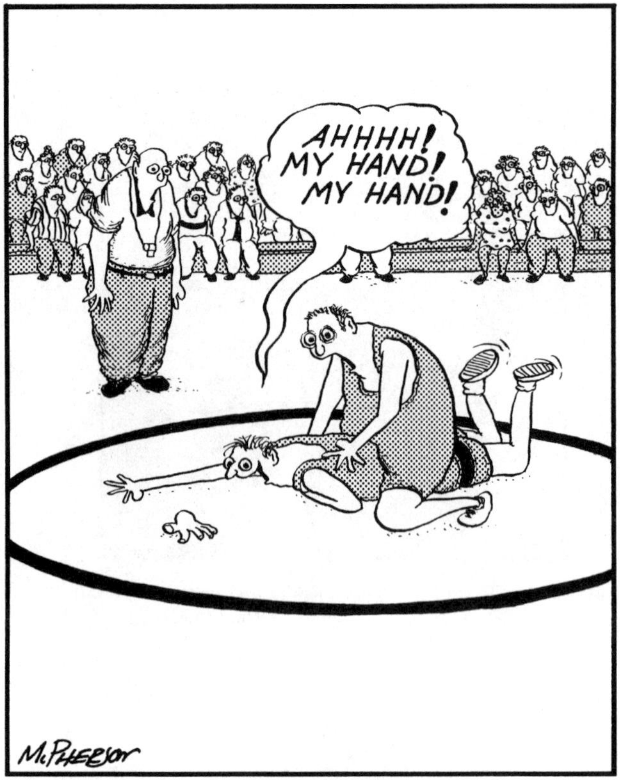
AHHHH!
MY HAND!
MY HAND!
McPHERSON

**Brian's clever rubber-hand trick chalks up yet another come-from-behind victory.**

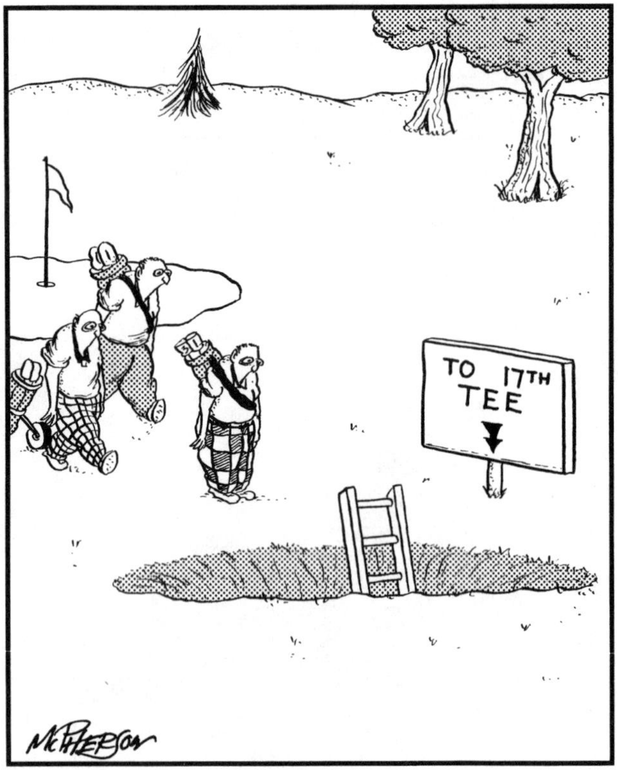
TO 17TH TEE
McPHERSON

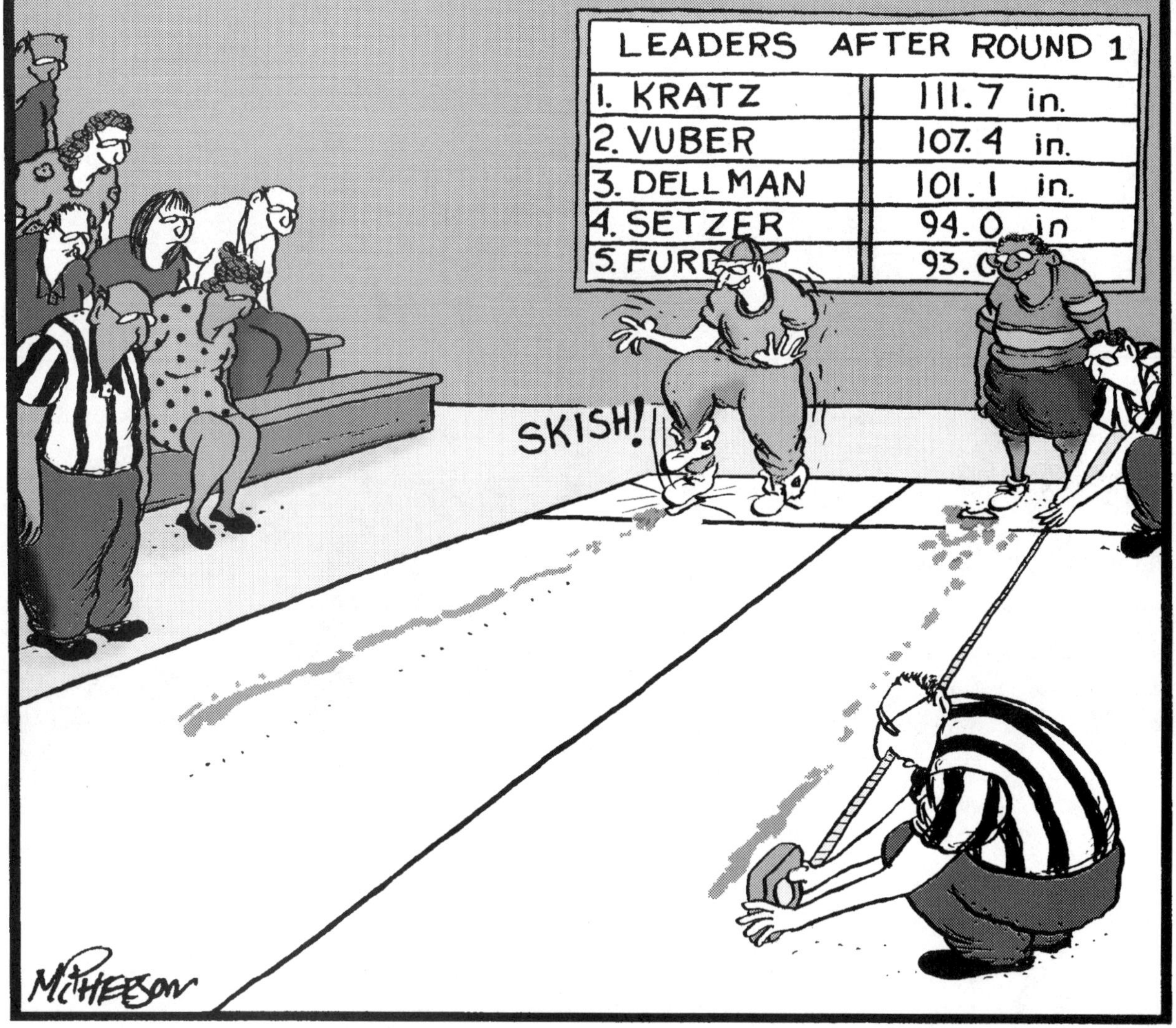
LEADERS AFTER ROUND 1
1. KRATZ 111.7 in.
2. VUBER 107.4 in.
3. DELLMAN 101.1 in.
4. SETZER 94.0 in
SKISH!
MCPHERSON

**At the National Ketchup Packet Stomping Championships, Junior High Division**

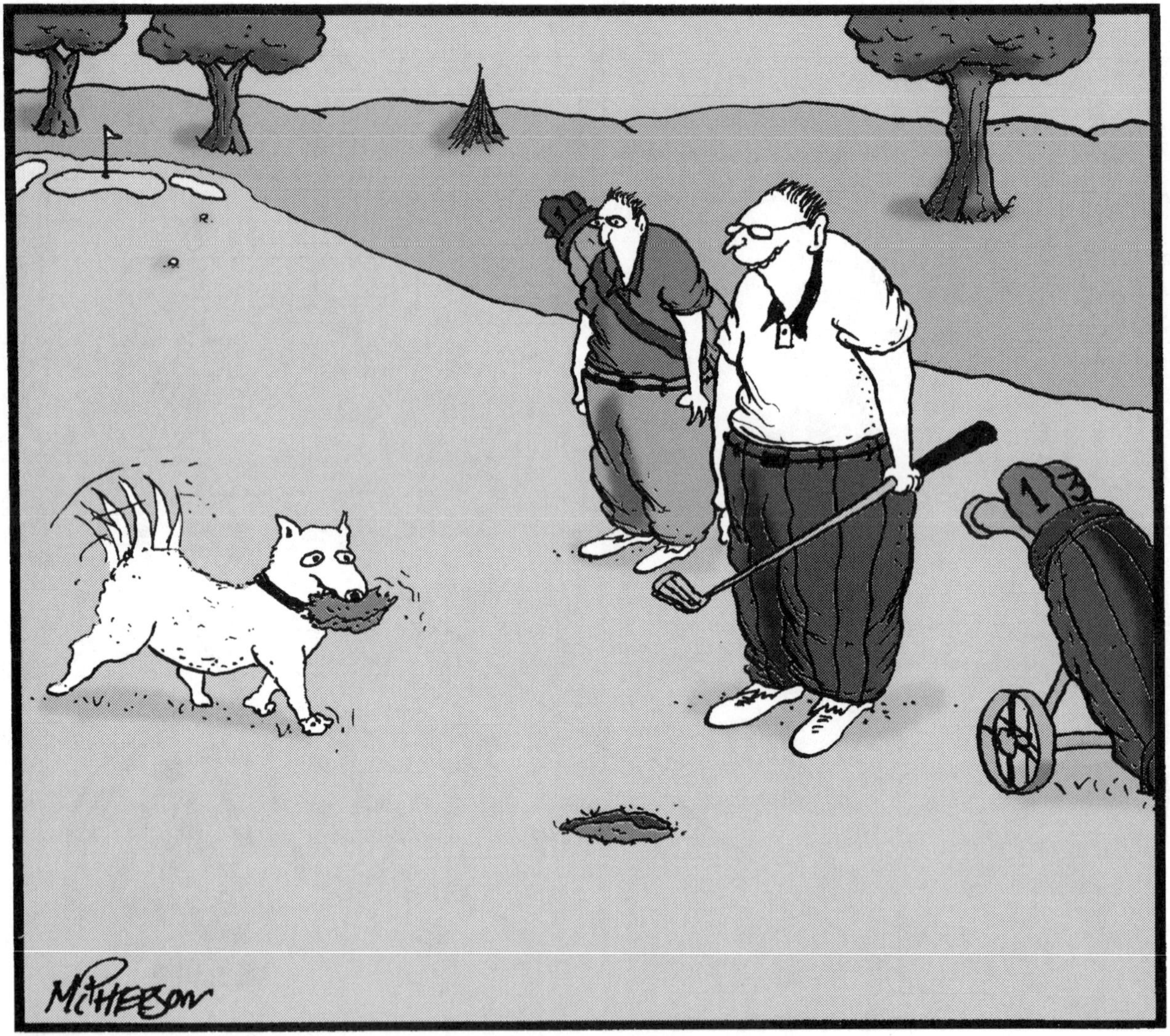

**Darren never played a round without the aid of his trusty Divot Terrier.**

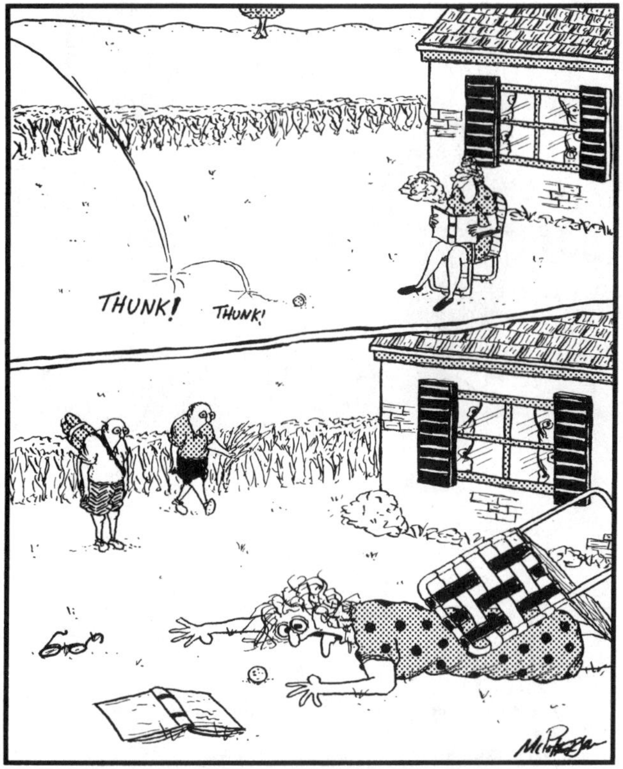
THUNK!
THUNK!

Throughout the seventeen years that she had lived next to the golf course, Linda simply couldn't resist pulling this stunt whenever the opportunity arose.

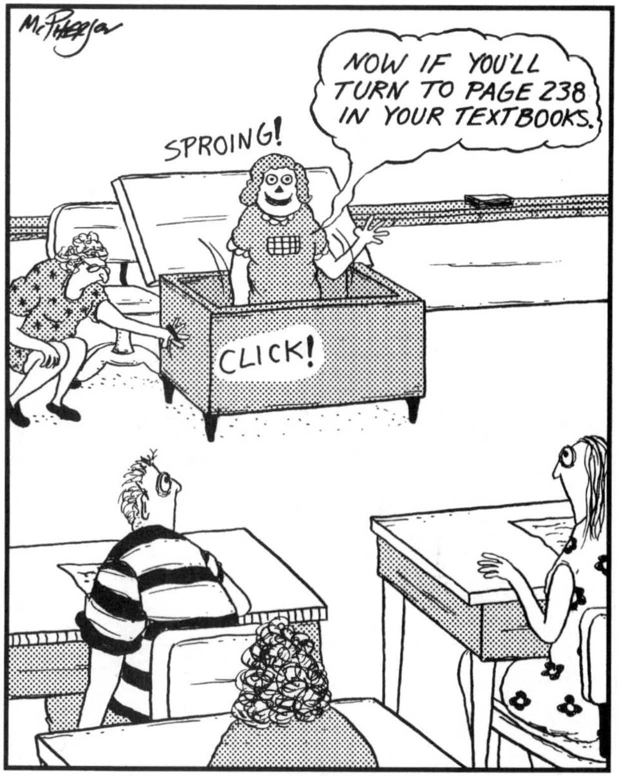
SPROING!
NOW IF YOU'LL TURN TO PAGE 238 IN YOUR TEXTBOOKS.
CLICK!

Stricken by a sudden case of laryngitis, Mrs. Gurtley switches to autoteacher.

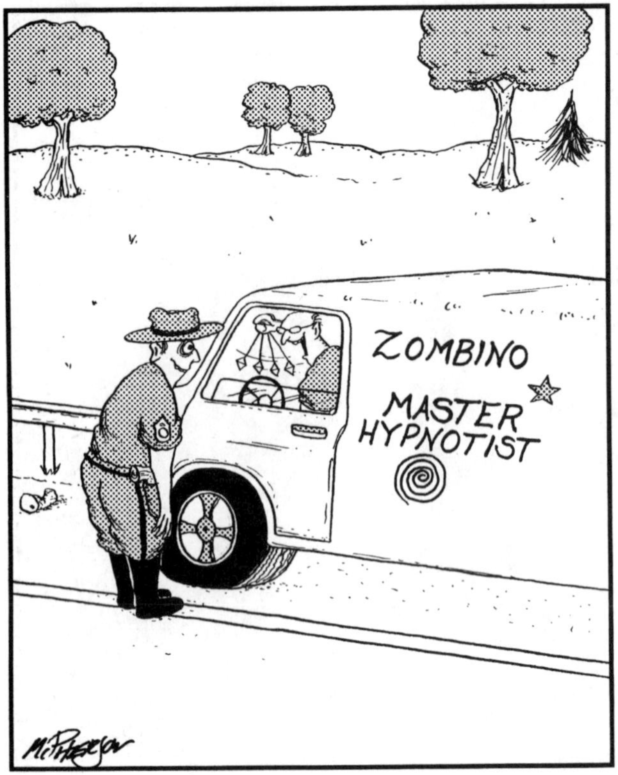
ZOMBINO
MASTER HYPNOTIST

"... and when I snap my fingers, you will completely forget that I was doing 87 in a 45 mph zone ..."

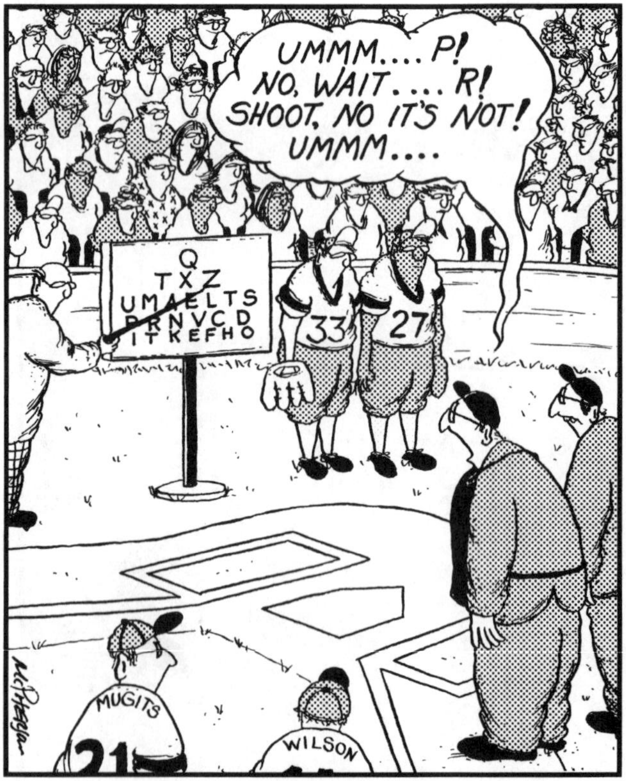
UMMM.... P! NO, WAIT.... R! SHOOT, NO IT'S NOT! UMMM....
Q
TXZ
UMAELTS
PRNVCD
ITKEFHO
33
27
MUGITS
21
WILSON

To appease the fans, major-league umpires are now required to take eye exams during the seventh-inning stretch.

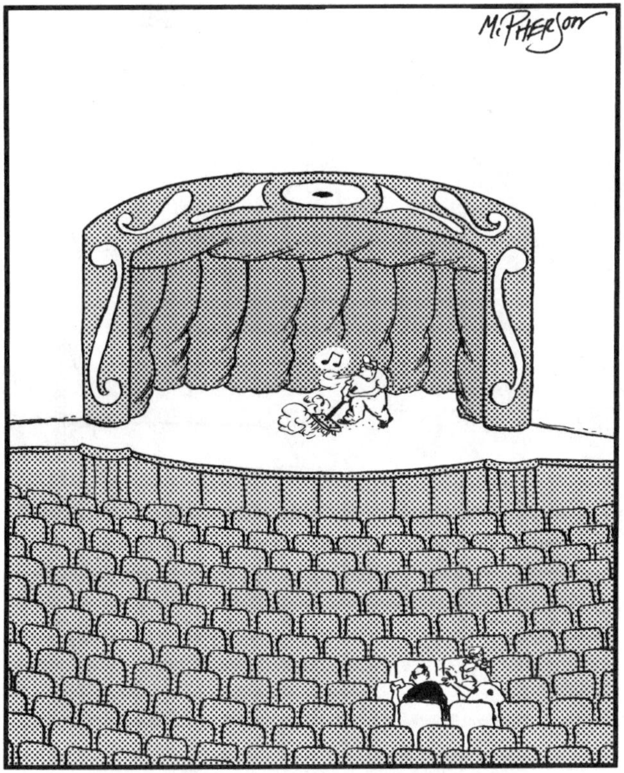
McPherson

"What do you *mean* it was last night?!
Let me see the tickets!"

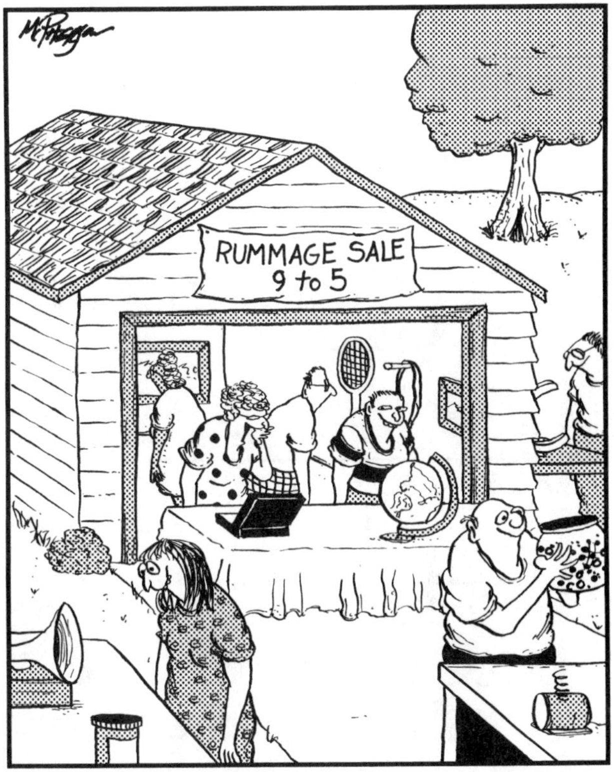
McPherson
RUMMAGE SALE
9 to 5

"Pssst, Bill . . . the sale's going great, but we're getting low on stuff. Make another run to the landfill and bring back whatever you can get your hands on."

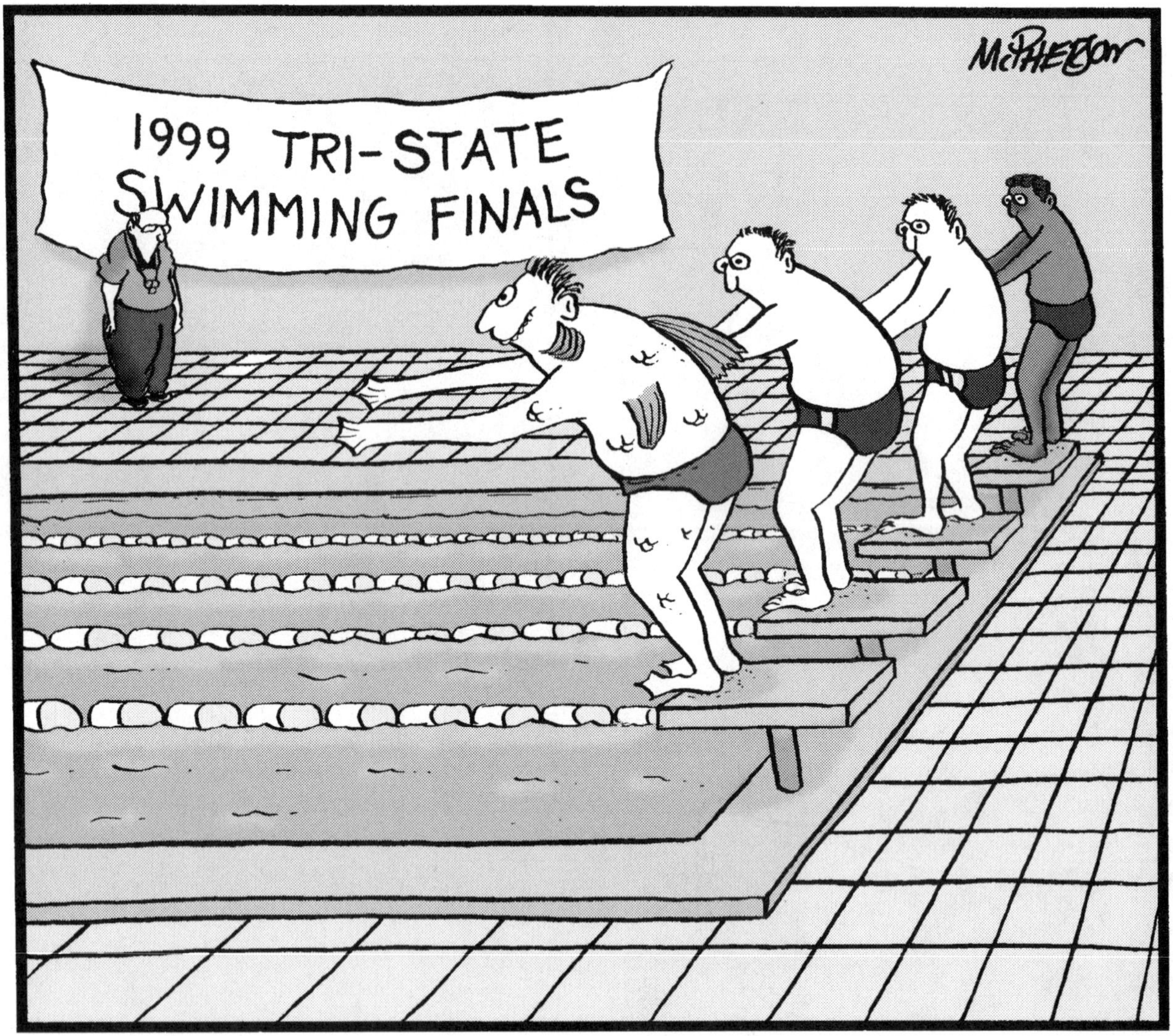
McPHERSON
1999 TRI-STATE SWIMMING FINALS

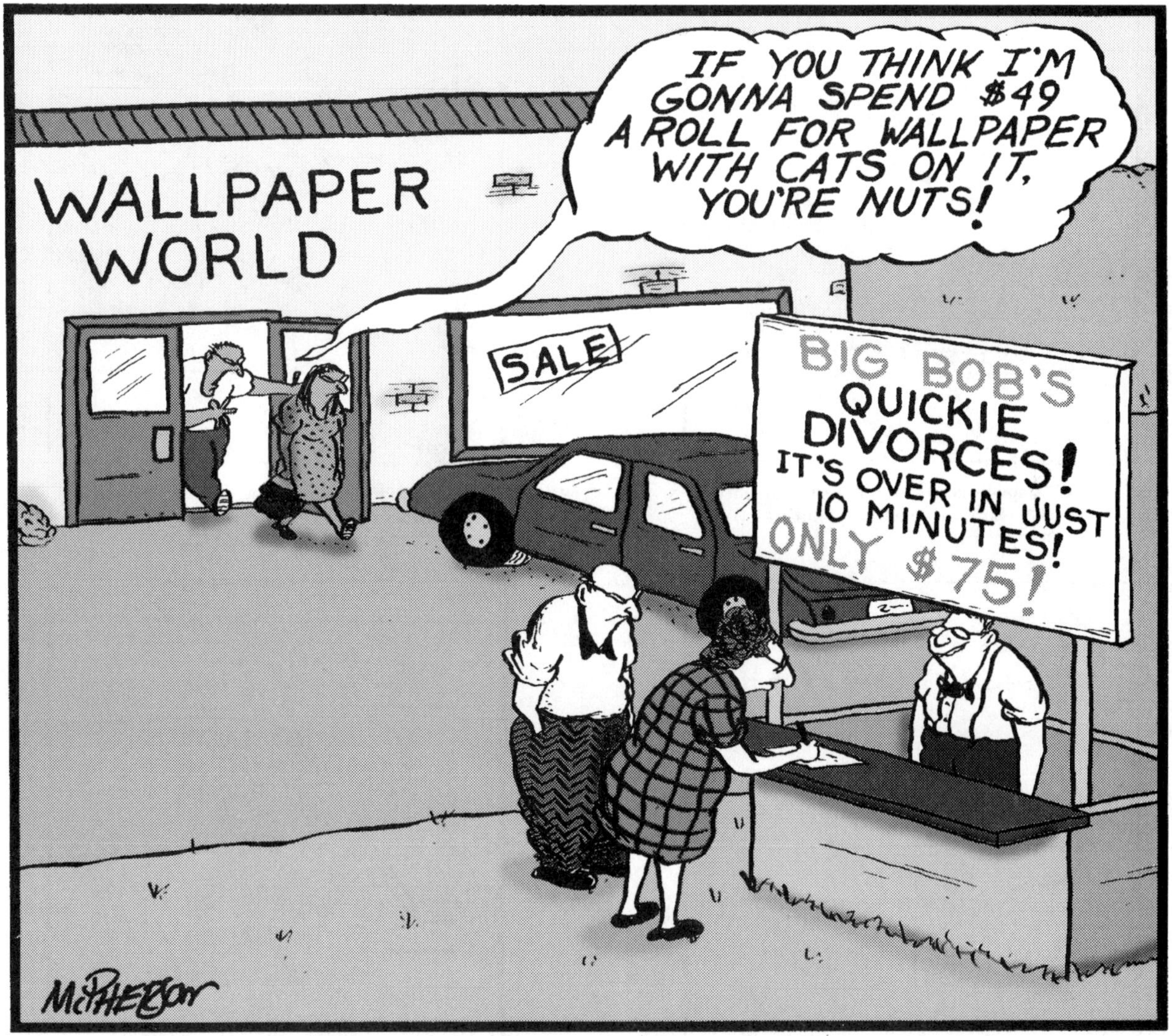
IF YOU THINK I'M GONNA SPEND $49 A ROLL FOR WALLPAPER WITH CATS ON IT, YOU'RE NUTS!
WALLPAPER WORLD
SALE
BIG BOB'S QUICKIE DIVORCES! IT'S OVER IN JUST 10 MINUTES! ONLY $75!
McPHERSON

**Bob stumbles onto a gold mine.**

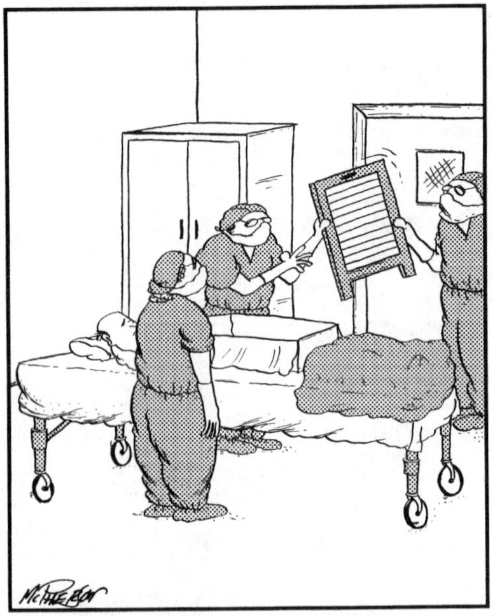

Chris Rhinebeck: the world's first recipient of a washboard stomach implant

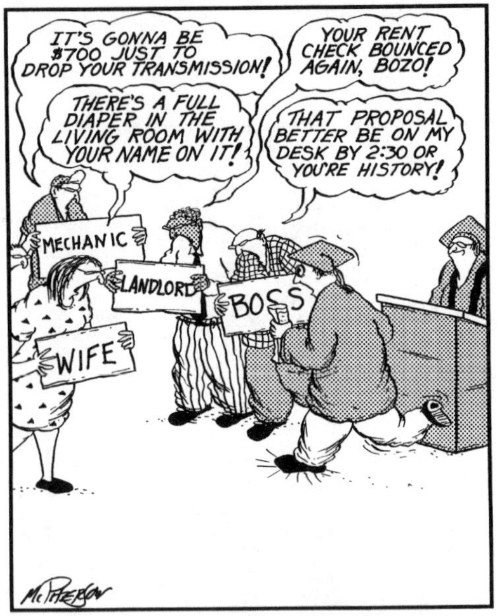

IT'S GONNA BE $700 JUST TO DROP YOUR TRANSMISSION!
YOUR RENT CHECK BOUNCED AGAIN, BOZO!
THERE'S A FULL DIAPER IN THE LIVING ROOM WITH YOUR NAME ON IT!
THAT PROPOSAL BETTER BE ON MY DESK BY 2:30 OR YOU'RE HISTORY!
MECHANIC
LANDLORD
BOSS
WIFE


As a final rite of passage, graduates at Borsteen University were required to run the Real World Gantlet.

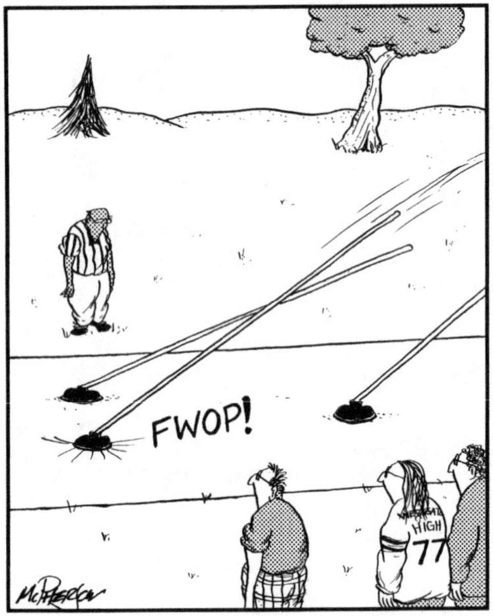

FWOP!
HIGH
77


For insurance purposes the Westgate High track program switches to safety-tipped javelins.

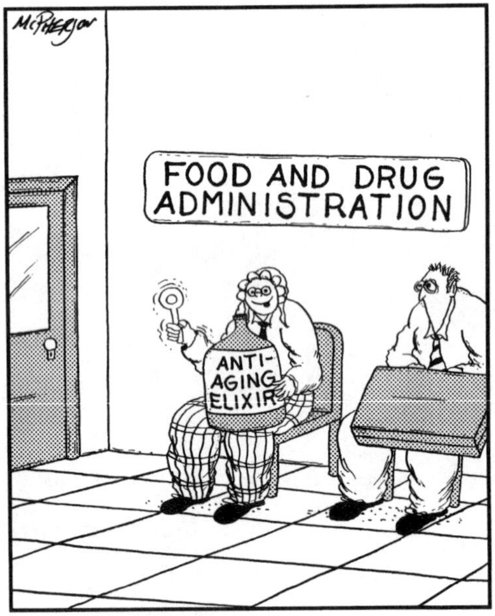

FOOD AND DRUG ADMINISTRATION
ANTI-AGING ELIXIR

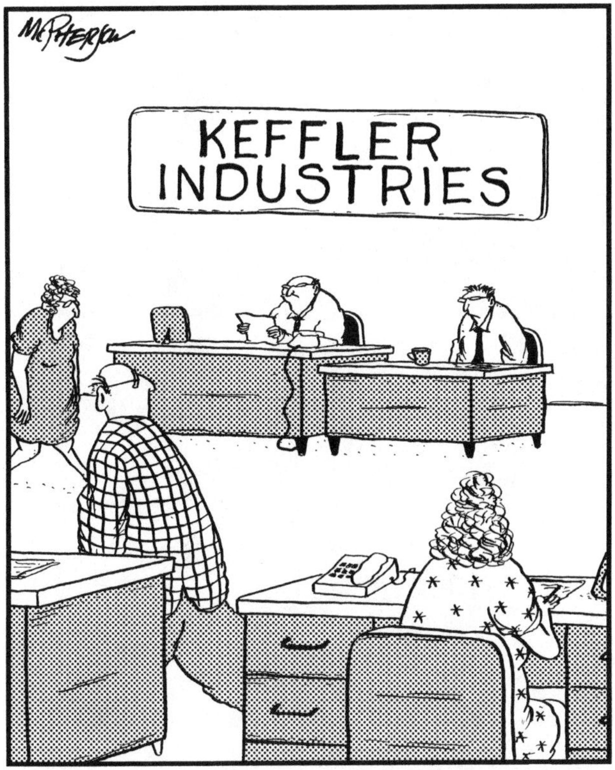
KEFFLER
INDUSTRIES
After being caught a fifth time making personal phone calls, Bruce was ordered to move his desk up next to Mr. Keffler's.

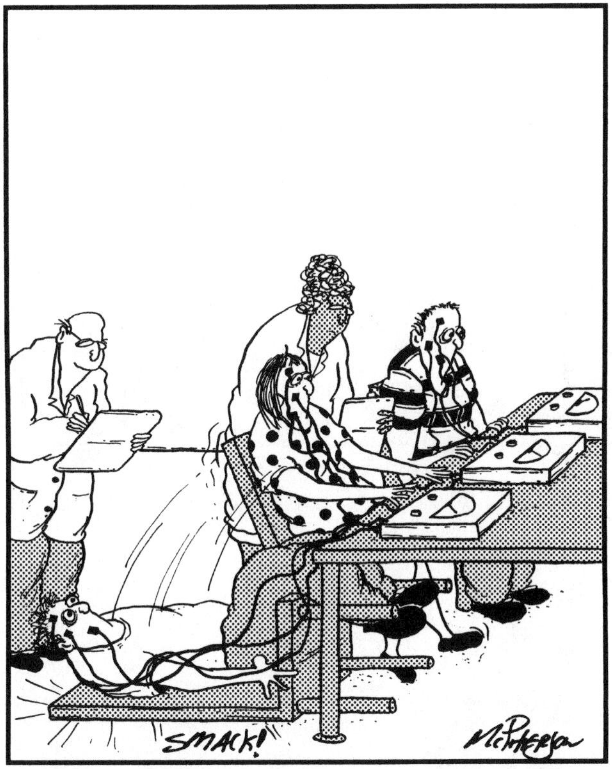
SMACK!
At the institute for the Study of That Scary Feeling You Get When You Start to Fall Backward in Your Chair but Catch Yourself at the Last Second

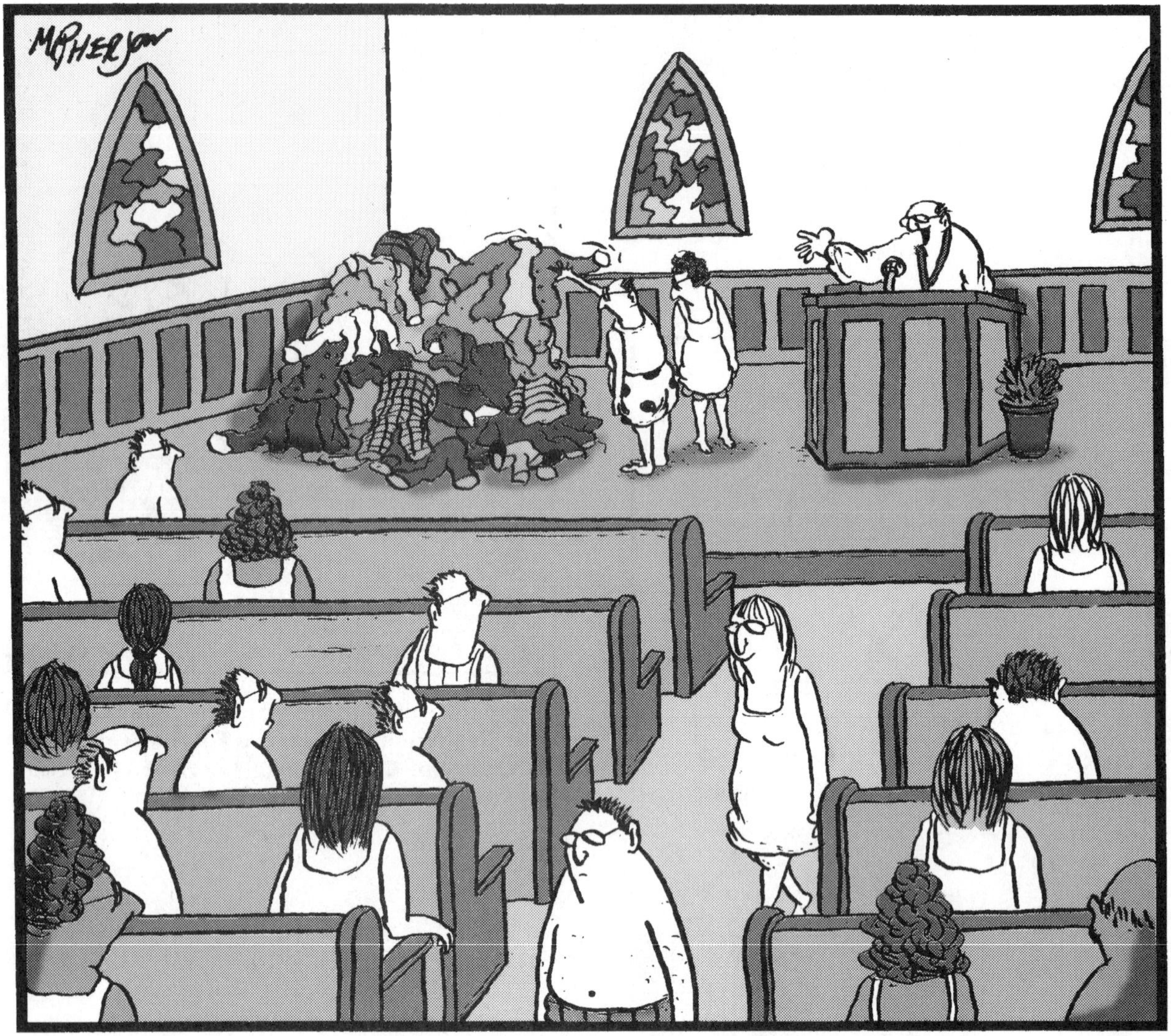
McPHERSON

**"I'd like to thank all of you for making this year's clothing drive a huge success."**

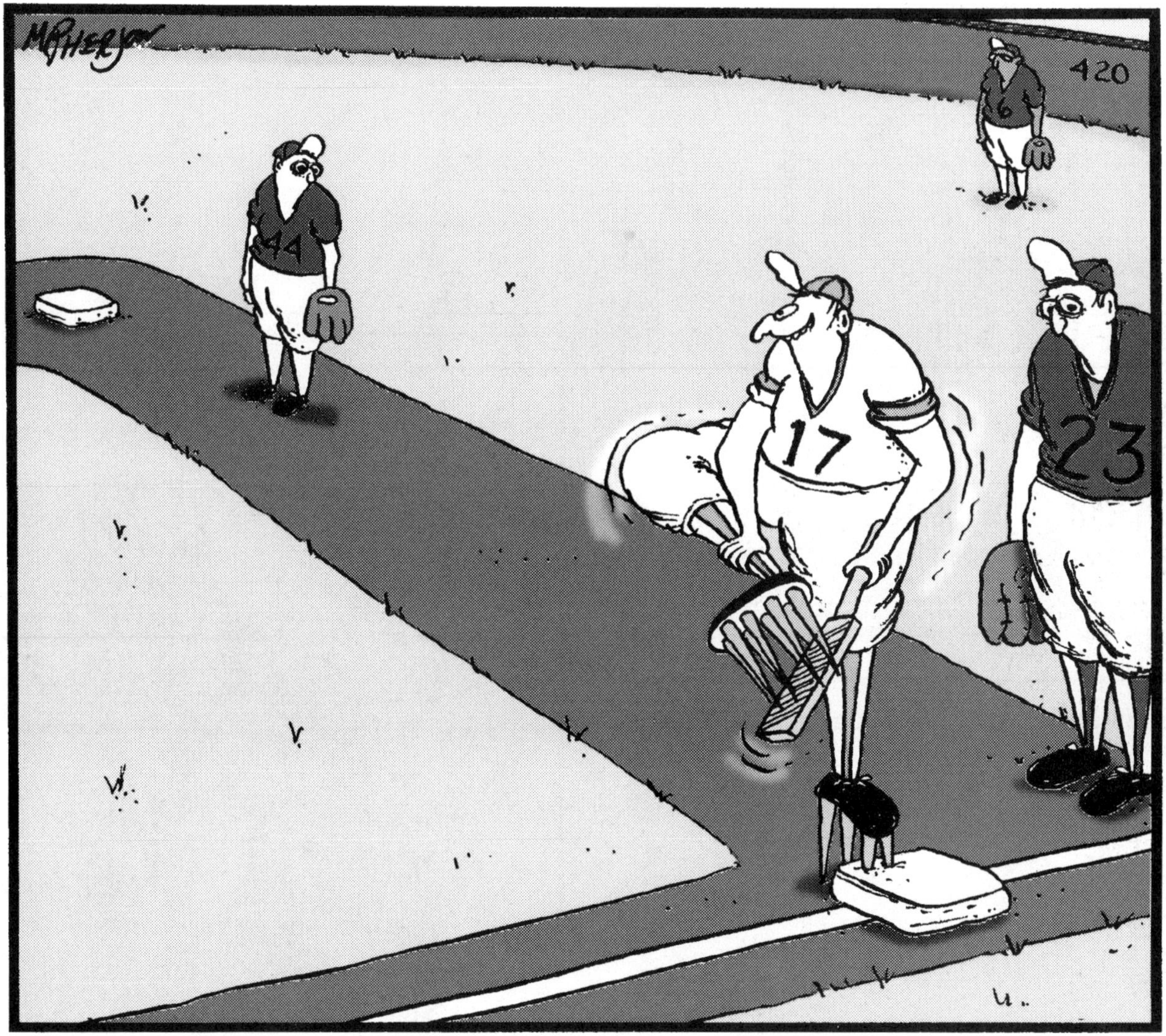
420
44
6
17
23

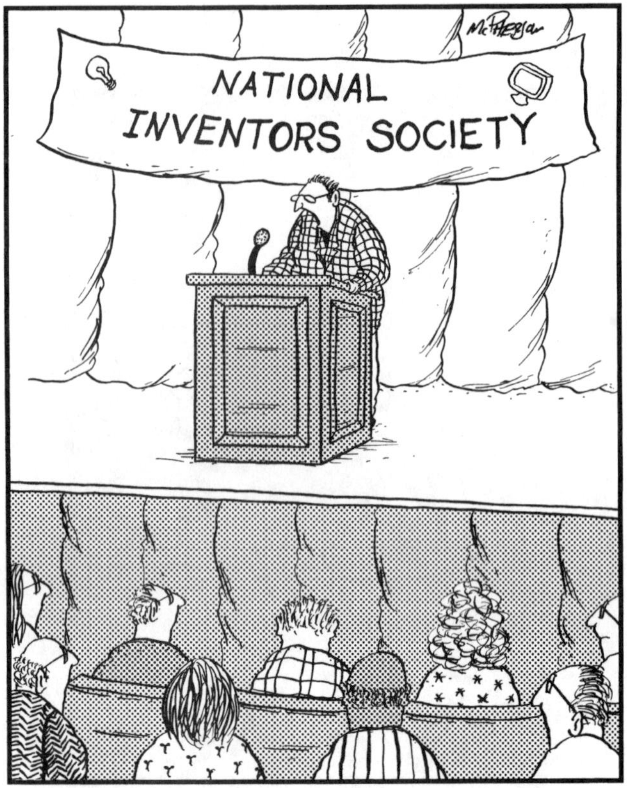

NATIONAL
INVENTORS SOCIETY


**"Unfortunately, this morning's guest speaker, Don Keppler, inventor of the snooze alarm, has not yet arrived."**

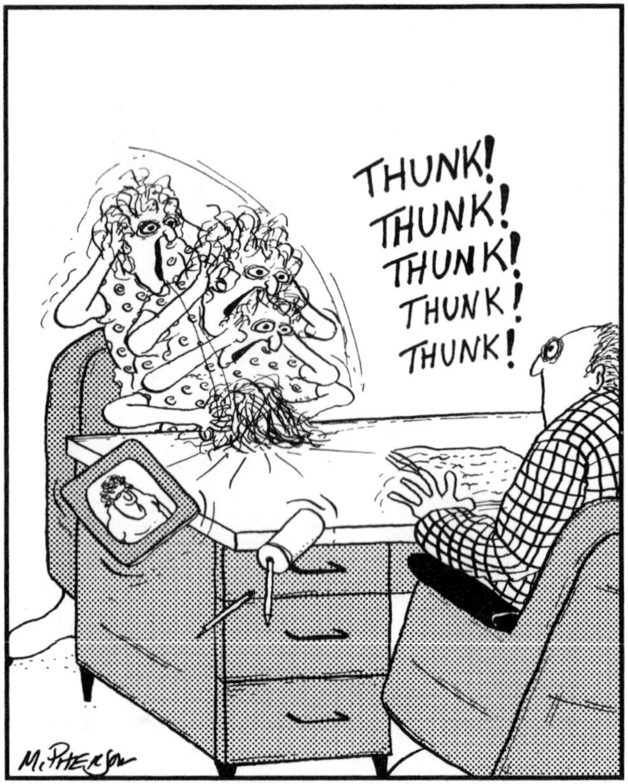

THUNK!
THUNK!
THUNK!
THUNK!
THUNK!


**Tina reacts to Principal Harstein's comment that her third-grader, Jenny, has difficulty handling criticism.**

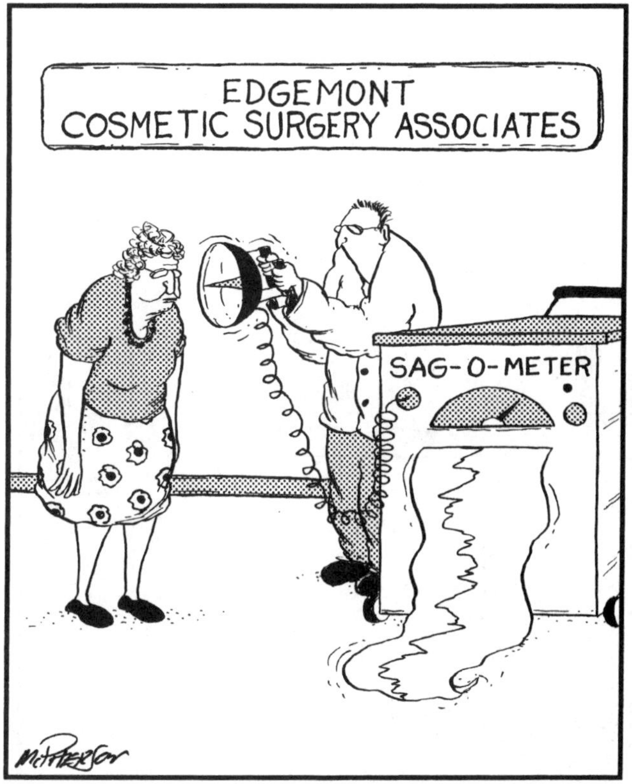
EDGEMONT
COSMETIC SURGERY ASSOCIATES
SAG-O-METER
McPHERSON

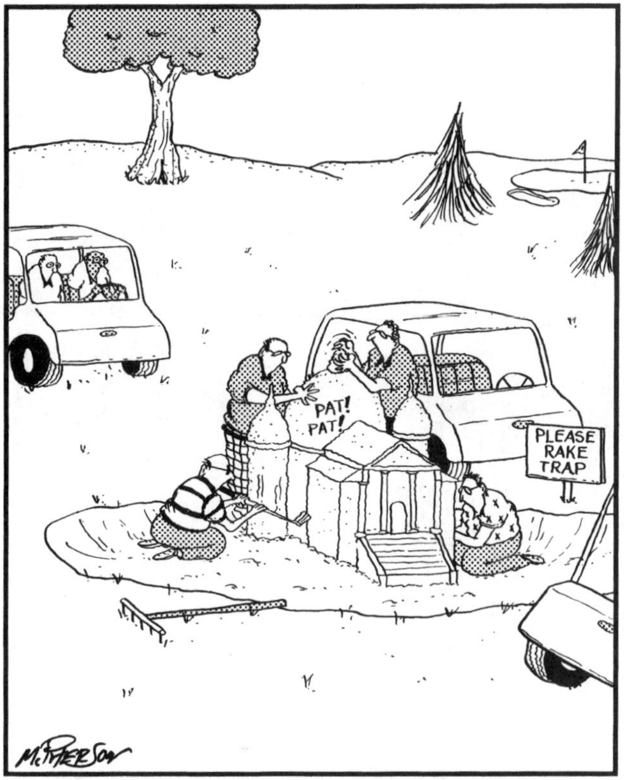
PAT!
PAT!
PLEASE
RAKE
TRAP
McPHERSON

**As they caught up to the foursome in front of them, Phil and Bob's hopes of finishing their round in four hours quickly faded.**

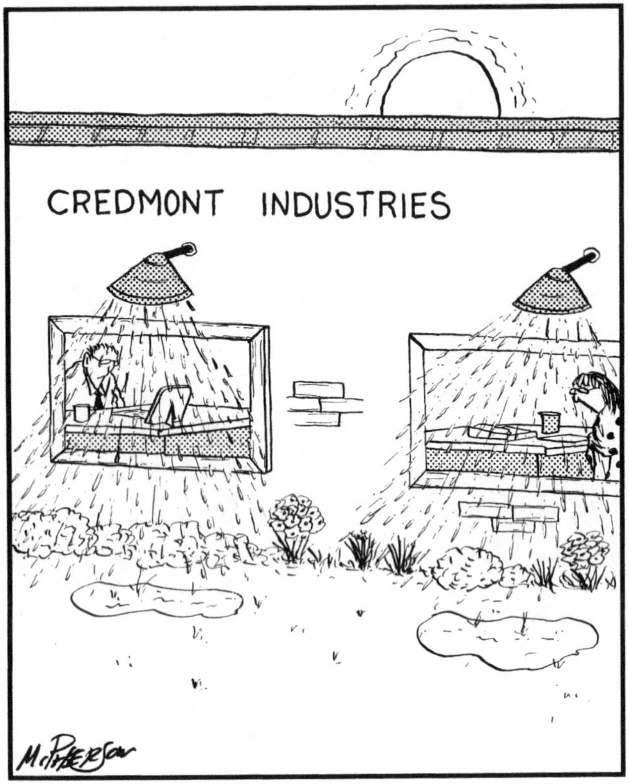
CREDMONT INDUSTRIES

To stave off spring fever among employees on sunny days, Credmont Industries wisely installed rain-simulation devices above all windows.

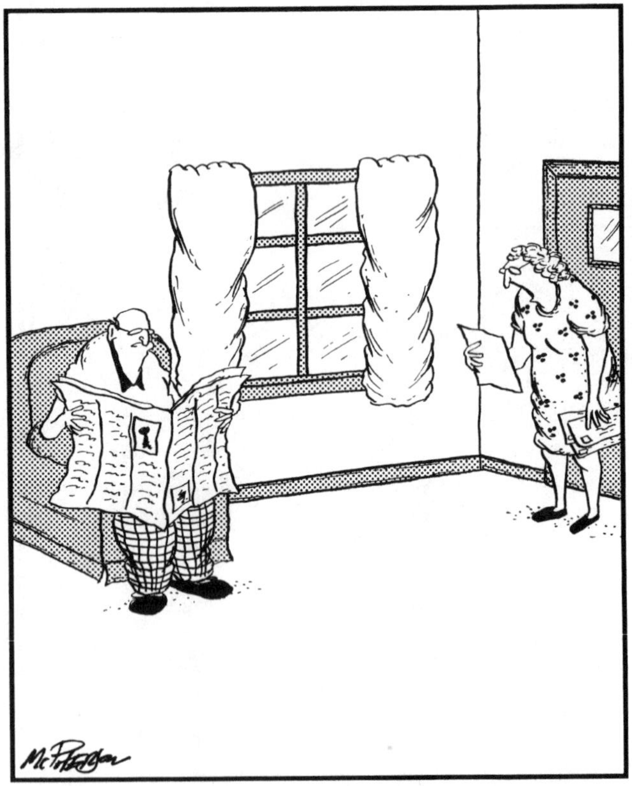

"It's a notice from our bank. Our mortgage was purchased by the First National Bank of Bangladesh, and our payments now have to be made in takas."

# Ideas

When things are really going my way, cartoon ideas will just pop into my head—while I'm driving, out to dinner, in the shower, while I'm getting a speeding ticket . . .

But most of the time I have to consciously try to come up with them. To get cartoon ideas, I try to really focus on something in particular. If I just sit there going "funny idea . . . funny idea . . ." I get nothing. So I try to really home in on something—maybe an angry guy at an airport ticket counter, an airplane filled with crying babies, a doctor who hates the sight of blood. I try to think of mixing things that just don't go together or situations that will cause stress, because I know that if I can put my characters in a stressful situation, something funny is not far behind. Hospital settings are great sources of stress, which is one reason I do so many medical cartoons. I'm not trying to make fun of people who are sick, rather, I'm trying to bring some humor into an upsetting predicament.

Often, I'll sift through magazines to help spark an idea. Photos can really trigger some goofy thoughts. And goofy thoughts are the key to good cartoons, I think.

But sometimes I can sift through a pile of stuff and still come up dry. When that happens, I just sit at my drawing table and draw some bizarre scene and then see if I can come up with captions to make sense of it. It's a pretty effective way to break through a block and has generated some pretty funny cartoons. (Well, at least my mom said they were funny.)

Here are some examples of that method at work.

I drew this sketch of some movers staring at a huge hole in the floor. There must be one hundred funny things that one of them could be saying here. So here are four that I came up with:

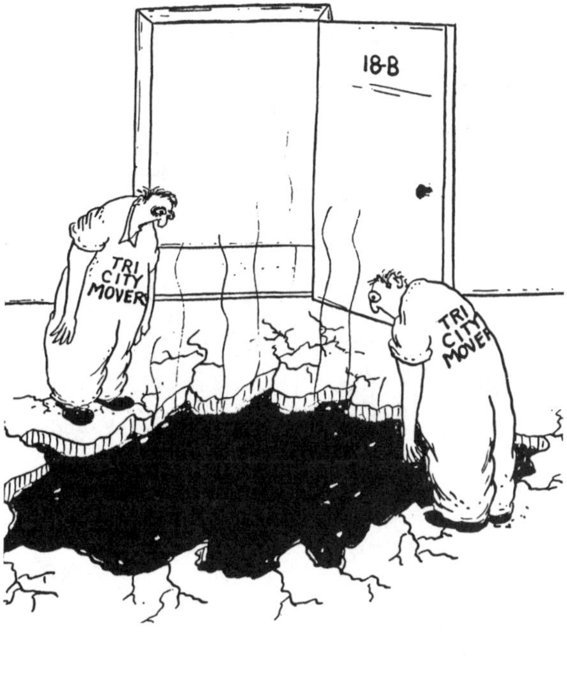
18-B
TRI CITY MOVERS
TRI CITY MOVER

1. "Man, they sure do build those Steinways great. That thing was in perfect tune right until it hit the fourth floor."

2. "For an elderly couple, they sure scrambled out of the way quickly."

3. "I say we bring in that big oriental rug next."

4. "I can't believe that nun down on the seventh floor actually tried to catch it!"

Now, not all of these are necessarily hilarious captions. I just sort of start writing. But the third and fourth ones work pretty well, I think. At this stage, I'll fax the cartoon over to my editor in Kansas City and he and I will try to decide which captions work best. He might even poll some other editors. And I might wander around a mall and stop perfect strangers to get their opinions. In this case, we liked the image of a nun trying to catch some large object that was hurtling at her. However, when I've shown this cartoon during speaking engagements, the crowd pleaser is always the oriental rug caption. Just goes to show you what my editor and I know.

Here's a great calamitous scene. A surgical lamp has fallen onto the patient's face.

1. "Cancel the anesthesiolgist."

2. "Well, looks like Mr. Gardner is going to get his money's worth out of *this* nose job!"

3. "Ten to one that when he's recovering tomorrow he tells one of those stories about seeing a bright light at the end of a tunnel!"

The first two are decent, but the clear winner is number three, and that's what we decided on.

# EMERGENCY

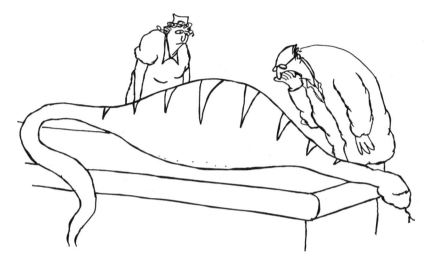

Here I drew a snake in an emergency room with a large lump that obviously contains a person. I stared at it for a while and then decided that it would be funnier if the doctor was holding a saw. Endless possibilities, and just a funny image in itself.

Here are four captions for it.

1. "Before we resort to surgery, Mrs. Sanders, I'd like you to try 'Open Sesame.'"

2 "It's not that simple, Mrs. Sanders. This snake is an endangered species."

3. "Everything's going to be fine, Mrs. Sanders. We've given the snake a laxative and you should be out of there in four hours."

4. "Okay, Mrs. Sanders, I need to have you scoot as *far* to your left as possible."

Now, my editor actually came up with the third caption, and we laughed for a good five minutes over it. So I said, "That's perfect! Let's run it." He said, nope, can't deal with snake diarrhea in the newspapers. I said, "Come on! No one's going to *see* snake diarrhea, it's just kind of inferred." But he felt it was just too gross an image—so he killed even his own caption!

We went with number four, which I also like. But it's hard to top snake diarrhea.

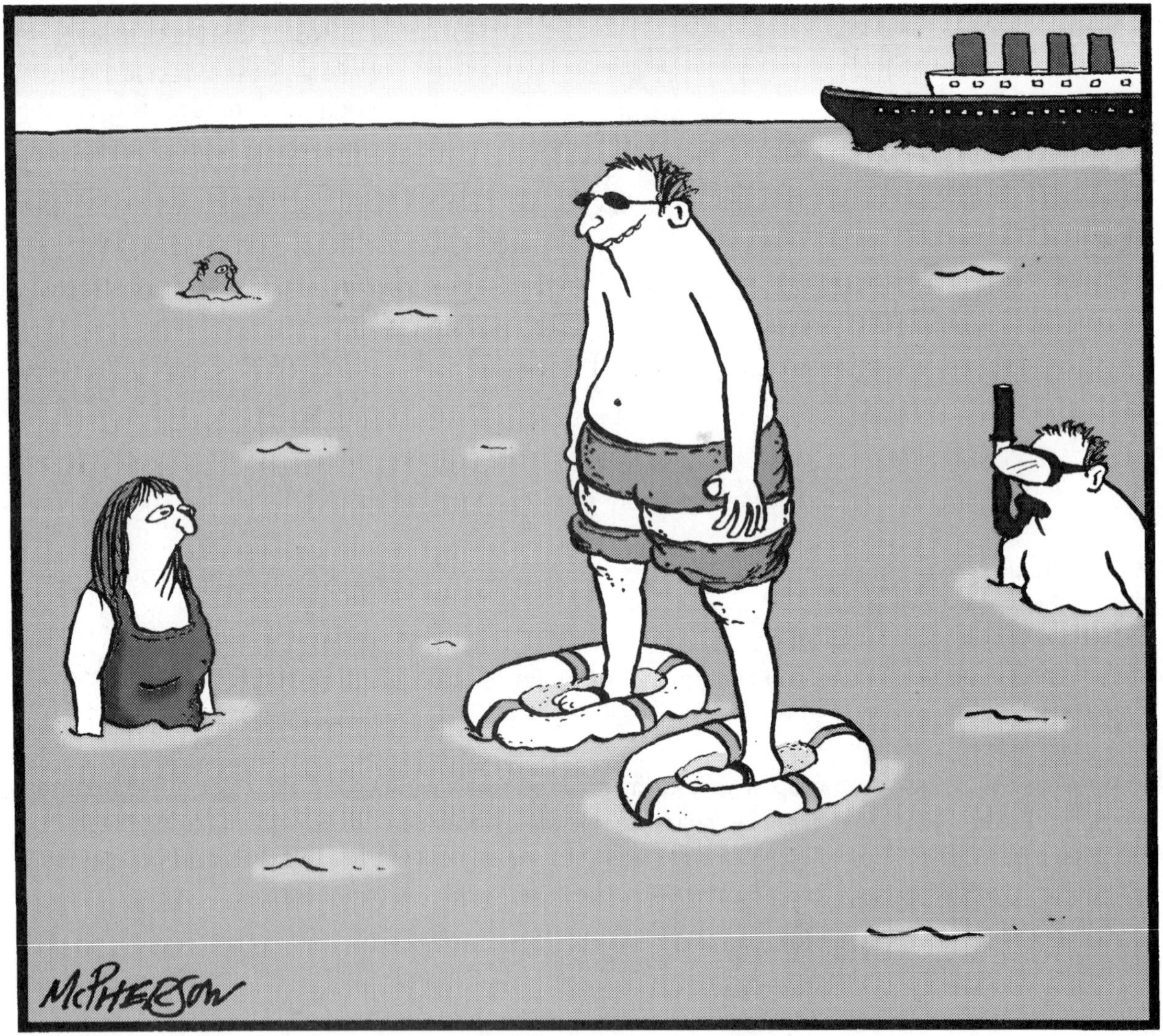
McPHERSON

**The latest in beachwear: pontoon shoes**

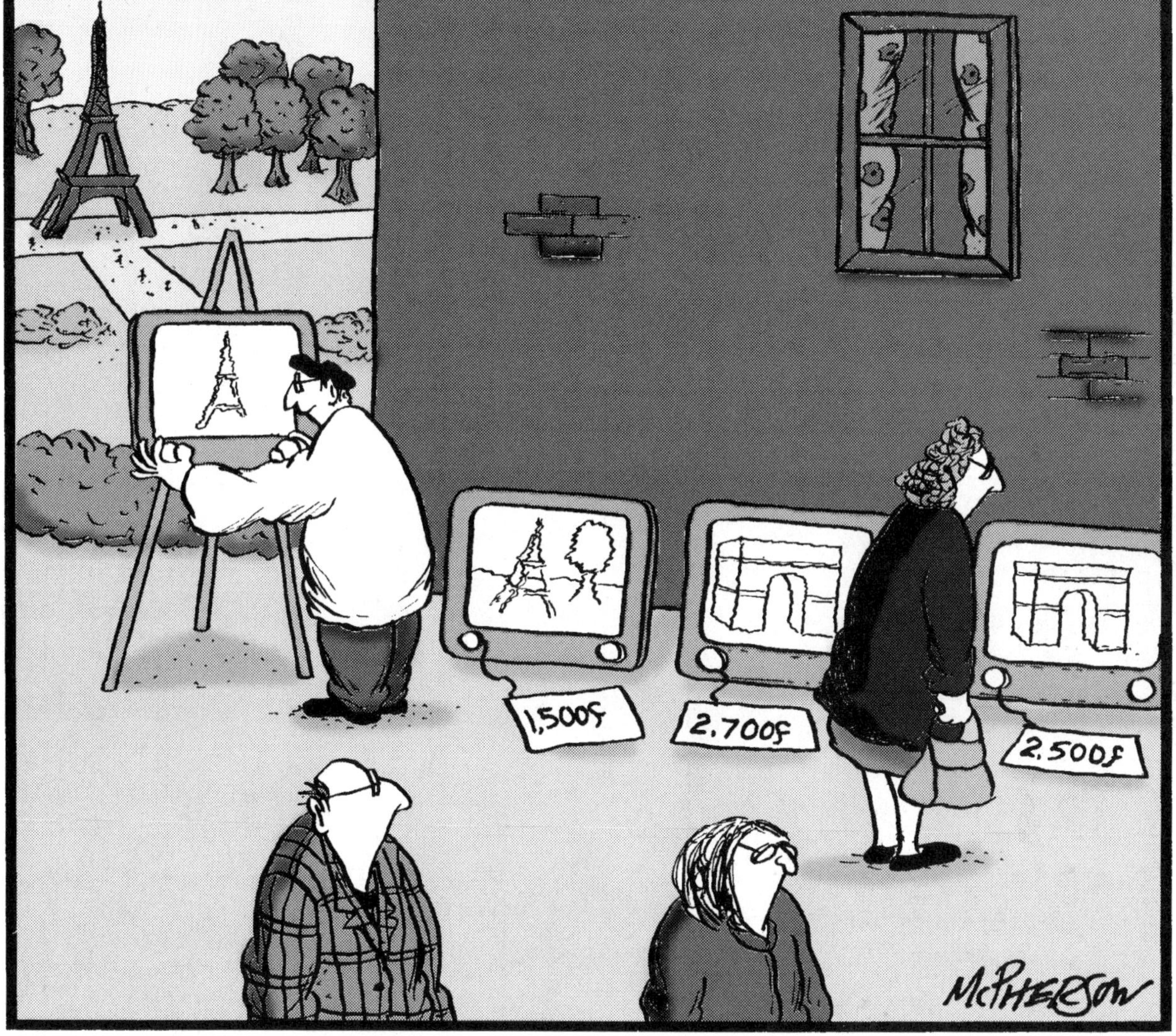
1,500f
2,700f
2,500f
McPHERSON

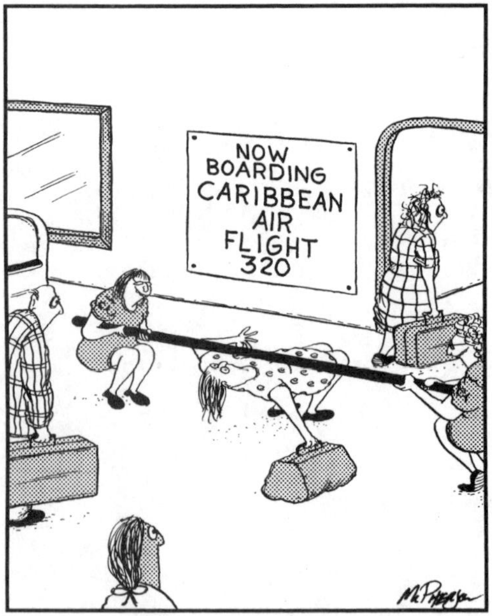
NOW
BOARDING
CARIBBEAN
AIR
FLIGHT
320

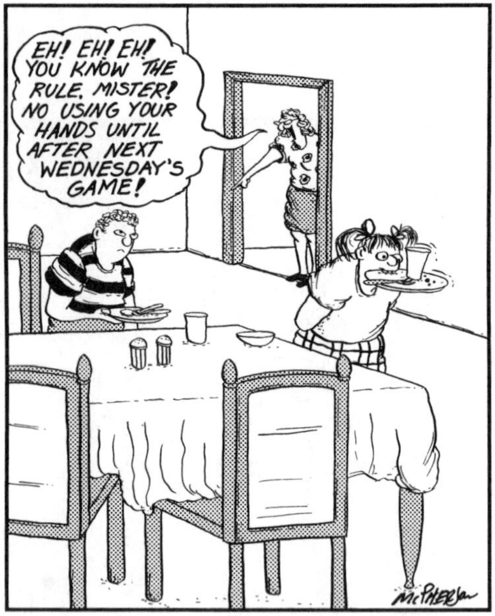
EH! EH! EH! YOU KNOW THE RULE, MISTER! NO USING YOUR HANDS UNTIL AFTER NEXT WEDNESDAY'S GAME!

When soccer moms go too far

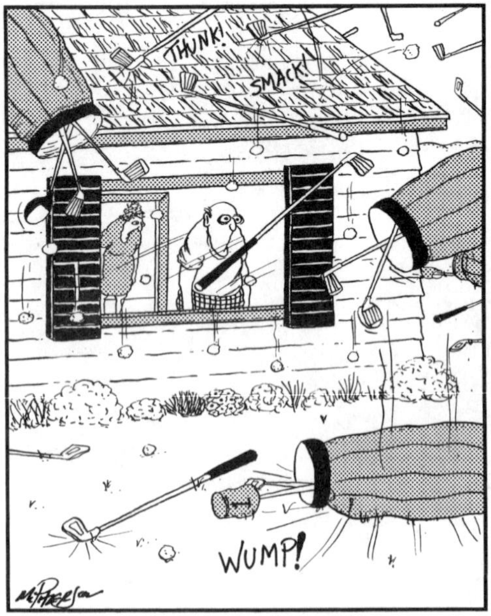
THUNK!
SMACK!
WUMP!

"Good heavens! What on earth is going on out there? I know they forecast golf-ball-sized hail, but this sounds more like baseballs!"

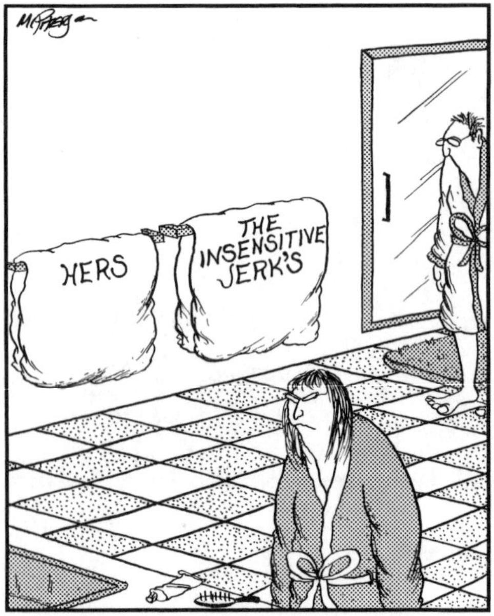
HERS
THE INSENSITIVE JERK'S

Yet another sign that the Bertmans' marriage counseling sessions had a long way to go

The new Snowboard Mow-Master meant the Gecklemans never again had to nag their thirteen-year-old to cut the grass.

Dr. Vortner tries to lighten the mood before performing Carol's C-section.

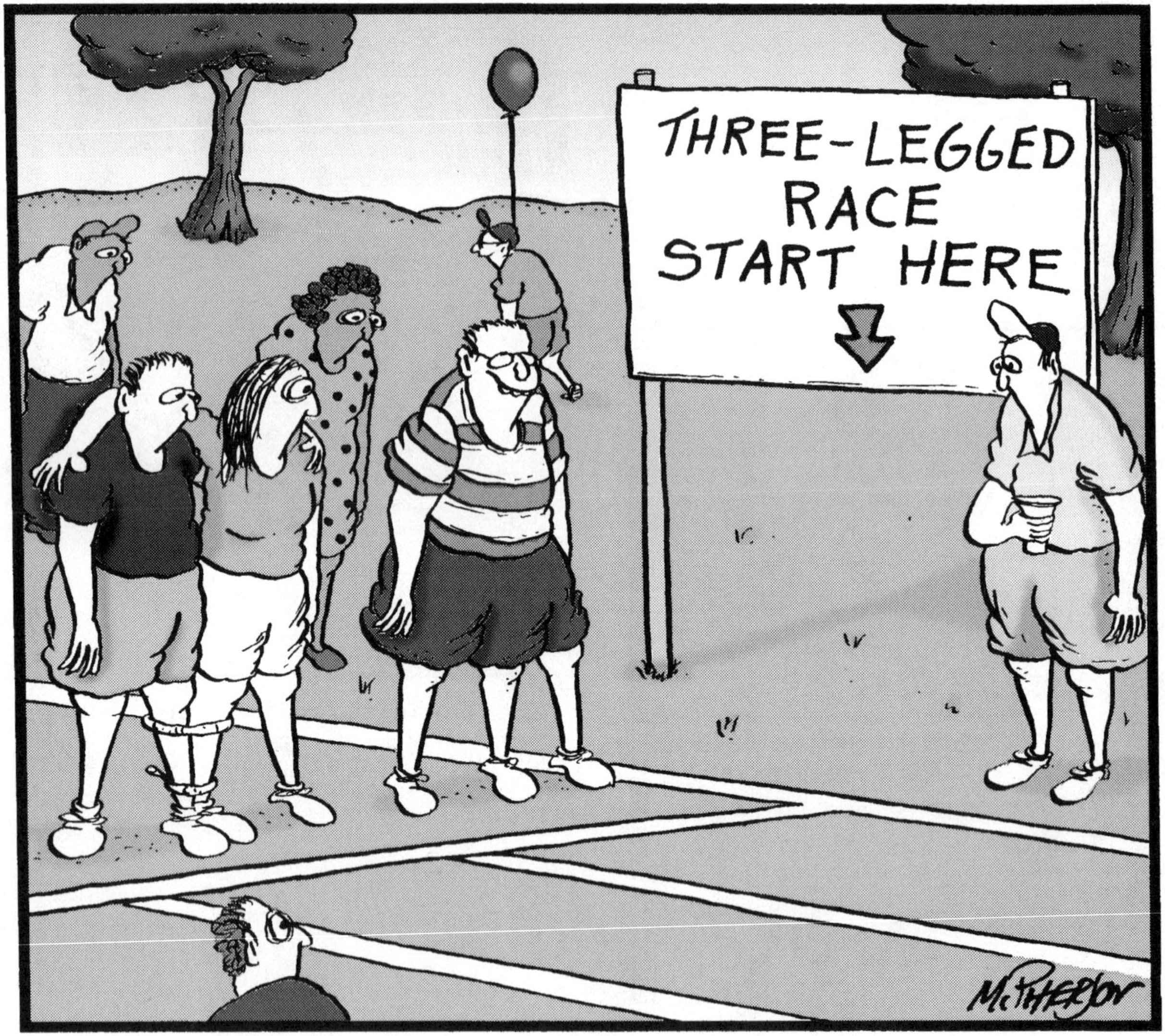
THREE-LEGGED
RACE
START HERE

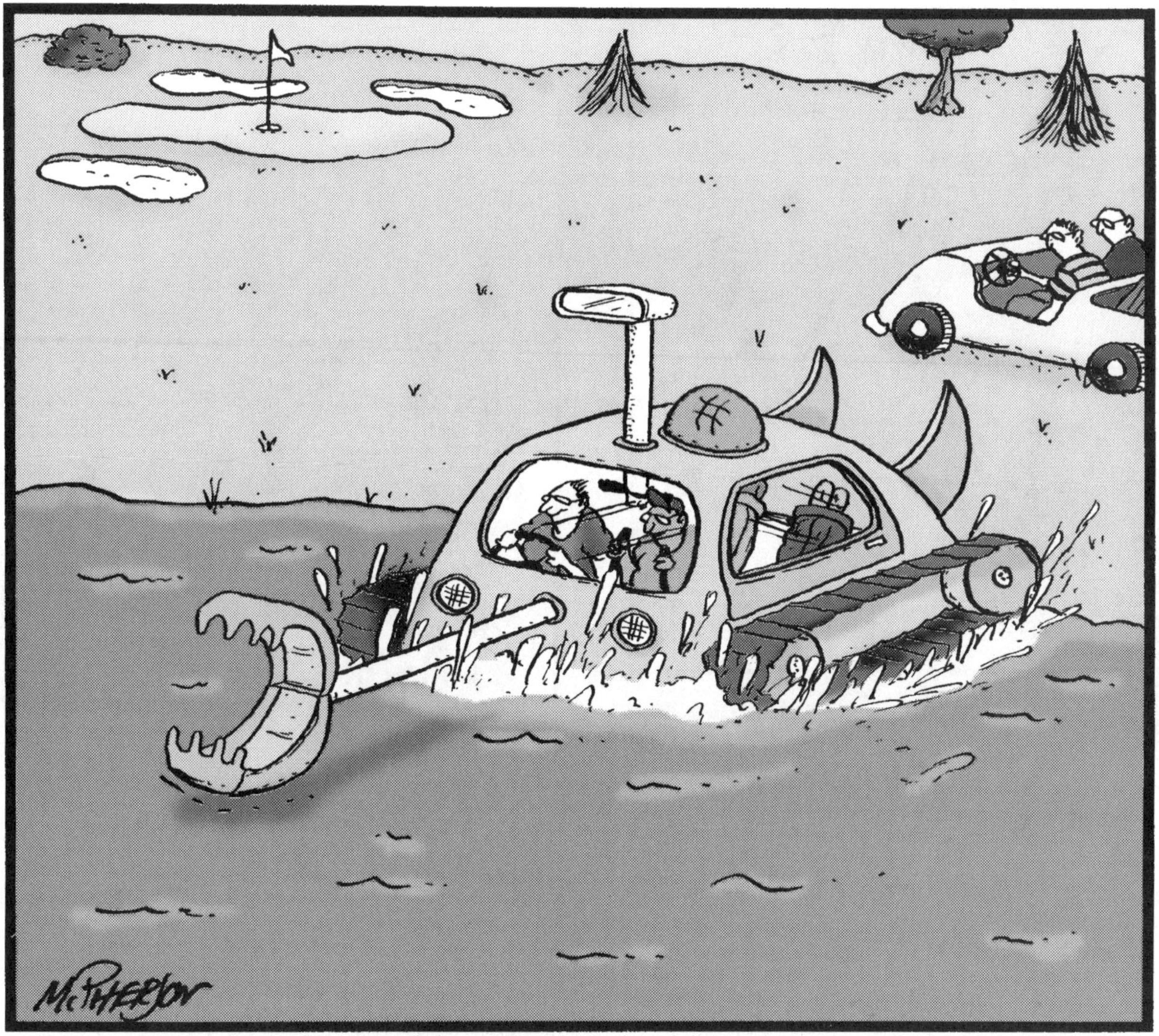
McPherson

**Tired of losing golf balls to water hazards, Ed and Brian opt for one of the new amphibious golf carts.**

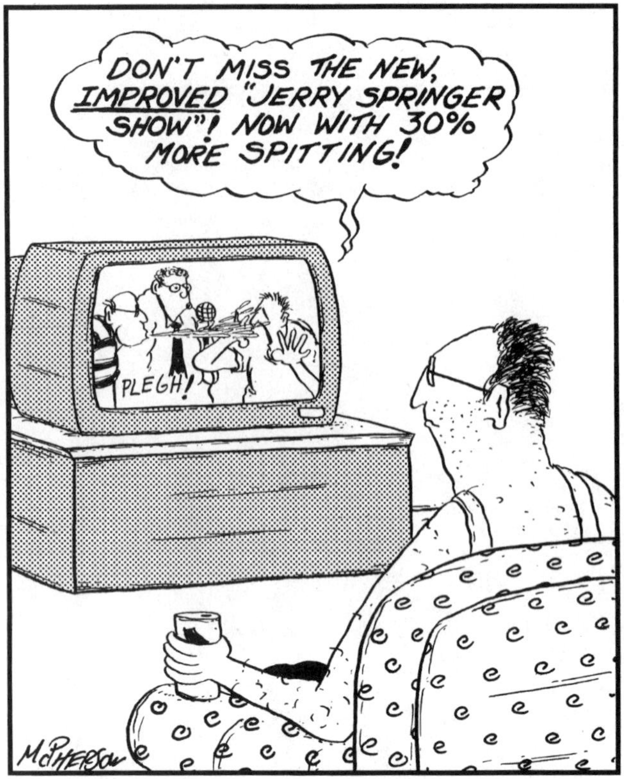
DON'T MISS THE NEW, IMPROVED "JERRY SPRINGER SHOW"! NOW WITH 30% MORE SPITTING!
PLEGH!

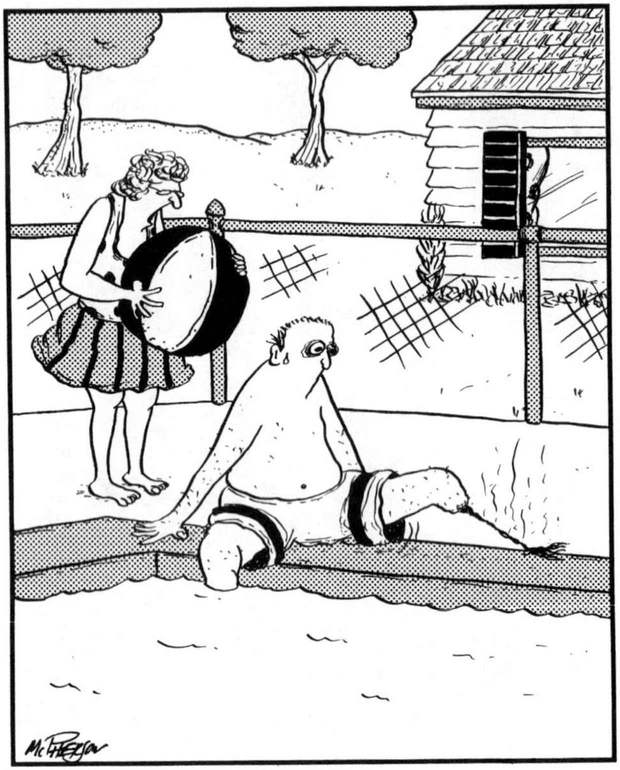

"I told you not to use so much chlorine."

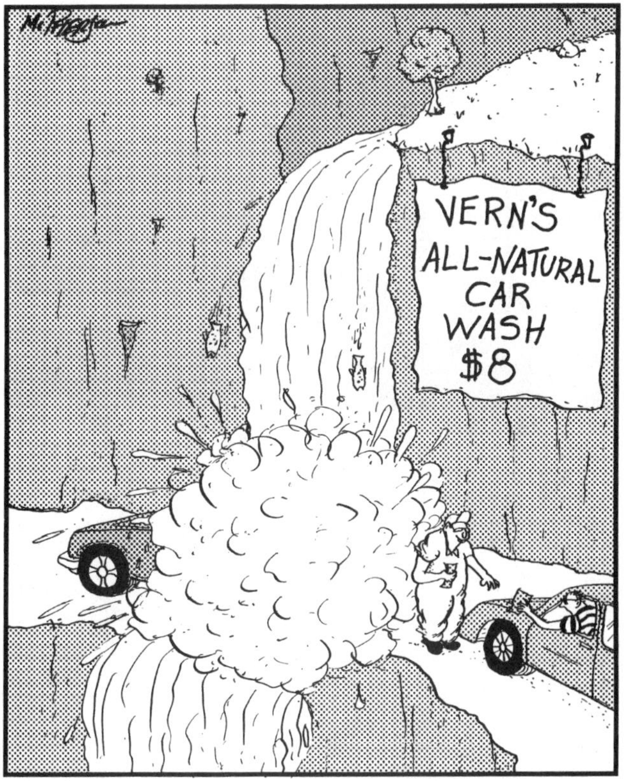
VERN'S
ALL-NATURAL
CAR
WASH
$8

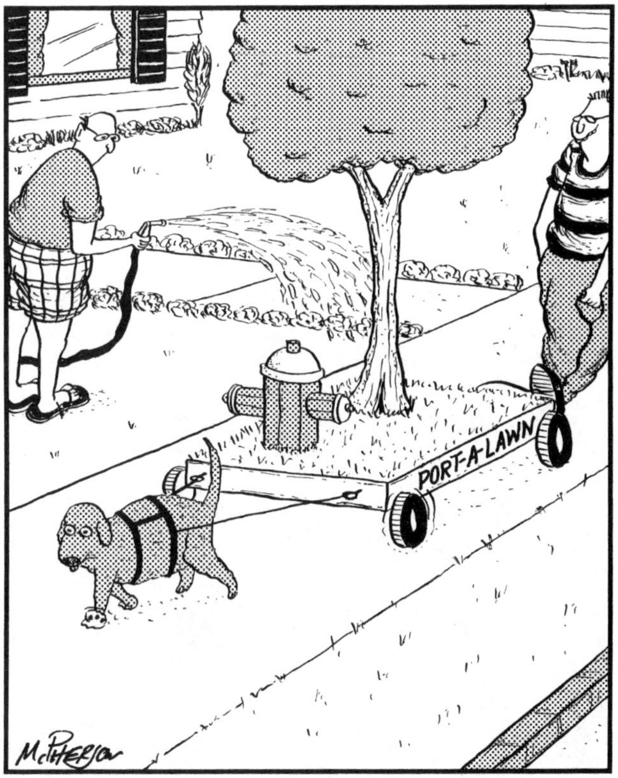
PORT-A-LAWN

Ron avoids the issue of pooper-scoopers altogether.

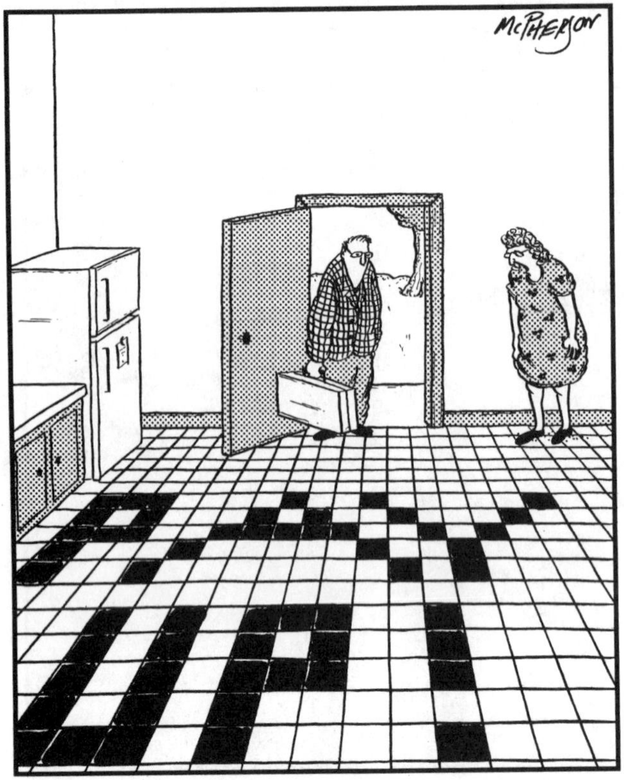

“The tile guy says he’ll come back and replace the black tiles when our check clears.”

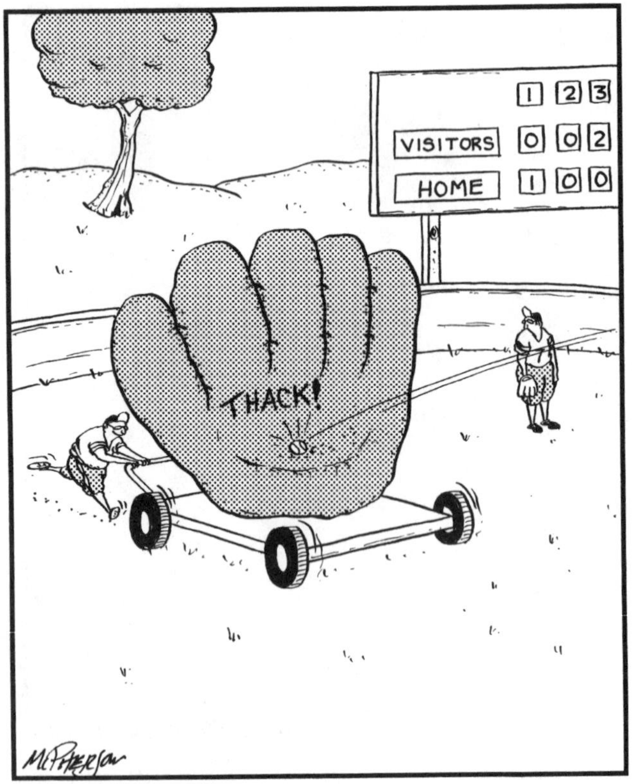
1 2 3
VISITORS 0 0 2
HOME 1 0 0
THACK!

Unwieldy though it was, Larry had yet to miss a fly ball with his new glove.

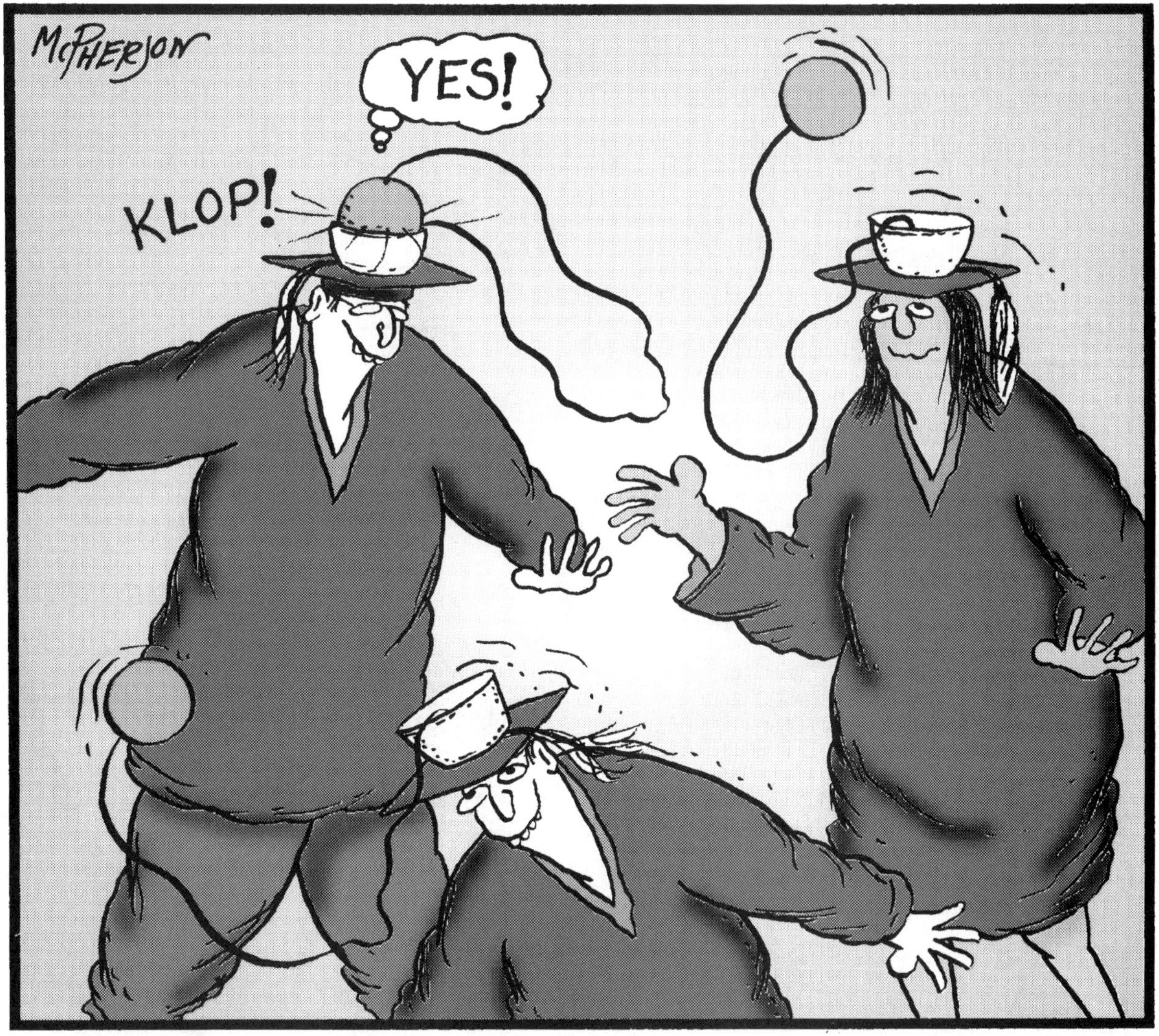
McPHERSON
YES!
KLOP!

**Inspired by the classic children's toy, the new graduation caps helped students pass the time during lengthy commencement speeches.**

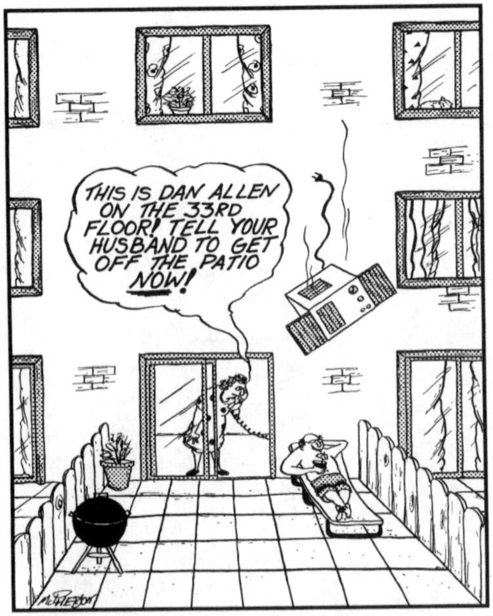
THIS IS DAN ALLEN ON THE 33RD FLOOR! TELL YOUR HUSBAND TO GET OFF THE PATIO NOW!

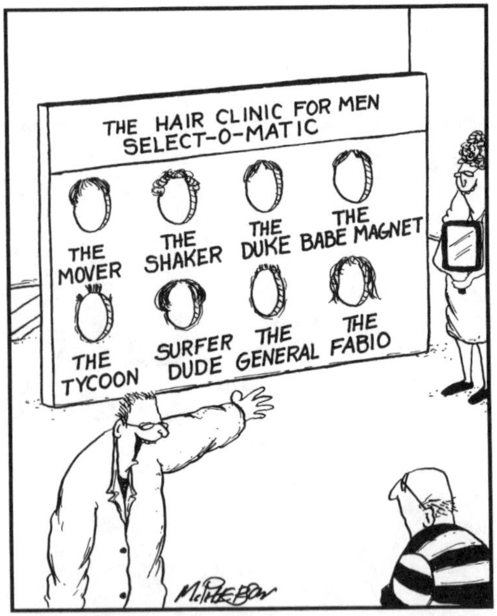
THE HAIR CLINIC FOR MEN
SELECT-O-MATIC
THE MOVER
THE SHAKER
THE DUKE
THE BABE MAGNET
THE TYCOON
SURFER DUDE
THE GENERAL
THE FABIO

"Now, Mr. Dawkins, if you'll just step over to our patented Selct-o-Matic, we'll help you decide which hair replacement system is best for you."

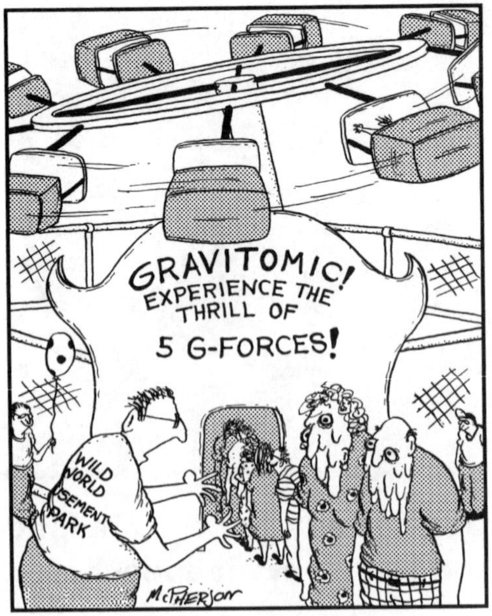
GRAVITOMIC!
EXPERIENCE THE THRILL OF
5 G-FORCES!

"Folks, you were given ample warning about the potential risks of the ride. Besides, your faces should return to normal in eighteen to twenty-four hours."

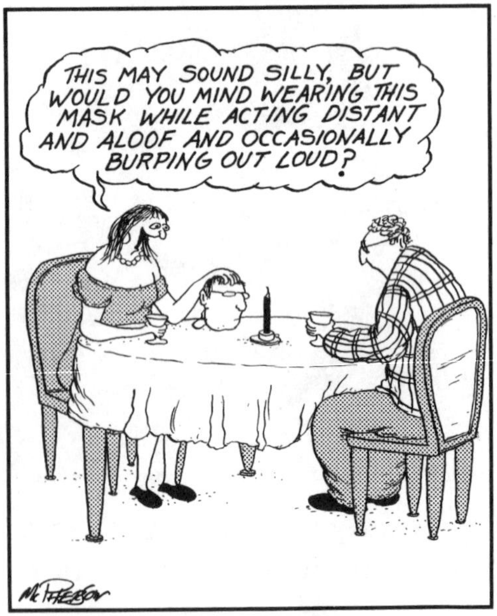
THIS MAY SOUND SILLY, BUT WOULD YOU MIND WEARING THIS MASK WHILE ACTING DISTANT AND ALOOF AND OCCASIONALLY BURPING OUT LOUD?

Dwayne sensed that his date hadn't quite gotten over her ex-boyfriend.

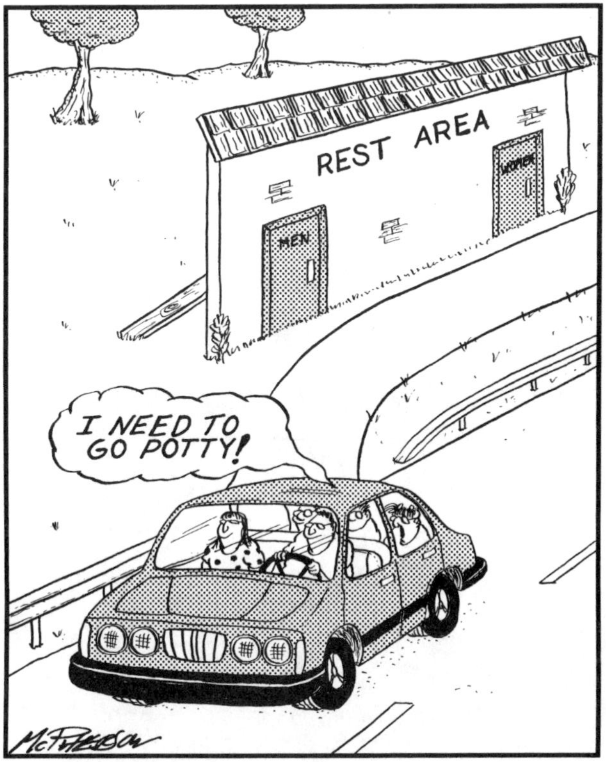
REST AREA
MEN
WOMEN
I NEED TO GO POTTY!
McPHERSON

To spare parents of small children much anguish on road trips, many highway departments have placed rest stop facades one mile before the real rest stops.

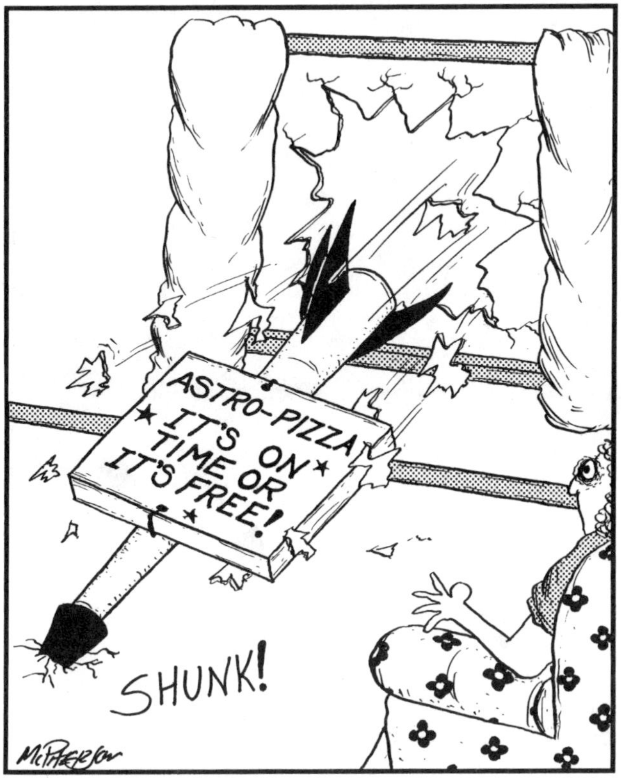
ASTRO-PIZZA
★ IT'S ON TIME OR IT'S FREE! ★
SHUNK!
McPHERSON

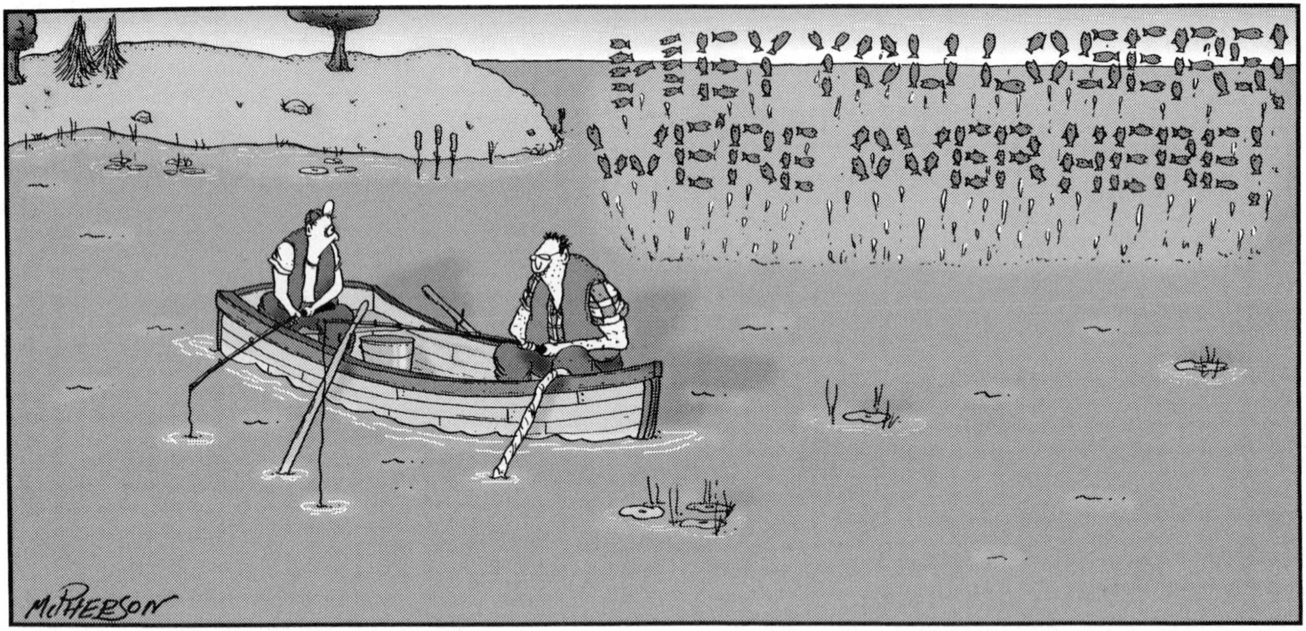
McPHERSON

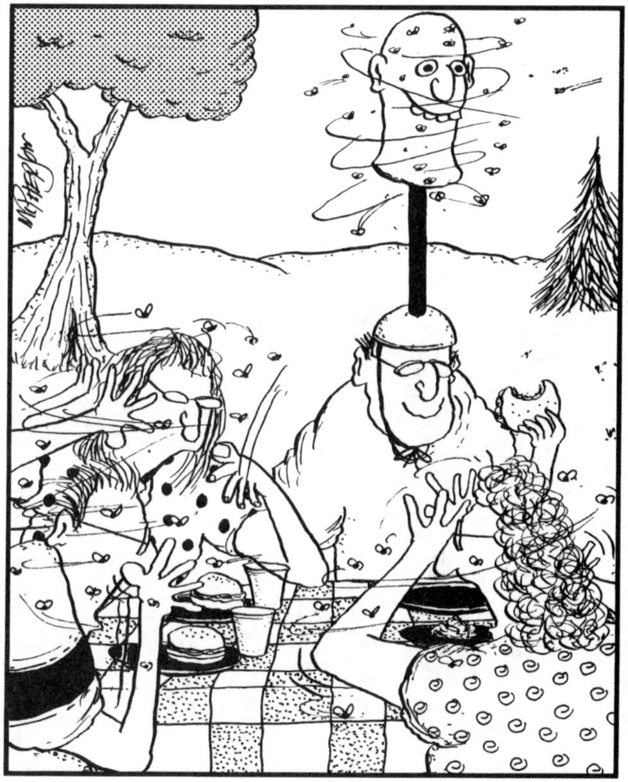

Thanks to his bug-decoy device,
Gerald was able to eat his meal in peace.

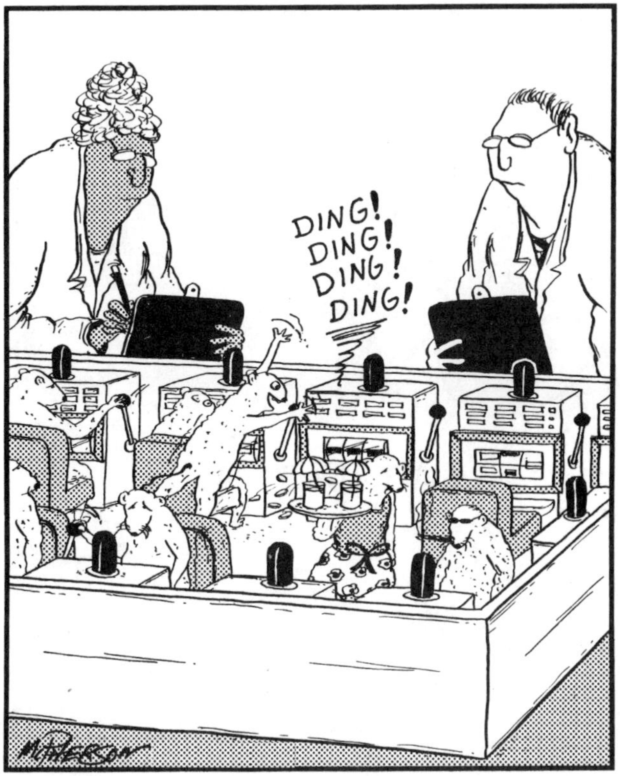
DING!
DING!
DING!
DING!

Researchers at MIT study the effects of
casino gambling on laboratory rats.

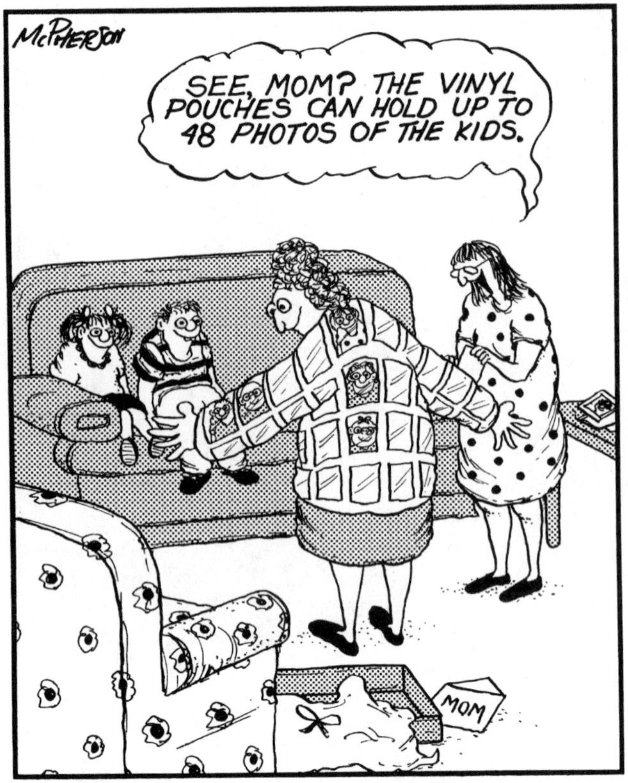
McPHERSON
SEE, MOM? THE VINYL POUCHES CAN HOLD UP TO 48 PHOTOS OF THE KIDS.
MOM

**Birthday gifts for grandmothers**

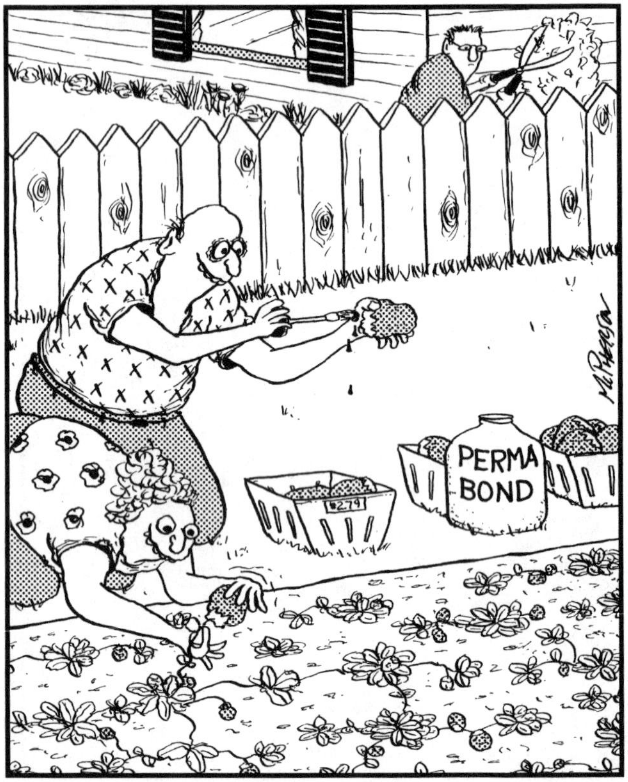
PERMA BOND
$2.79
McPHERSON

**The Wertners resort to treachery in their desperation to win the Hornby County Strawberry Growing Contest.**

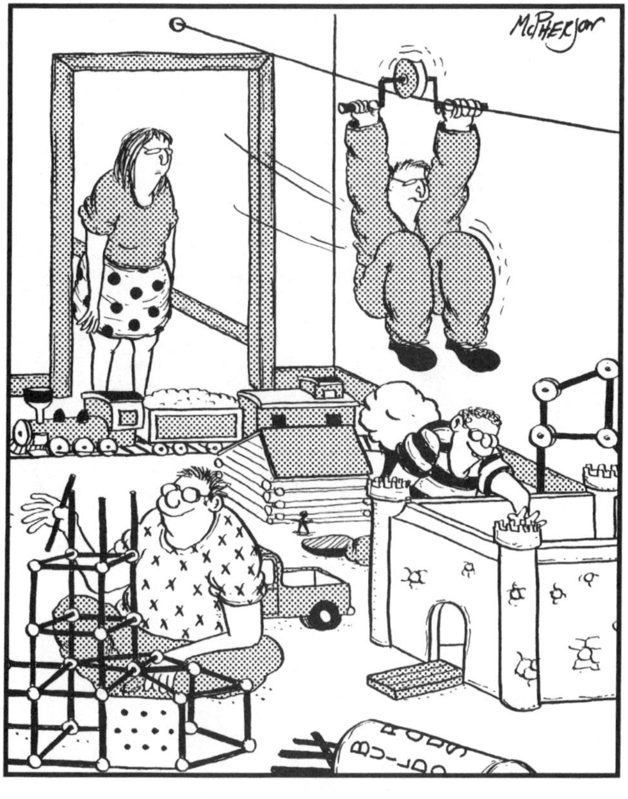

To avoid disturbing the kids' elaborate toy layouts, the Nortsteins wisely installed a zip-line in the family room.

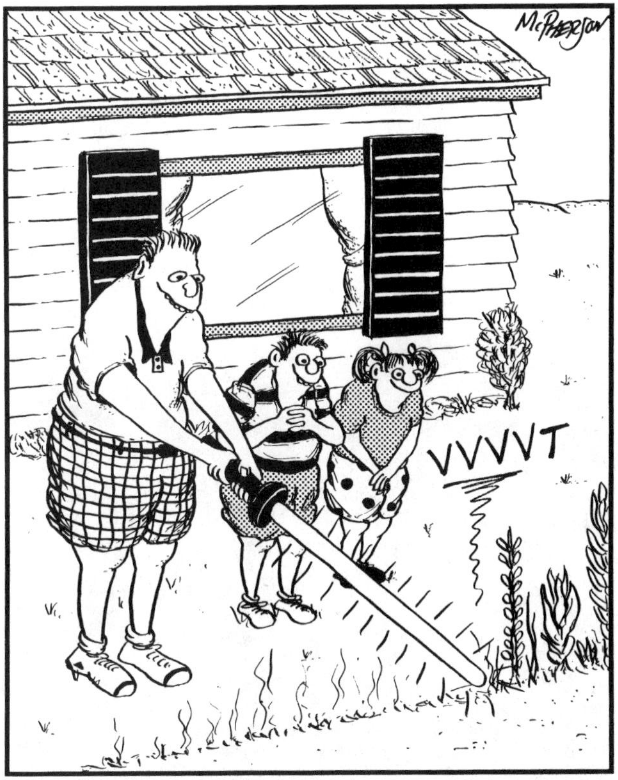
VVVVT

Hoping to cash in on *Star Wars* mania, a leading garden equipment manufacturer introduces its new Lightsaber Weed-Pro.

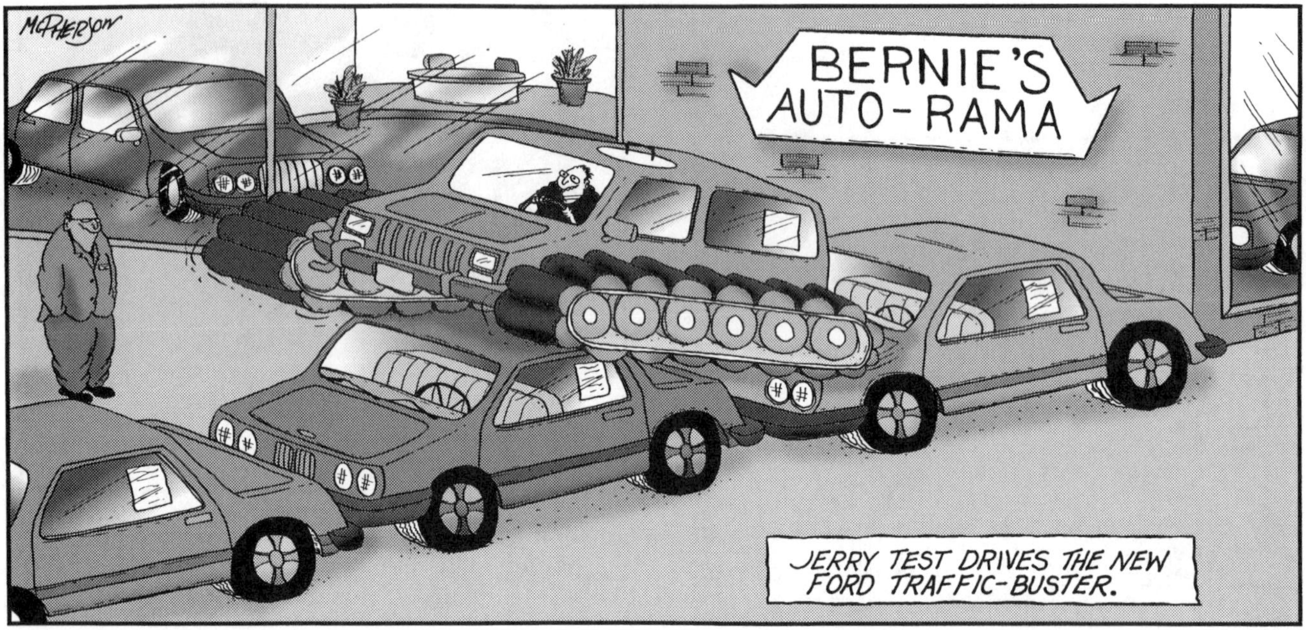
MCPHERSON
BERNIE'S
AUTO-RAMA
JERRY TEST DRIVES THE NEW
FORD TRAFFIC-BUSTER.

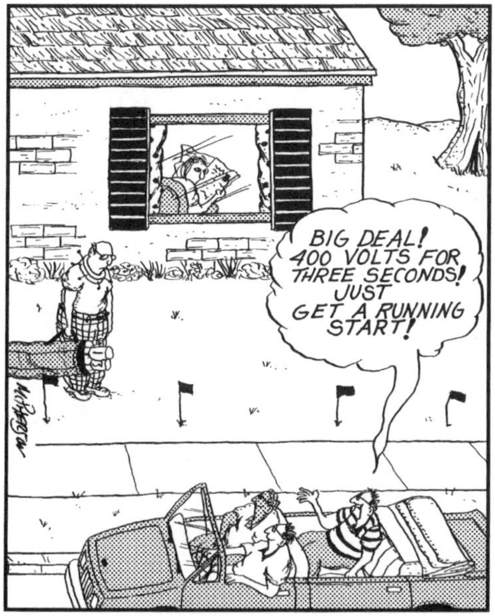
BIG DEAL! 400 VOLTS FOR THREE SECONDS! JUST GET A RUNNING START!
McPHERSON

Hoping to cure him of his golf addiction,
Ted's wife installs an invisible electric fence system.

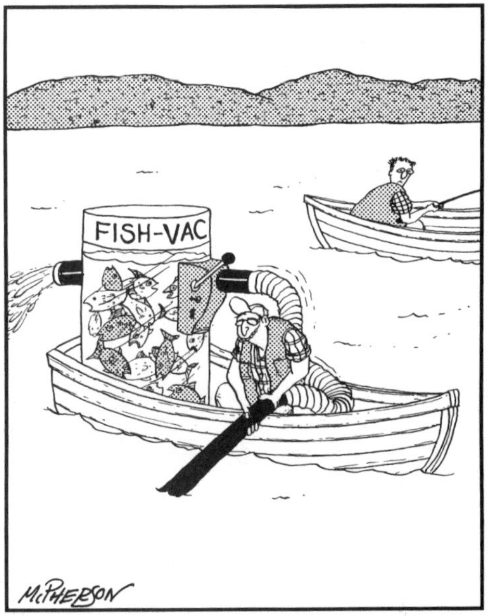
FISH-VAC
McPHERSON

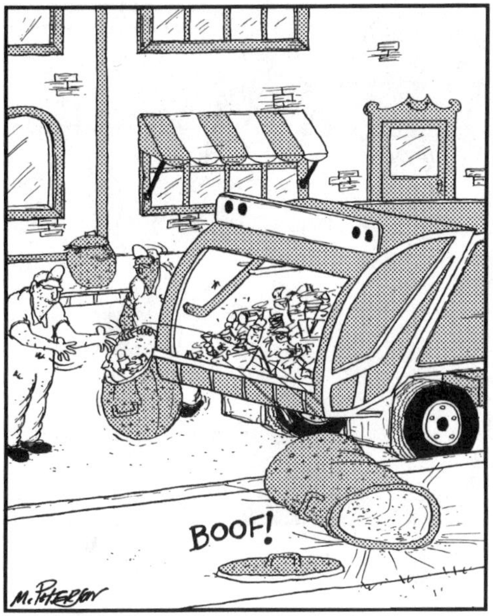
BOOF!
McPHERSON

City dwellers everywhere are sleeping better,
thanks to the advent of Nerf garbage cans.

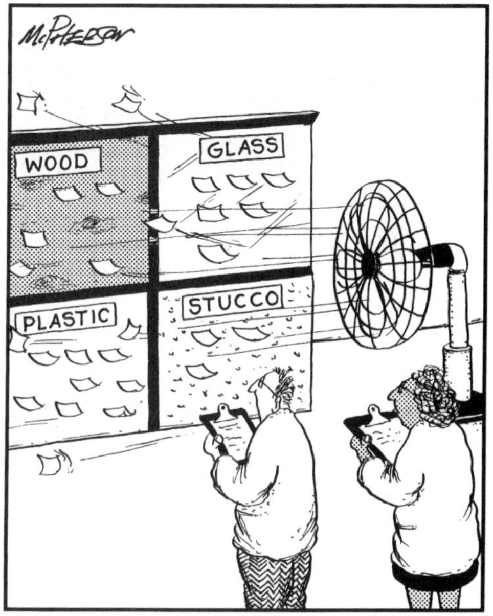
McPHERSON
WOOD
GLASS
PLASTIC
STUCCO

At the Post-it note research laboratory

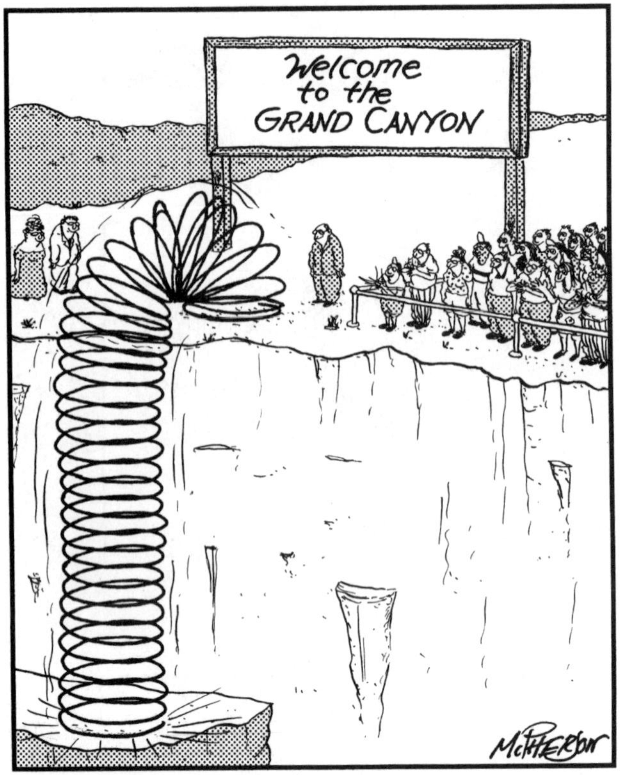
Welcome
to the
GRAND CANYON
McPHERSON

**The Slinky Corporation embarks on its most elaborate promotional campaign ever.**

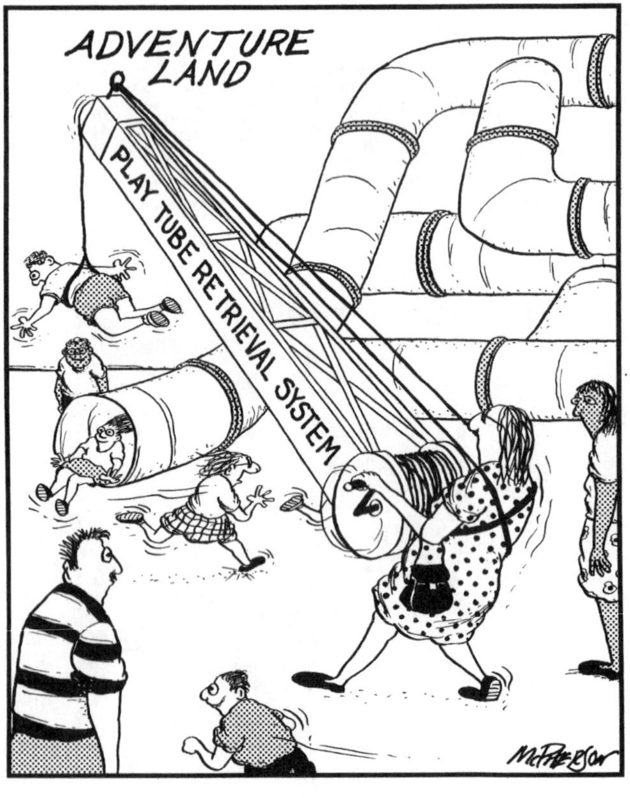
ADVENTURE
LAND
PLAY TUBE RETRIEVAL SYSTEM
McPHERSON

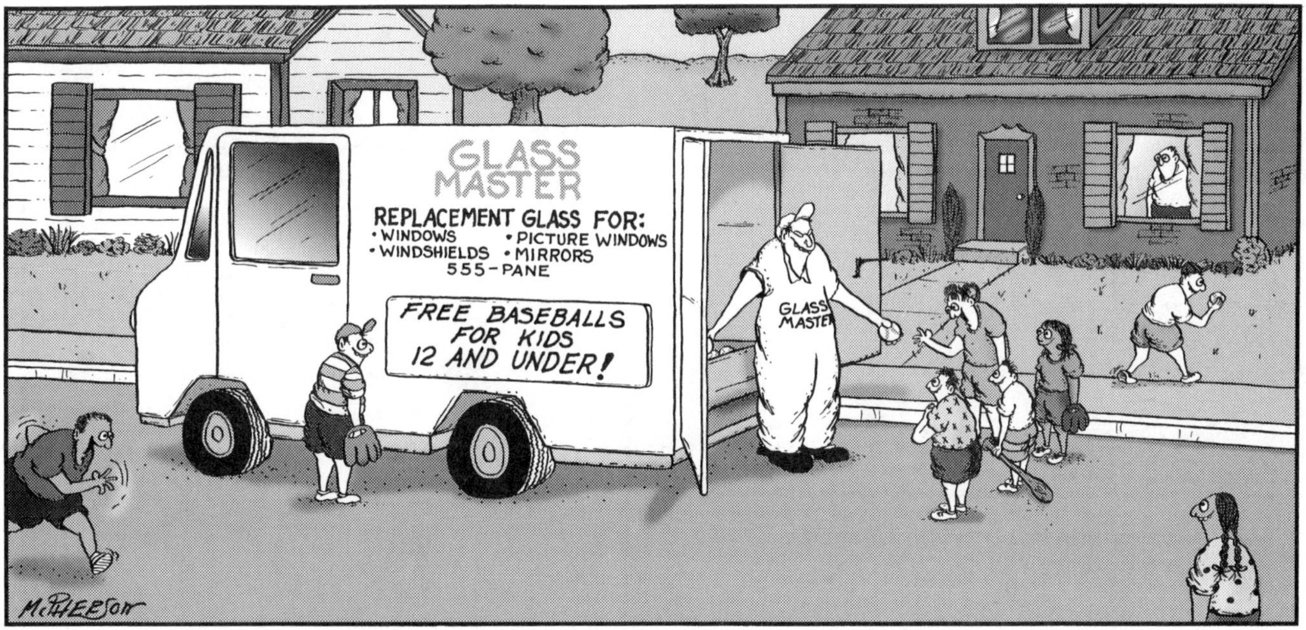
GLASS MASTER
REPLACEMENT GLASS FOR:
• WINDOWS • PICTURE WINDOWS
• WINDSHIELDS • MIRRORS
555-PANE
FREE BASEBALLS FOR KIDS 12 AND UNDER!
GLASS MASTER
McPHERSON

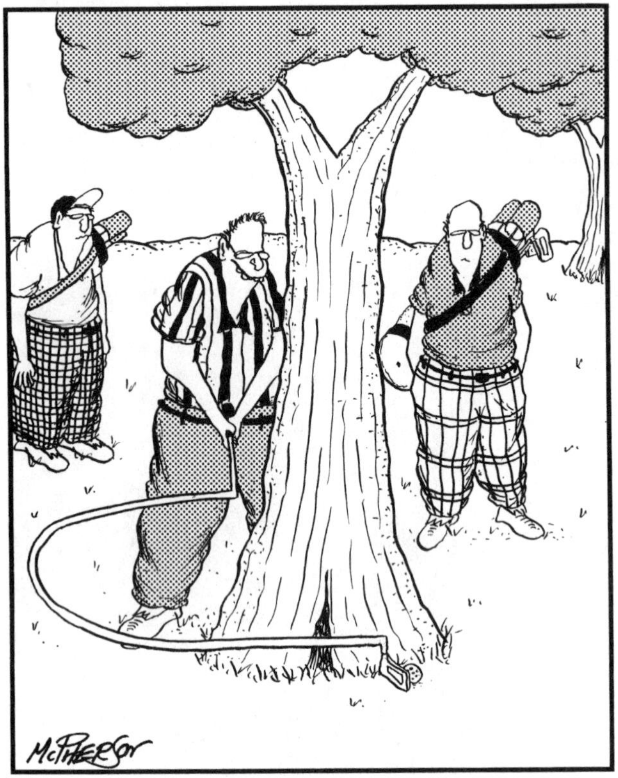

Fortunately, Roger just happened to have a tree wedge in his bag.

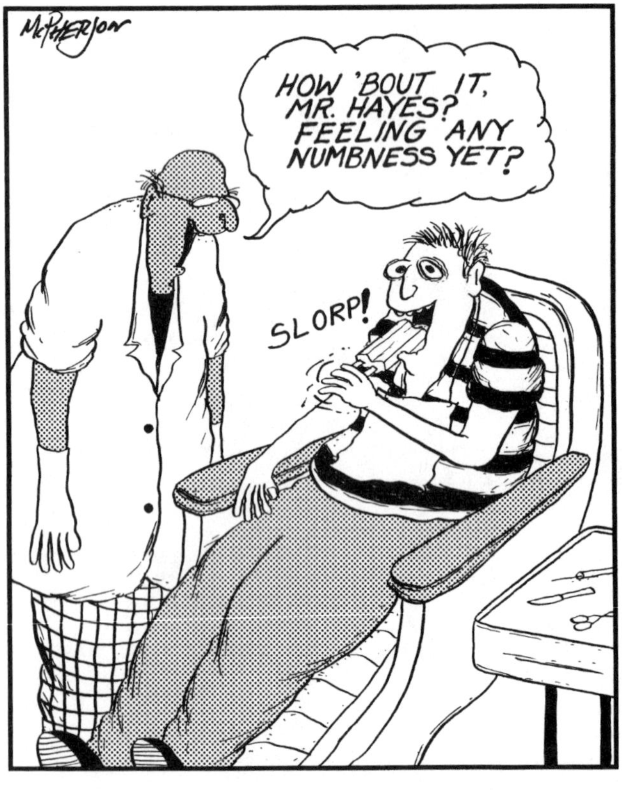
HOW 'BOUT IT, MR. HAYES? FEELING ANY NUMBNESS YET?
SLORP!

Dental technology takes a giant leap forward with the invention of the Novocain pop.

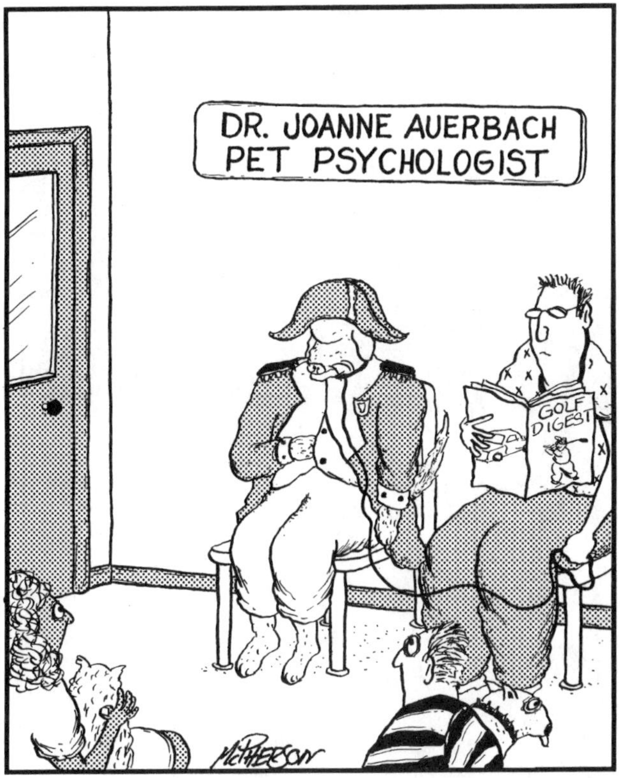
DR. JOANNE AUERBACH
PET PSYCHOLOGIST
GOLF DIGEST

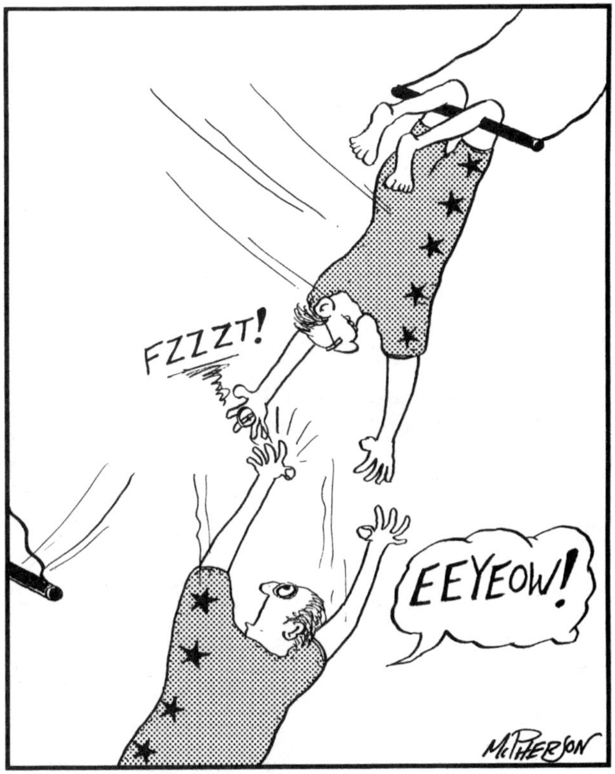
FZZZT!
EEYEOW!

**Pete chooses an inappropriate moment to pull the old joy-buzzer gag.**

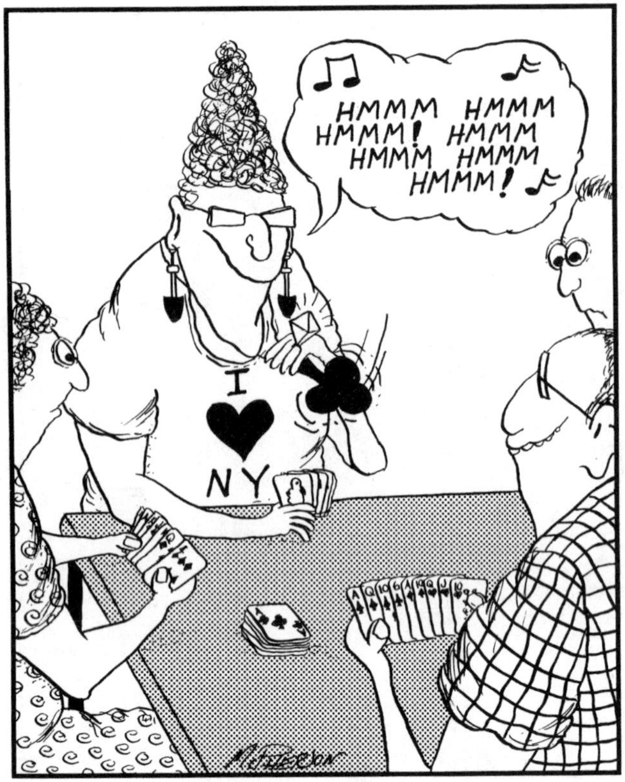
HMMM HMMM HMMM! HMMM HMMM HMMM HMMM!

After losing their eighth straight game of bridge, the Landrys began to suspect that the Morrisons were telegraphing signals to each other.

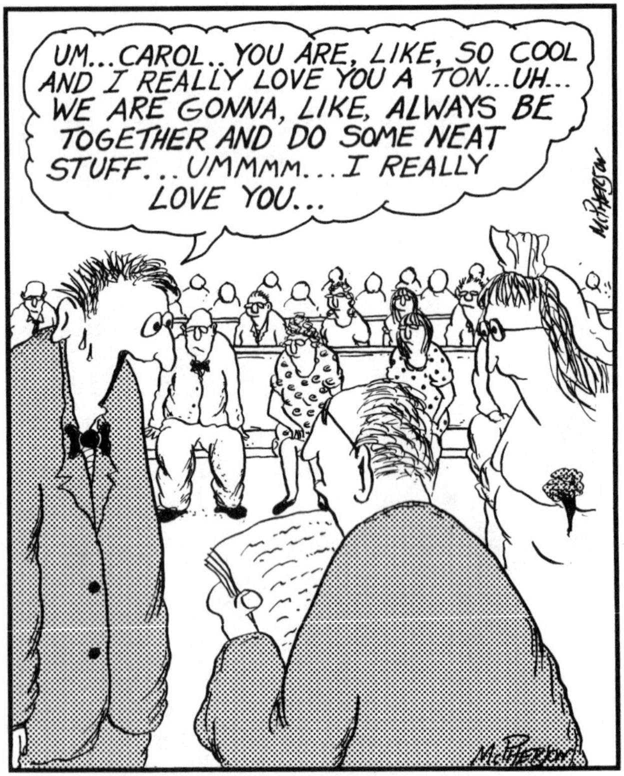
UM...CAROL.. YOU ARE, LIKE, SO COOL AND I REALLY LOVE YOU A TON...UH... WE ARE GONNA, LIKE, ALWAYS BE TOGETHER AND DO SOME NEAT STUFF...UMMMM...I REALLY LOVE YOU...

Within seconds, it was painfully obvious to everyone in the church that Brian had forgotten he was supposed to write his own vows.

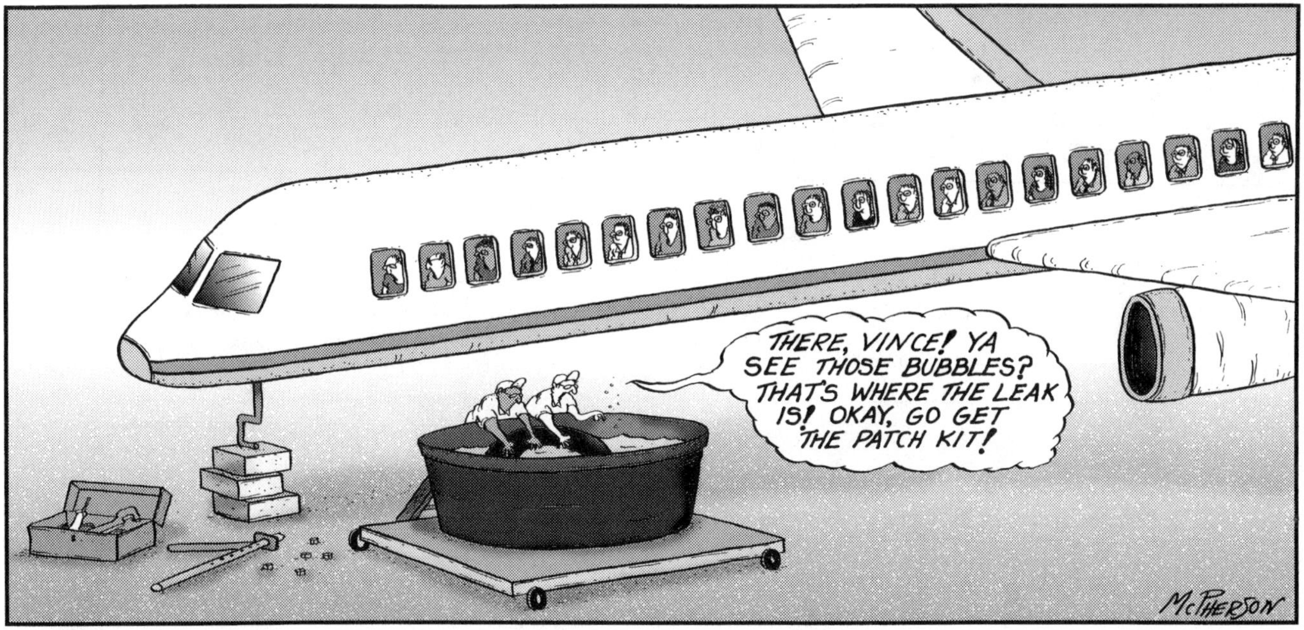
THERE, VINCE! YA SEE THOSE BUBBLES? THAT'S WHERE THE LEAK IS! OKAY, GO GET THE PATCH KIT!
McPHERSON

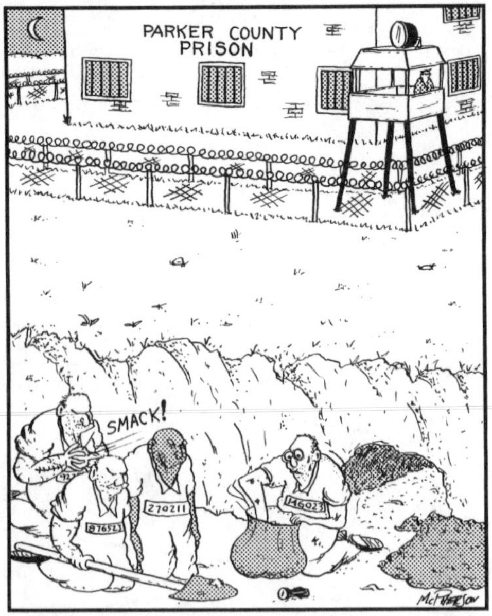
PARKER COUNTY PRISON
SMACK!
270211
146023
McPHERSON

After they emerged from the tunnel, Bruce felt the deathly cold stares of the others as they all realized he had forgotten to pack the juice boxes.

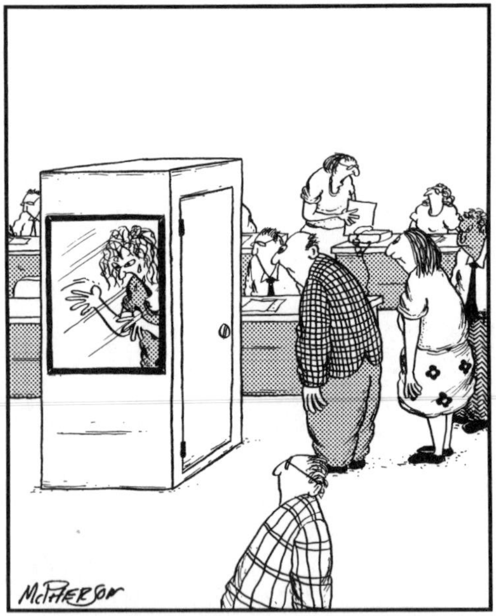
McPHERSON

As part of its new anger-management program, Zorcon Industries installed a soundproof primal scream booth in every office.

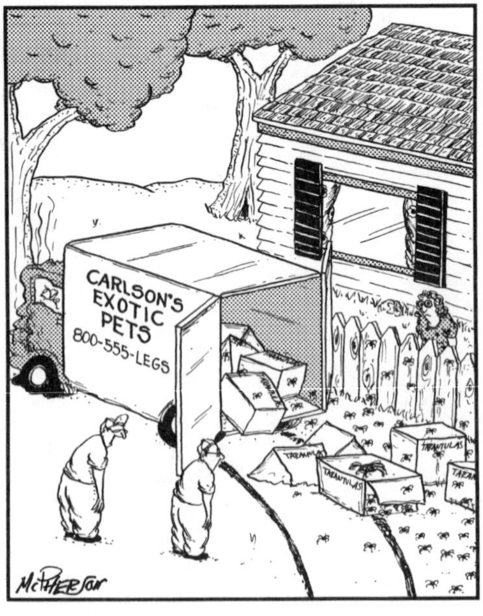
CARLSON'S EXOTIC PETS
800-555-LEGS
TARANTULAS
TARANTULAS
McPHERSON

"Yeah, right, Dave! Like we're gonna scramble around and try to recapture 180,000 tarantulas! Forget about 'em! The insurance will cover it."

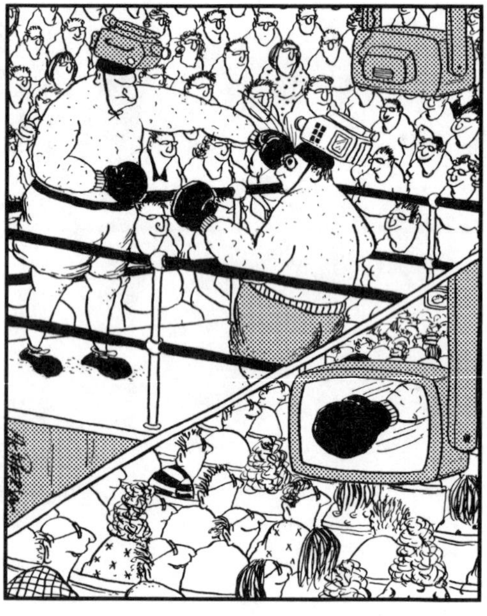

The latest innovation for heavyweight fans: boxer cam

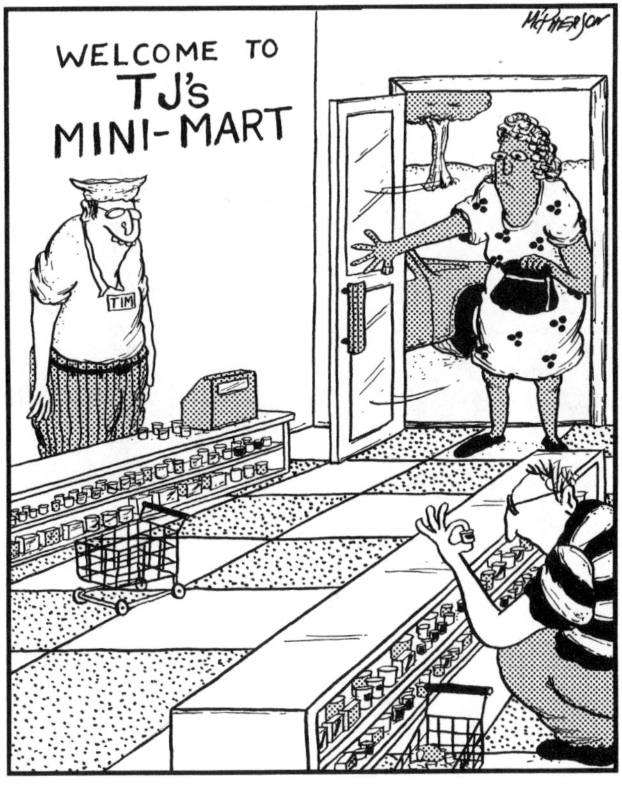
McPHERSON
WELCOME TO
TJ's
MINI-MART
TIM

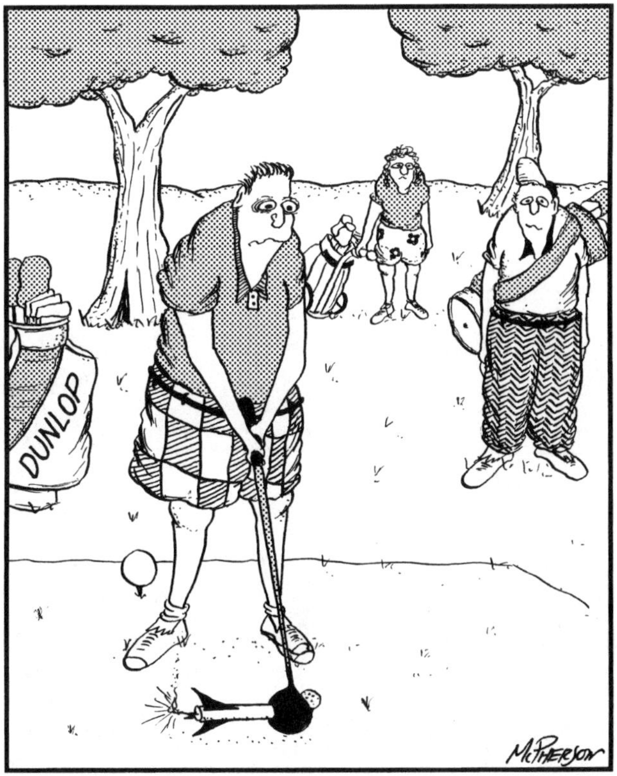
DUNLOP
McPHERSON

**Dwight knew that timing was essential for success with his new Ka-blam™ driver.**

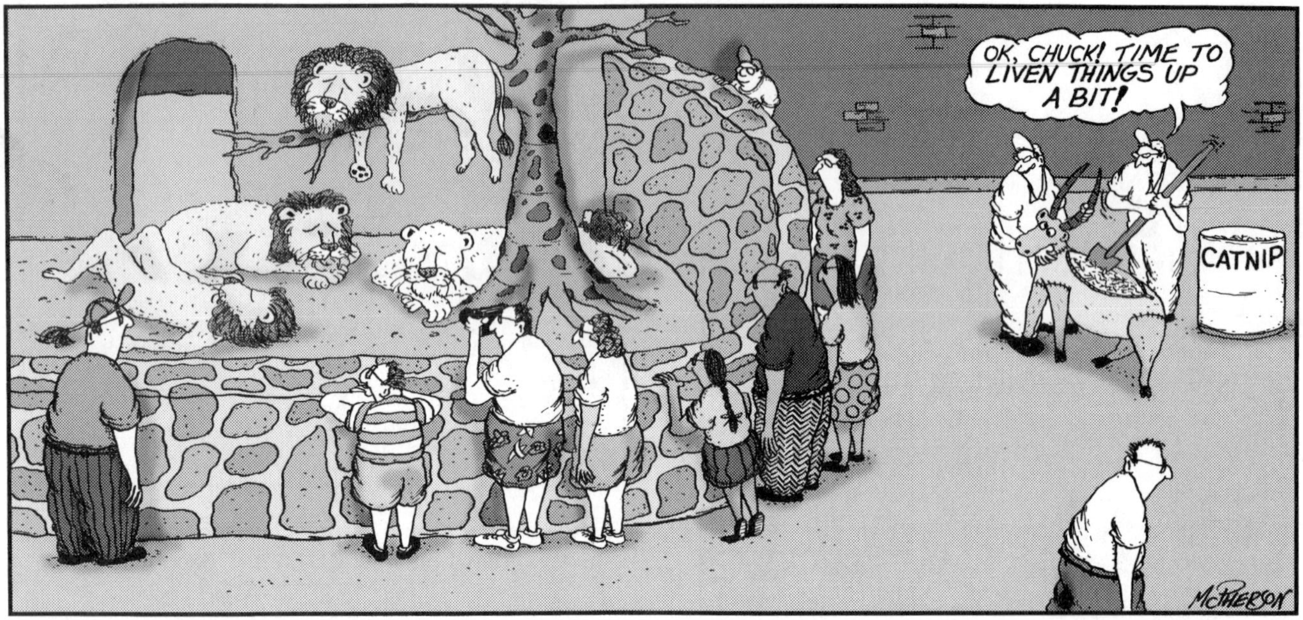
OK, CHUCK! TIME TO LIVEN THINGS UP A BIT!
CATNIP
McPHERSON

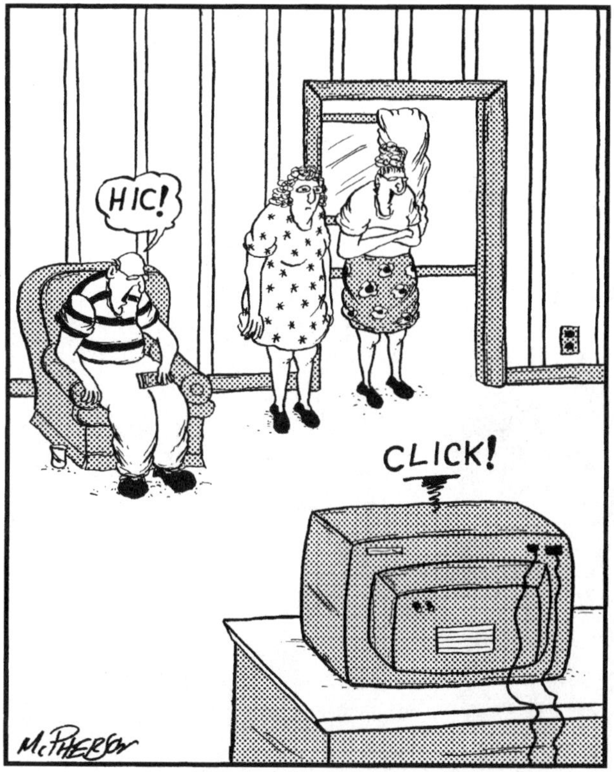
HIC!
CLICK!
McPHERSON

"He's recovering fine. The only problem is that when he hiccups, his pacemaker changes the channel on the TV."

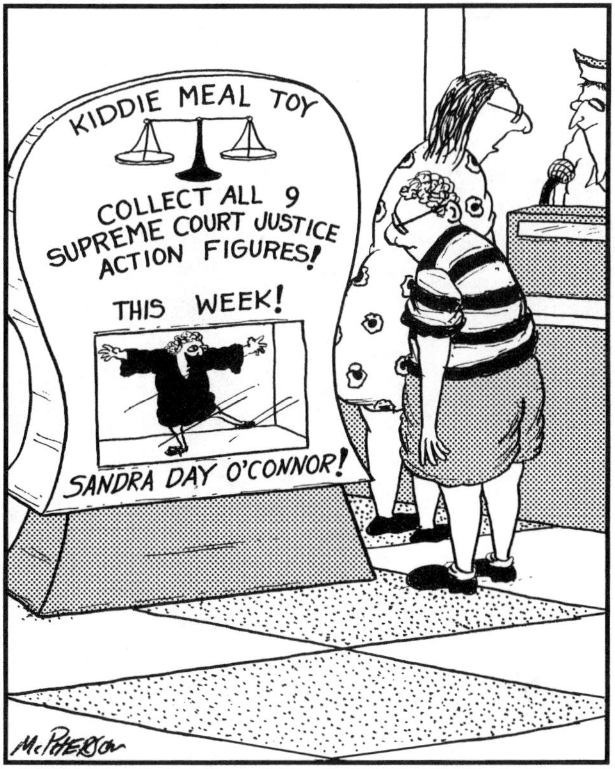
KIDDIE MEAL TOY
COLLECT ALL 9 SUPREME COURT JUSTICE ACTION FIGURES!
THIS WEEK!
SANDRA DAY O'CONNOR!
McPHERSON

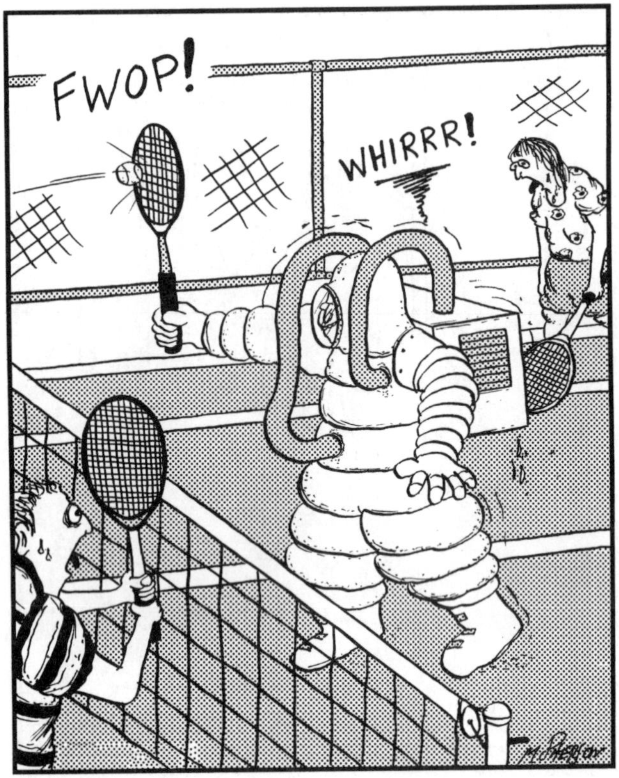
FWOP!
WHIRRR!
McPHERSON

As the others sweltered in the ninety-five-degree heat, Darren's personal air-conditioning system kept him cool and comfortable.

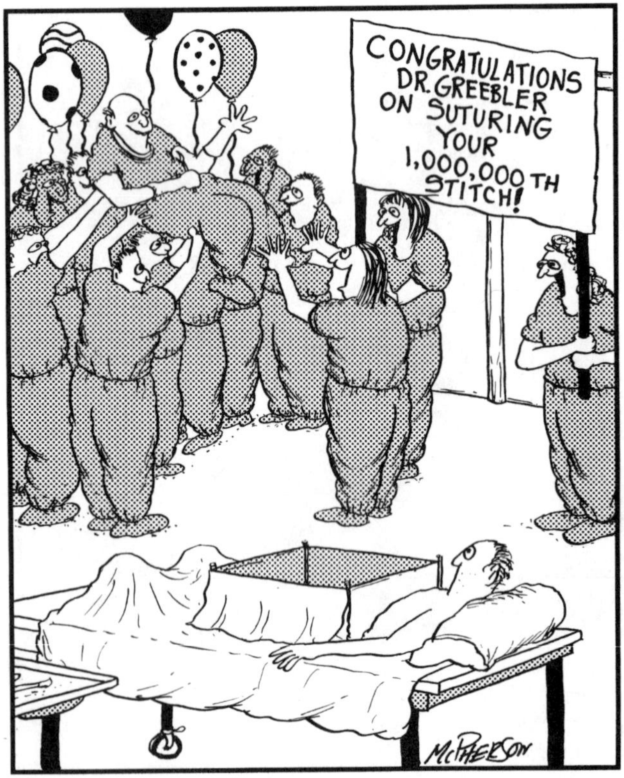
CONGRATULATIONS DR. GREEBLER ON SUTURING YOUR 1,000,000TH STITCH!
McPHERSON

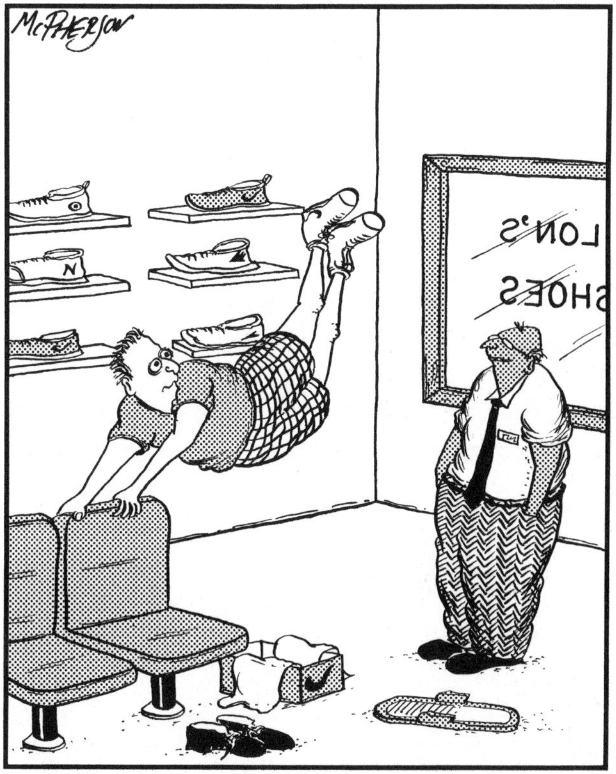
LON'S
SHOES

Gus tries on a pair of the new Helium Nikes.

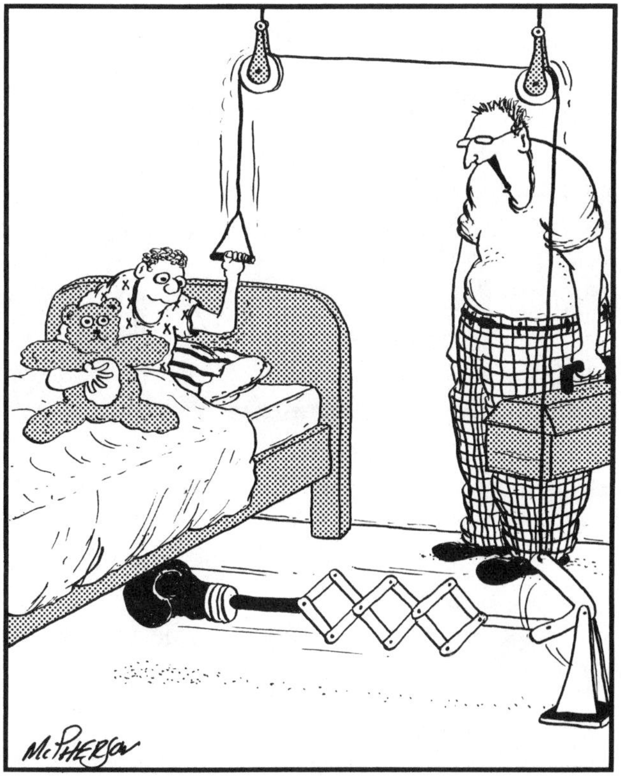

"There now. The next time you think there are monsters under your bed, just yank on that cord and you'll knock those old monsters out cold."

# Angry Letters

One thing I've learned as a cartoonist is that no matter how tame a cartoon may seem, someone out there will be offended by it. Having my e-mail address on my cartoons drives this point home even more clearly. What truly amazes me is not so much that people get upset about cartoons, but that they have the time to write to me about it. And the cartoons that set people off are rarely the ones that I'm expecting to get people a bit riled. Understand, I never set out to upset people with my cartoons. I'm trying to entertain people and get them to laugh. But what is funny to one person is an outrage to another. I think all cartoonists have a fantasy of drawing the perfect cartoon that everyone who sees it would agree is very funny. It'll never happen.

So here are some cartoons that *really* ticked people off and the responses that I got.

Here is a pretty simple, straightforward cartoon. A passenger gets on an airplane and sees that instead of the usual five hundred dials and gauges, this plane just has a big lever that says "Fly" and "Land." What could be upsetting to someone about this?

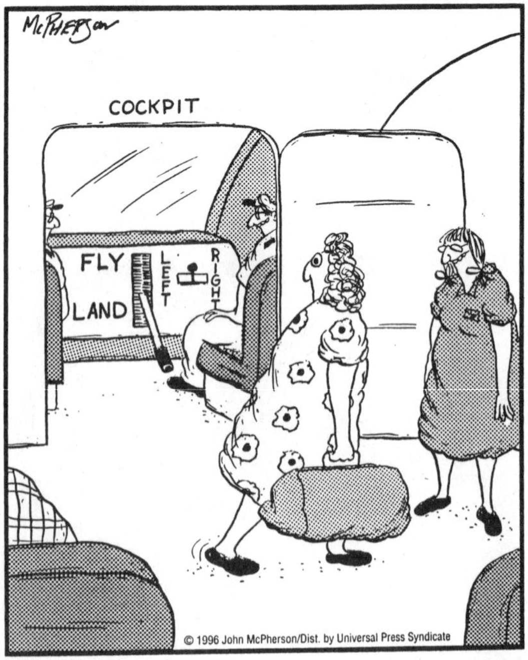
McPherson
COCKPIT
FLY
LAND
LEFT
RIGHT
© 1996 John McPherson/Dist. by Universal Press Syndicate

*Dear Mr. McPherson:*

*I am a pilot for TWA. NEVER in my entire life have I been so offended and disgusted by a cartoon! How dare you insinuate that my job is so mindless as to be performed by the simple switching of a lever. Obviously, you have never seen the inside of an airliner's cockpit. Rather than the simplistic machine you show it to be, an airplane has hundreds of controls that require years of study to master. We pilots train relentlessly so that people like you can be carried safely to your destination.*

*In the future I hope you will pause and reflect before you so thoughtlessly hurt people with your attempt at humor.*

*Sincerely,*

*Phil, TWA pilot*

You can imagine what I wanted to say to this guy, but I try to wait a day before I respond to a nutty e-mail. I wrote back the next day and told him that yes, I understood that airplanes have hundreds of dials and gauges, but wouldn't it be funny if there was just this *one* airplane that was controlled by a big lever? I schmoozed a bit about what a great job pilots do and the following day got this response:

*Dear John:*
*I looked at the cartoon again. I can't believe what a jerk I was. Please accept my apologies and keep up the great work.*

I was pretty stunned, I have to say. Nice to get a little vindication.

This next cartoon got me more outraged e-mails than any I have ever done. It's really kind of a weird cartoon. Sometimes I'm not even sure what I was trying to say with it, but man, did ferret owners get ticked. Here is one of over three hundred angry e-mails that I got after this appeared.

*Dear Mr. McPherson:*
*Today's cartoon is a vile and heinous depiction of ferrets! Ferrets are warm and loving creatures who would never harm a soul. Your cartoon cruelly perpetuates a stereotype of ferrets as being vicious animals.*
*SHAME ON YOU!*
*Disgustedly,*
*A reader in Worcerster, Massachussetts*

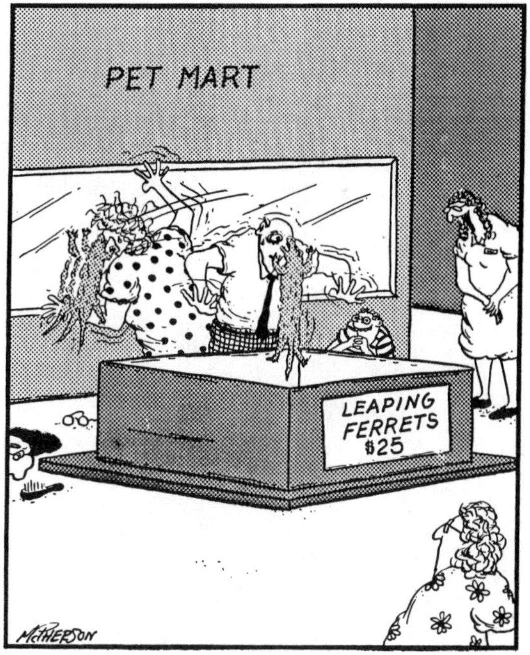
PET MART
LEAPING FERRETS $25
McPHERSON
"Those are 20 percent off."

Now, honestly, I knew nothing about ferrets at the time. I didn't know if they bit people or not. I just kind of liked the phrase "leaping ferrets." But apparently it's a pretty sensitive topic. I remember some of the e-mails said, "Die, ferret-hating scum!!" After I'd gotten about one hundred or so angry e-mails, I got the following e-mail:

*Dear Mr. McPherson:*
*Today's cartoon about the ferrets was fantastic! We used to own two ferrets but we had to get rid of them because they constantly bit the snot out of our noses!*
*Thanks for showing what ferrets are truly like.*
*Sincerely,*
*A reader in Ohio*

Now I realized there were two sides to the ferret debate. And as more angry e-mails poured in about how cuddly and nice ferrets are, I would just forward this guy's e-mail on to them. Along with the 350 or more angry e-mails, I also received about 250 e-mails telling stories about ferrets biting their owners.

I really don't know what ferrets are like and wasn't trying to ferret-bash. I've often done cartoons about toddlers who throw tantrums, so am I saying that all little kids are raging monsters? Of course not. Likewise, I wasn't inferring that all ferrets bite. It's just pretty amazing how many ferret owners got their hackles up over this.

I do cartoons on all kinds of medicine, and rarely if ever do I get an upset letter from medical people—except for chiropractors. I guess for some reason they are sensitive about the legitimacy of their work (hey, I go to a chiropractor!) so when a cartoon appears, some of them feel they are being mocked, which they *are*. But then again, I mock everyone and try to be an equal-opportunity mocker. I'm just trying to get people to laugh, not make sweeping statements about someone or some profession, except chiropractors. (I'M KIDDING! I'M KIDDING!).

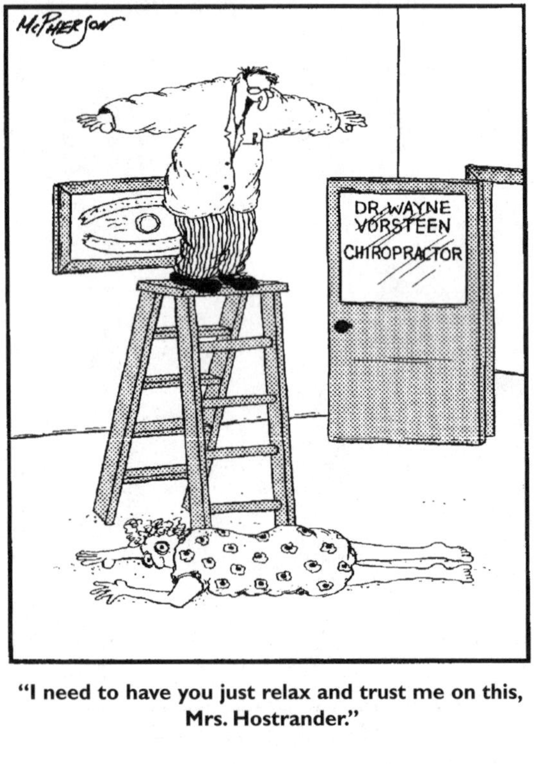
McPherson
DR. WAYNE VORSTEEN
CHIROPRACTOR
**"I need to have you just relax and trust me on this, Mrs. Hostrander."**

Anyway, several chiropractors were upset by this cartoon, but I thought this e-mail was the best of them.

*Dear Sir:*

*While I understand your intent at humor regarding this cartoon, we in the chiropractic field have worked long and hard to educate the public about the benefits of properly applied spinal manipulative therapy and dispel scary myths and stereotypes. One little cartoon in a syndicated feature like yours does more to undermine our efforts than you can imagine!*

*On the day that this cartoon appeared in our local paper, a seventy-six-year-old female patient failed to show up for her weekly appointment. We called her home and grew concerned when she did not answer. About an hour later, one of my staff members found her in our hallway. She was sobbing and held up a copy of your cartoon, and*

*said she was not going to come for her appointment because she did not want THIS to happen to her.*

*It took my staff and me forty-five minutes to calm her and convince her that I was not going to jump off a stepladder onto her back. . . .*

He continued with more rhetoric, but that was the meat of the letter.

Here was my response:

*Dear Dr. Miller* (the name has been changed to protect the nutty):

*Do you honestly expect me to believe that because of my cartoon, readers across America now think that chiropractors routinely jump off stepladders as part of their treatment? If that's the case, you have not done nearly the job of educating the public that you think you have.*

*Regards,*

*John McPherson*

He actually wrote back a few days later to tell me that seven more patients had fearfully brought in my cartoon and were afraid to receive treatment. What could I even say to that? There are some real nuts out there.

Meanwhile, I received scores of e-mails from other chiropractors telling me how much they liked the cartoon.

What could be upsetting about this cartoon? Read on.

*Dear Mr. McPherson:*

*Bathroom humor is NOT acceptable in a family newspaper! I do not choose to have such in my paper!*

*CLEAN UP YOUR ACT!*

*Disgustedly,*

*A reader in Washington, D.C.*

This woman was upset not by the snake coming out of the toilet, but by the fact that there was a drawing of a toilet in the cartoon. When you consider the fact

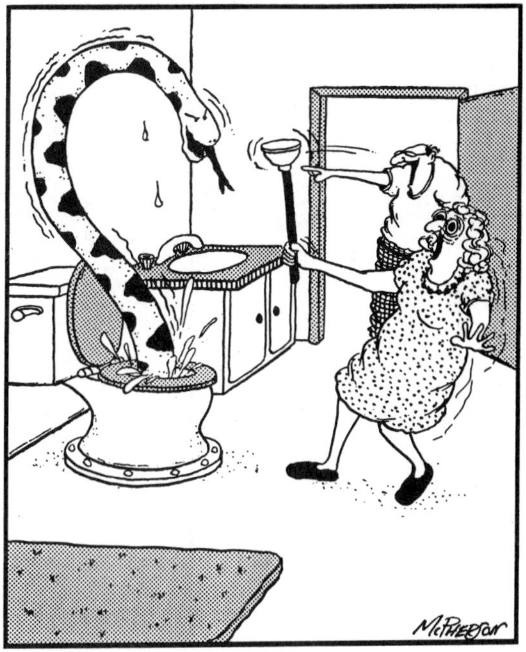
McPherson

**"Calm down, Lois! You're getting all worked up over nothing! Look at the shape of its head. That snake's not poisonous!"**

that most papers only run *Close to Home* about three inches high, she was offended by a ¼-inch drawing of a toilet. Which makes me wonder what seeing a *real* toilet up close must do to her. I considered this one too nutty to even respond to.

In addition to upset letters, I do get some really cool letters as well. It's always fun to get feedback from people all over the world and know that people are out there tuning in.

This cartoon got a lot of very favorable responses. A lot of people who had had angioplasty wrote to tell me how much they appreciated the humor. But one man in particular made my day. He wrote to tell me that on the day that this cartoon appeared in his paper, he was scheduled for angioplasty following a heart attack. When the surgical team saw the cartoon in the paper that day, they took the cartoon, blew it up to poster size, and plastered it all over the operating room. When he was wheeled in for the surgery, he saw the cartoon and started laughing and everyone in the OR broke out laughing as well. He wanted me to know how the cartoon helped defuse the tension of the moment and helped get him through a harrowing time in his life.

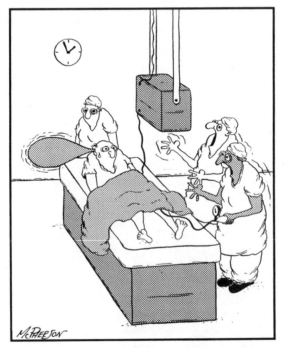

**Ted's balloon angioplasty procedure gets off to a rough start.**

Soon after this cartoon ran, I got a letter from the public information office at the Supreme Court, saying they loved this cartoon and asked if it would be possible to get the original. So, of course I whisked it over to them.

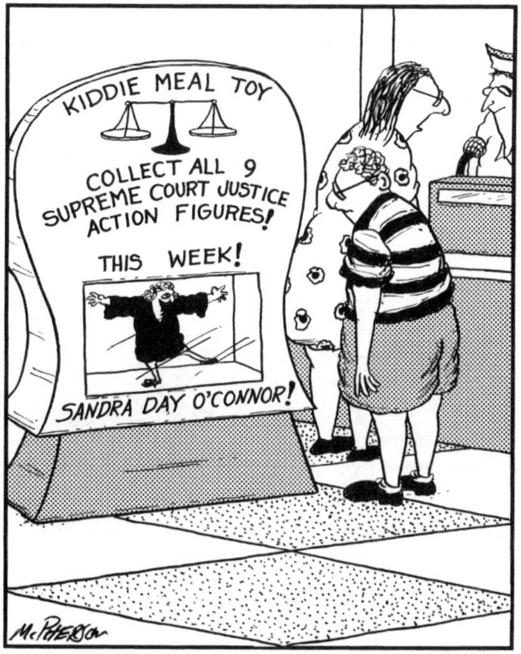
KIDDIE MEAL TOY
COLLECT ALL 9 SUPREME COURT JUSTICE ACTION FIGURES!
THIS WEEK!
SANDRA DAY O'CONNOR!
McPHERSON

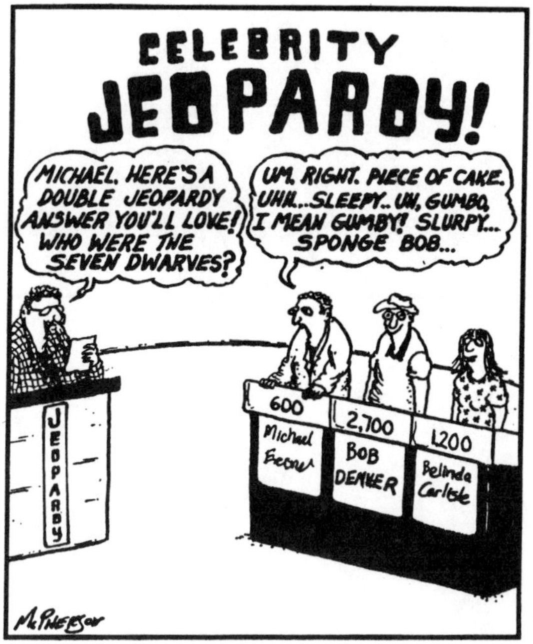
CELEBRITY
JEOPARDY!
MICHAEL, HERE'S A DOUBLE JEOPARDY ANSWER YOU'LL LOVE! WHO WERE THE SEVEN DWARVES?
UM, RIGHT. PIECE OF CAKE. UHH...SLEEPY.. UH, GUMBO, I MEAN GUMBY! SLURPY... SPONGE BOB...
JEOPARDY
600
Michael Eisner
2,700
BOB DENVER
1,200
Belinda Carlisle
McPHERSON

An awkward moment for Michael Eisner

The day after this cartoon ran I got a call from Disney saying that an anonymous buyer wished to purchase the cartoon. I said, anonymous, eh? They refused to reveal who the buyer was. So I sold it to them, and then a few weeks later got a very nice letter from Michael Eisner, thanking me for featuring him in a cartoon and for the original. Very cool of him, I thought.

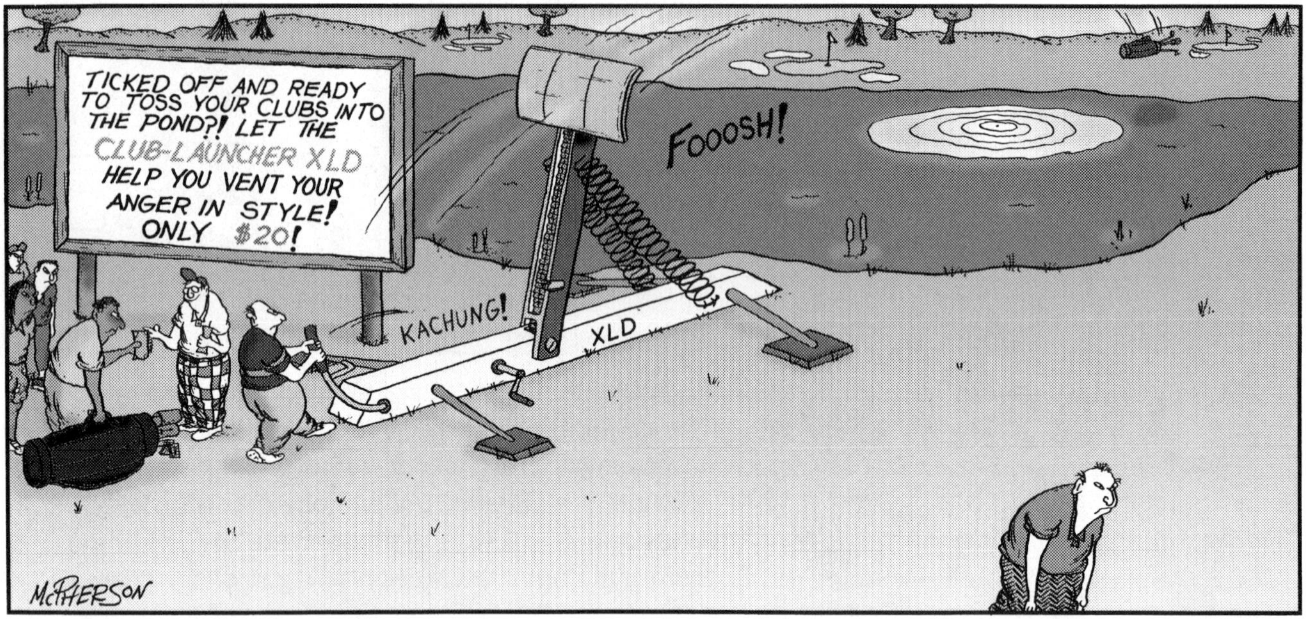
TICKED OFF AND READY TO TOSS YOUR CLUBS INTO THE POND?! LET THE CLUB-LAUNCHER XLD HELP YOU VENT YOUR ANGER IN STYLE! ONLY $20!
FOOOSH!
KACHUNG!
XLD
McPHERSON

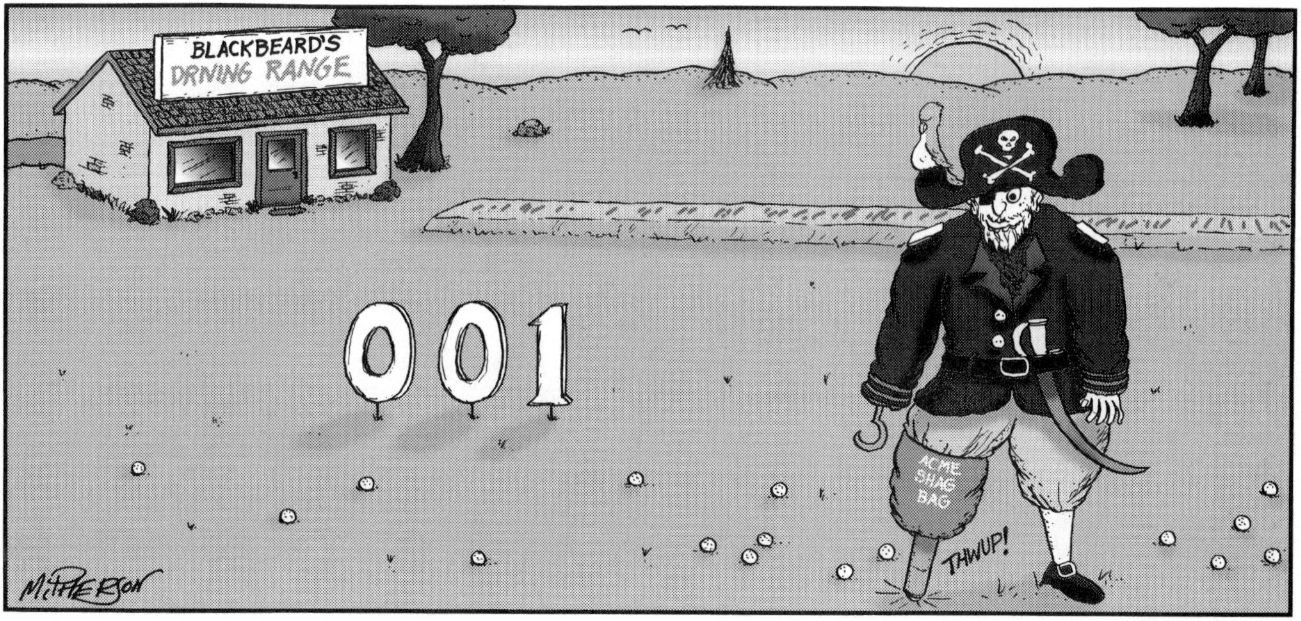
BLACKBEARD'S
DRIVING RANGE
001
ACME
SHAG
BAG
THWUP!
McPHERSON

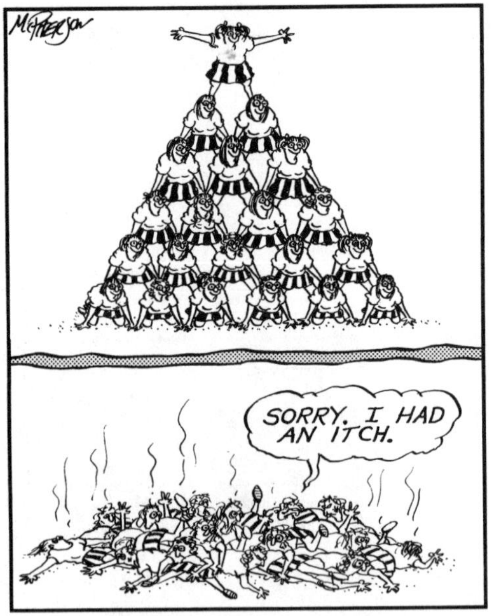
McPHERSON
SORRY, I HAD AN ITCH.

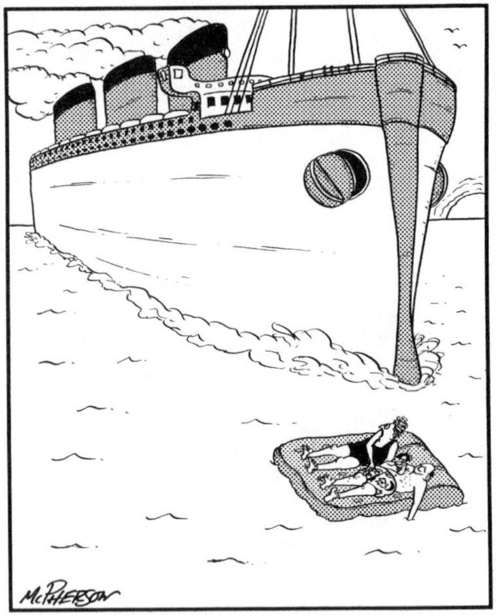
McPHERSON

"Bert, wake up! *Wake up!*"

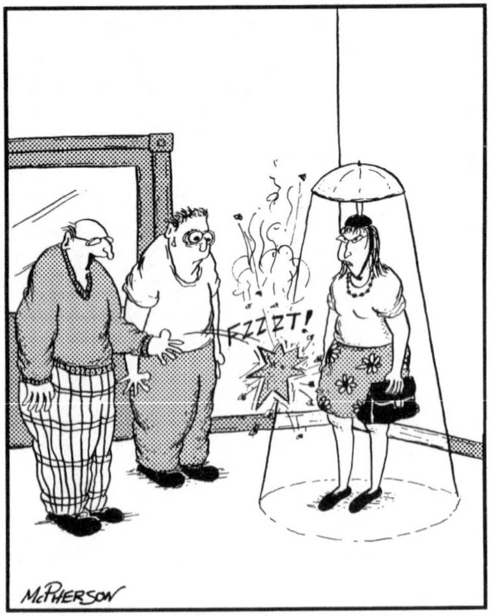
FZZZT!
McPHERSON

"Mike, watch me demonstrate how the force field around my daughter works using this old shoe. Oooo! Look at that. Totally disintegrated."

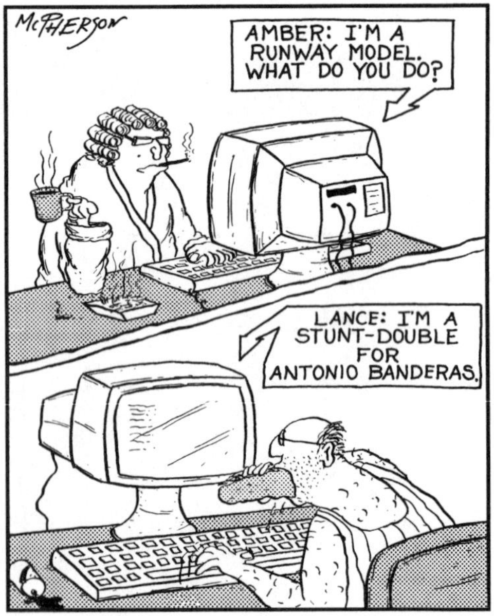
McPHERSON
AMBER: I'M A RUNWAY MODEL. WHAT DO YOU DO?
LANCE: I'M A STUNT-DOUBLE FOR ANTONIO BANDERAS.

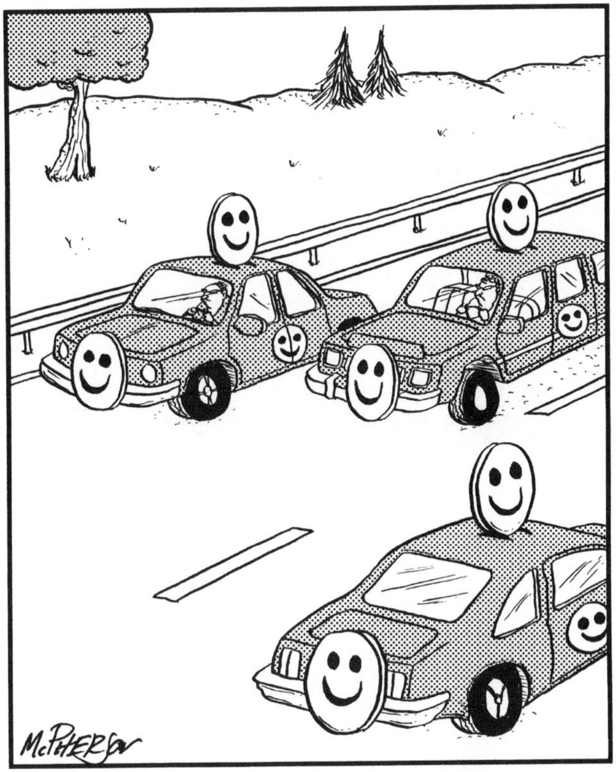
McPHERSON

Hoping to reduce road rage, many states now issue mandatory goodwill decals for all vehicles.

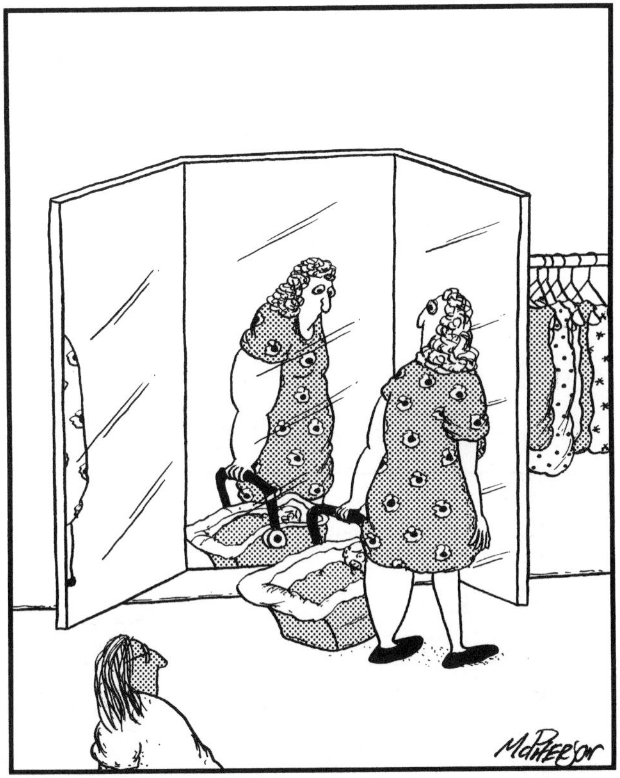
McPHERSON

Suddenly, Velma realized the effect that eight months of car-seat-hauling had had on her.

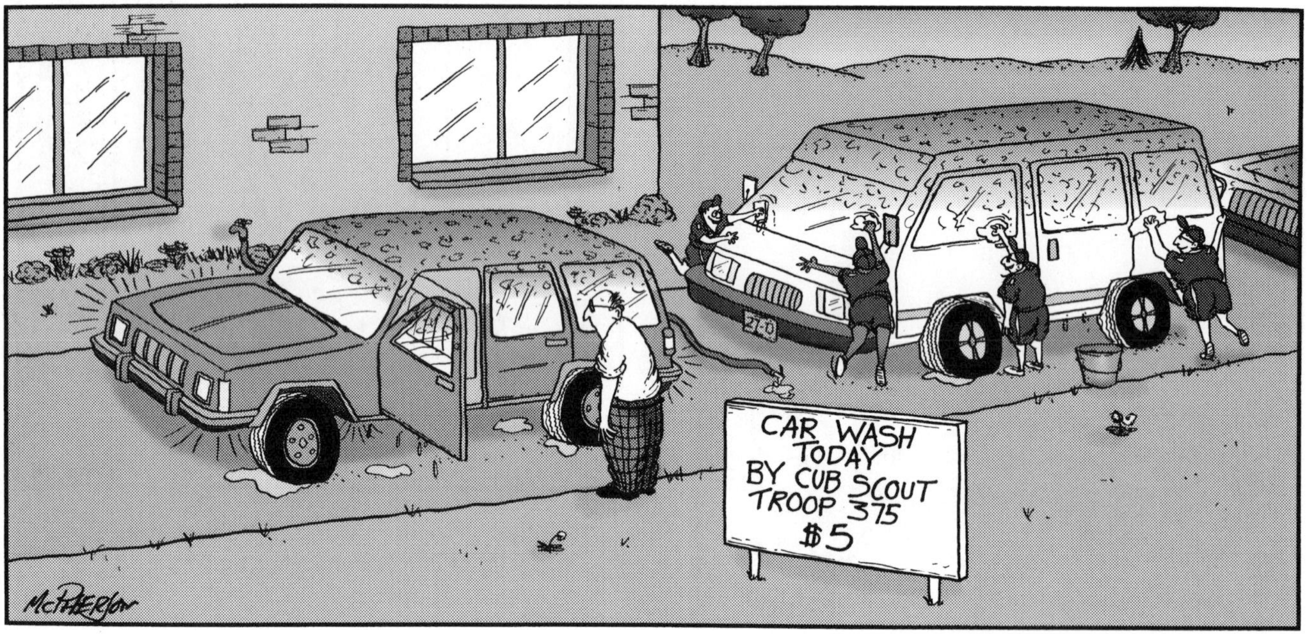
CAR WASH
TODAY
BY CUB SCOUT
TROOP 375
$5
McPHERSON

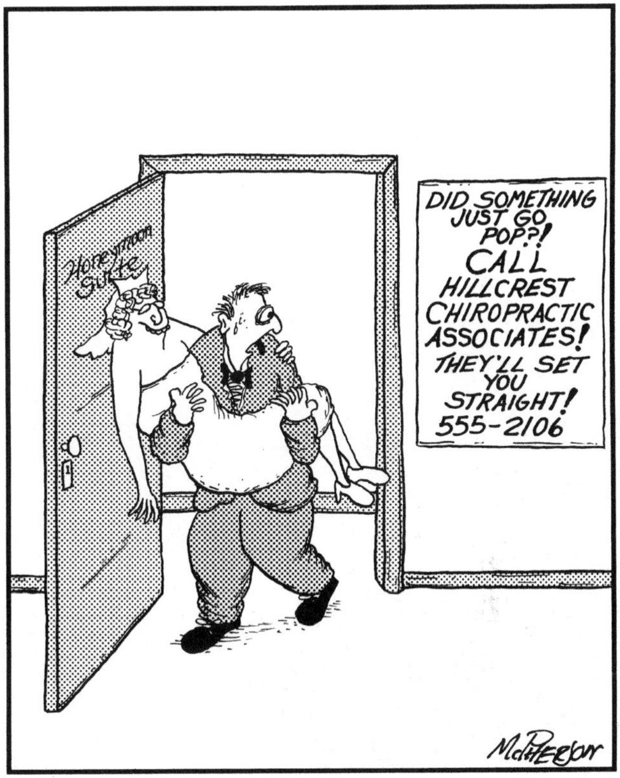
Honeymoon Suite
DID SOMETHING JUST GO POP?!
CALL HILLCREST CHIROPRACTIC ASSOCIATES!
THEY'LL SET YOU STRAIGHT!
555-2106

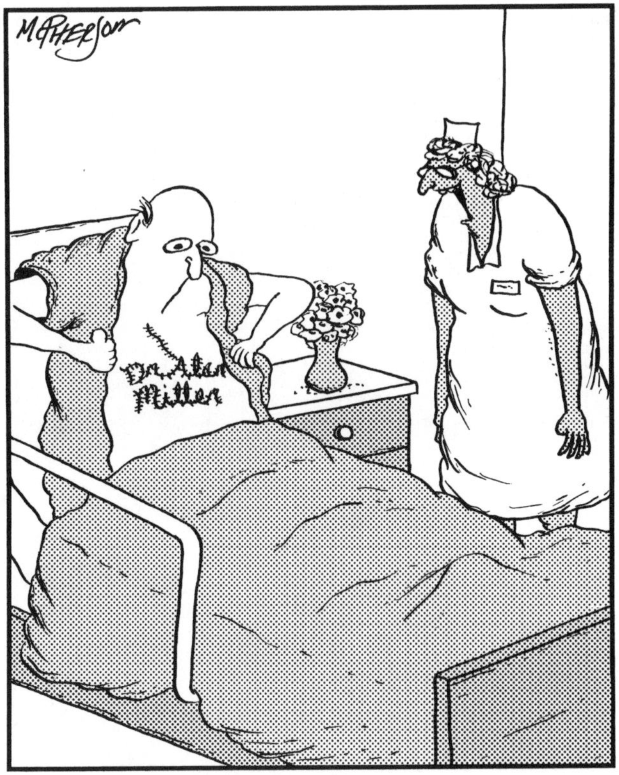
Dr. Alan Miller

"Do you have any idea how much an original Dr. Miller scar will be worth someday?"

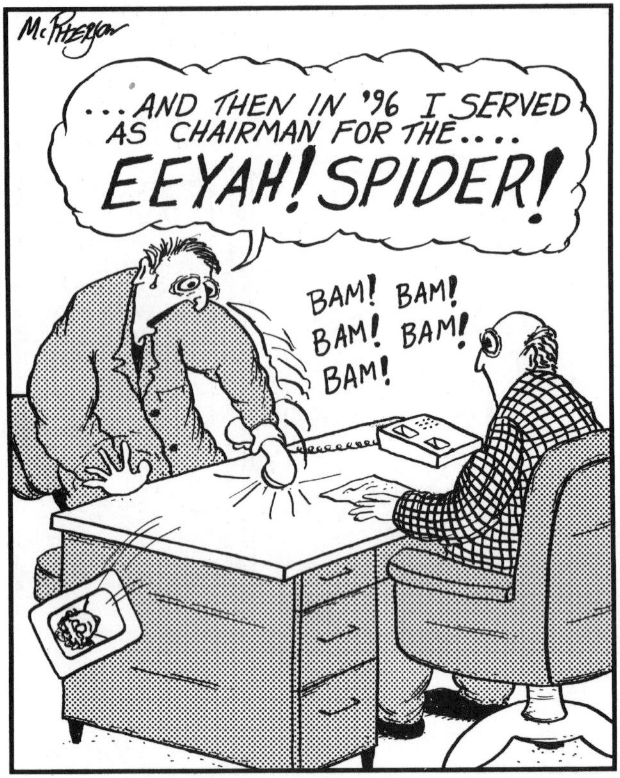
McPHERSON
...AND THEN IN '96 I SERVED AS CHAIRMAN FOR THE....
EEYAH! SPIDER!
BAM! BAM! BAM! BAM! BAM!

**Ted's bid to become director of the Entomology department at Penn State goes awry.**

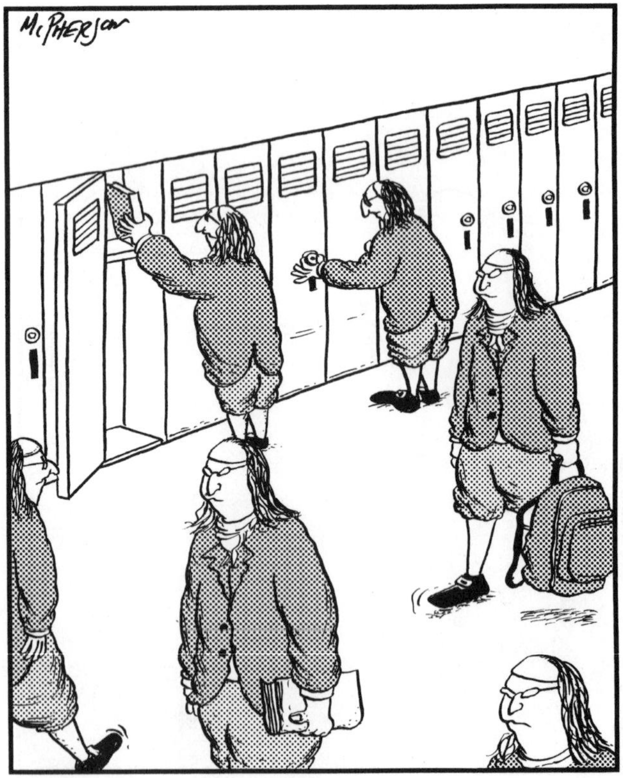
McPHERSON

**Nobody at Ben Franklin Senior High was too psyched about the school's new dress code.**

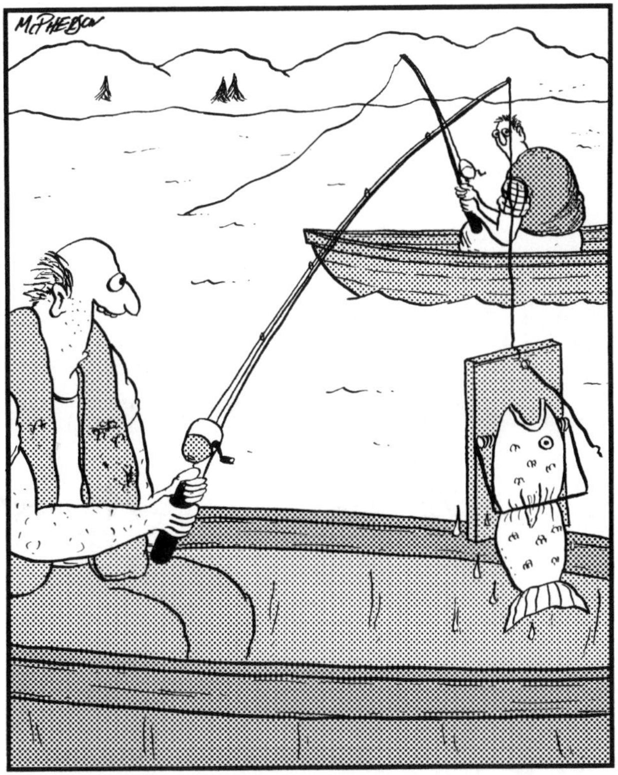
McPHERSON

"Takin' 'em off the hook gives me the creeps."

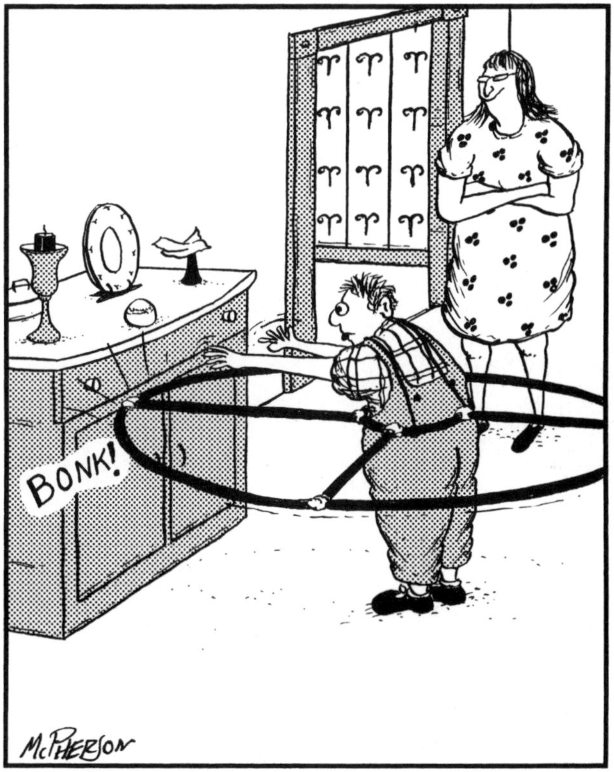
BONK!
McPHERSON

Thanks to a hula hoop and some ingenuity, Diane was able to toddler-proof her entire house in no time flat.

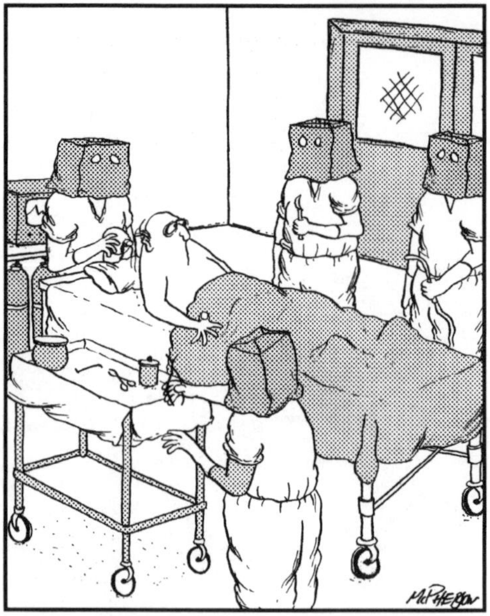
McPherson

"Calm down, Mr. Metzler. We're all out of surgical masks, that's all."

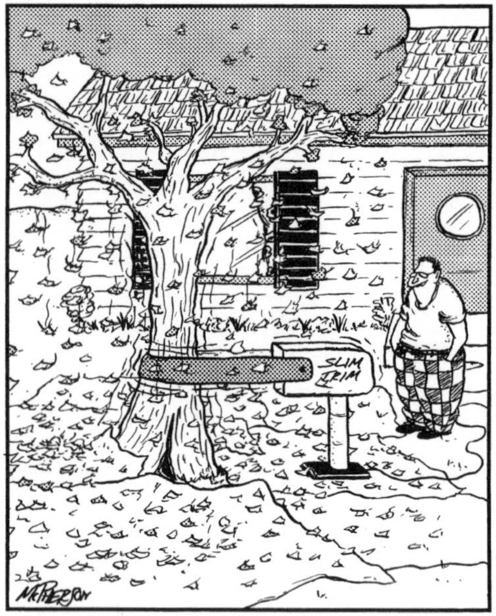
SLIM TRIM
McPherson

Wade finds a simple alternative to raking leaves.

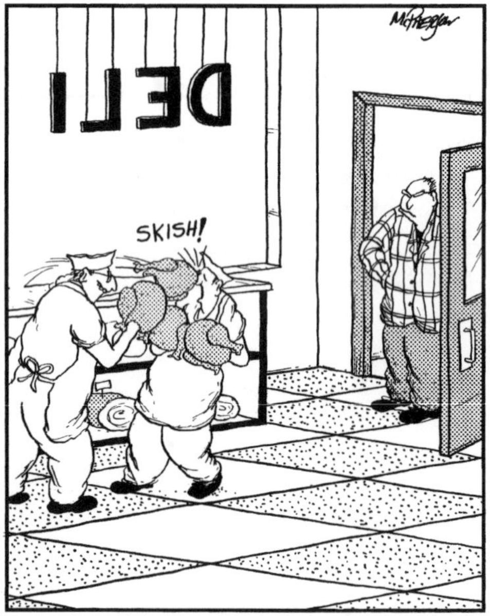
McPherson
DELI
SKISH!

Unbeknownst to them, Bruce and Rodney's sparring days were history.

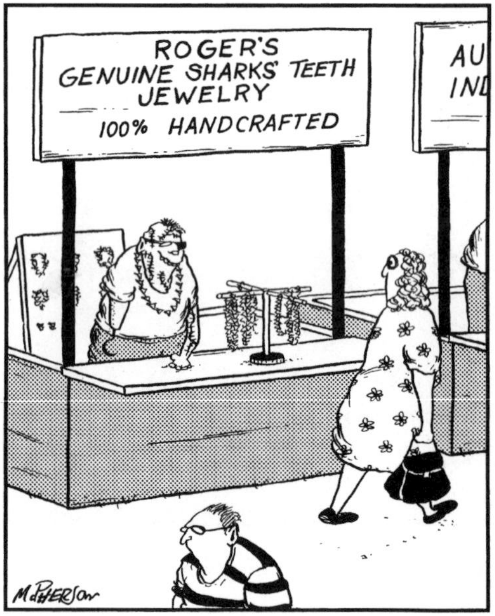
ROGER'S
GENUINE SHARKS' TEETH
JEWELRY
100% HANDCRAFTED
McPherson

"Well, I'd like to see how well you could drive
if a Japanese beetle landed on *your* knee!"

Veteran hot dog vendor Lenny Piltz does
his best to stave off job burnout.

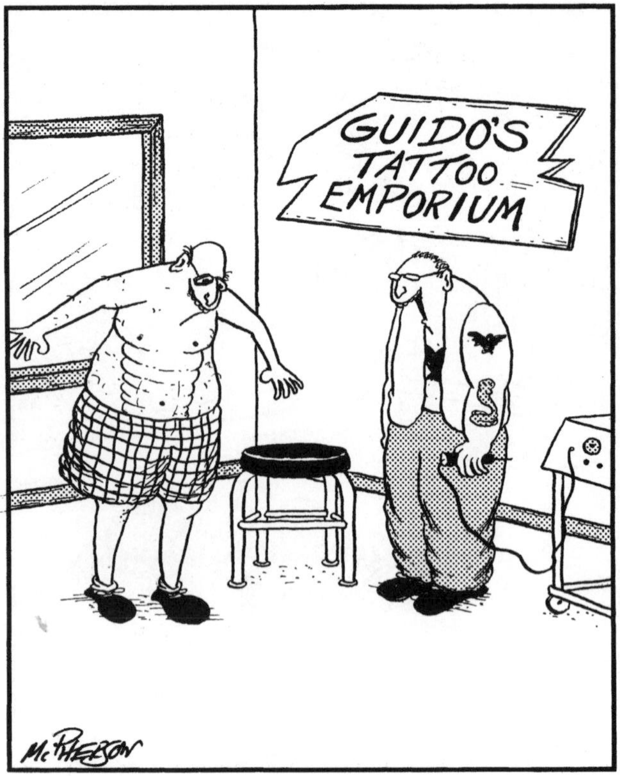
GUIDO'S
TATTOO
EMPORIUM
McPHERSON

"From thirty yards away nobody will be able to tell it's a tattoo."

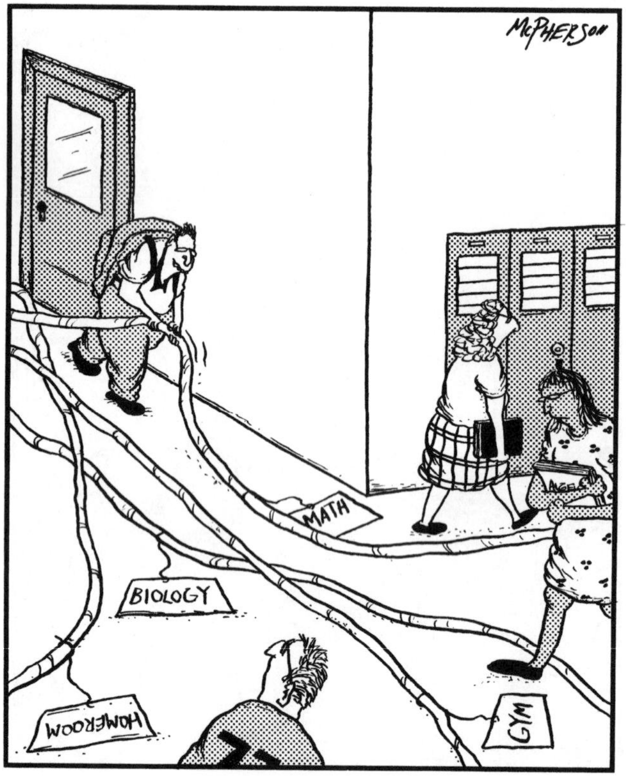
McPHERSON
MATH
BIOLOGY
HOMEROOM
GYM

Freshman Romney Yorp devised a foolproof way to keep himself from getting lost.

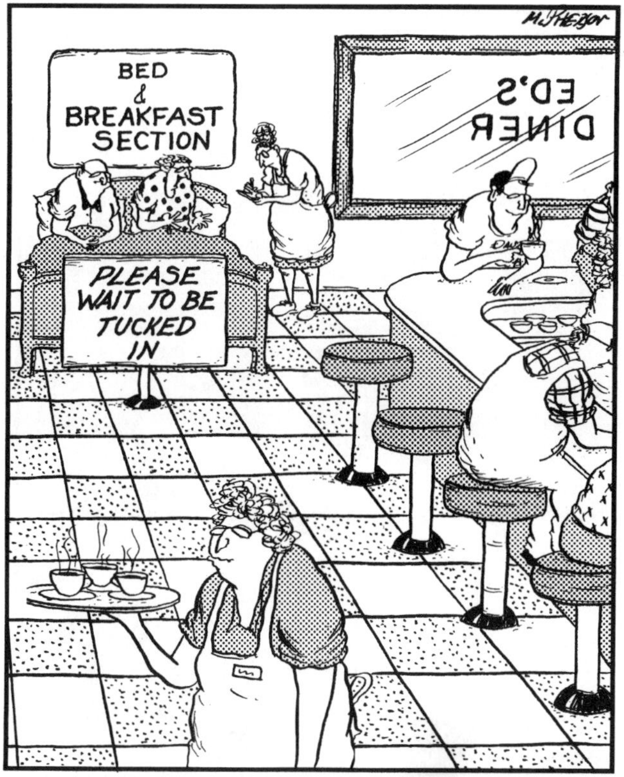
BED
&
BREAKFAST
SECTION
ED'S
DINER
PLEASE
WAIT TO BE
TUCKED
IN

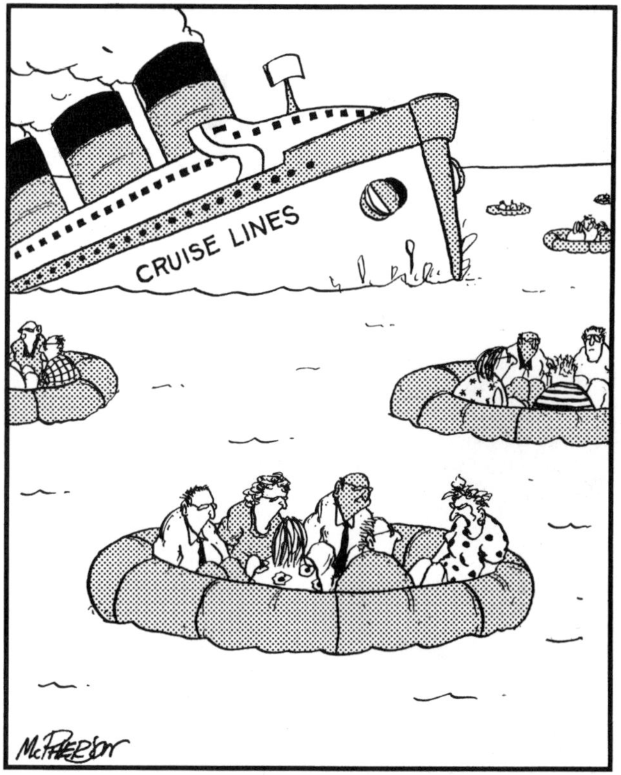
CRUISE LINES

**"Well, it figures! One more square and I would've had bingo!"**

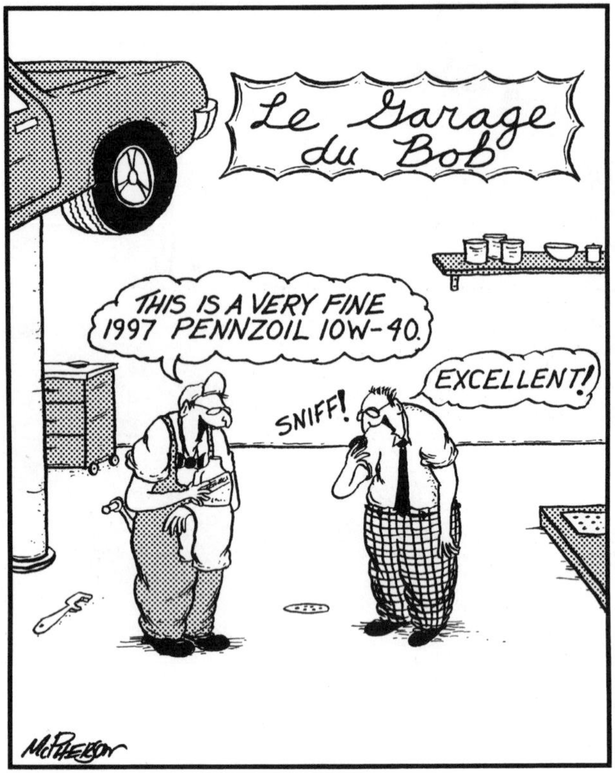
Le Garage du Bob
THIS IS A VERY FINE 1997 PENNZOIL 10W-40.
SNIFF!
EXCELLENT!
McPHERSON

Upscale garages

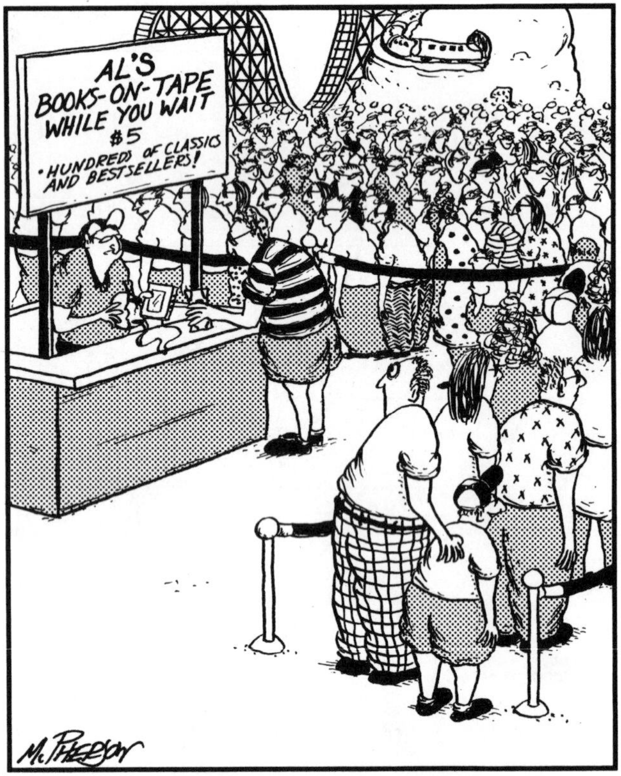
AL'S BOOKS-ON-TAPE WHILE YOU WAIT
$5
• HUNDREDS OF CLASSICS AND BESTSELLERS!
McPHERSON

How to tell when the amusement park line you're waiting in is way too long.

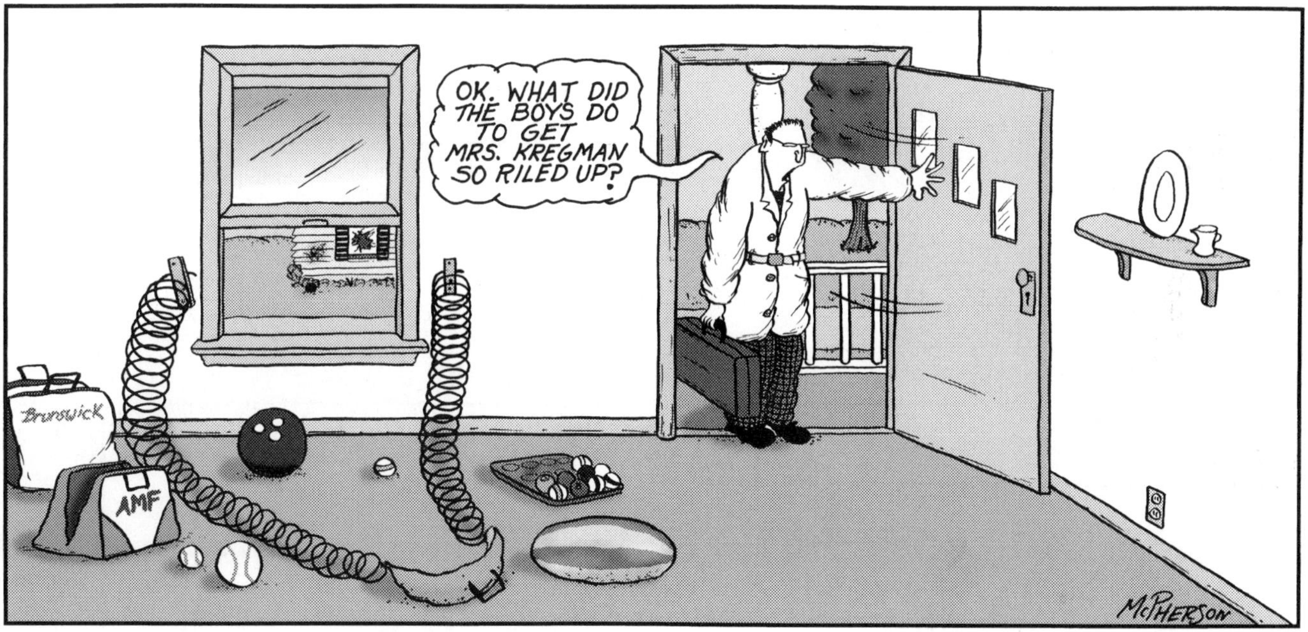
OK. WHAT DID THE BOYS DO TO GET MRS. KREGMAN SO RILED UP?
Brunswick
AMF
McPHERSON

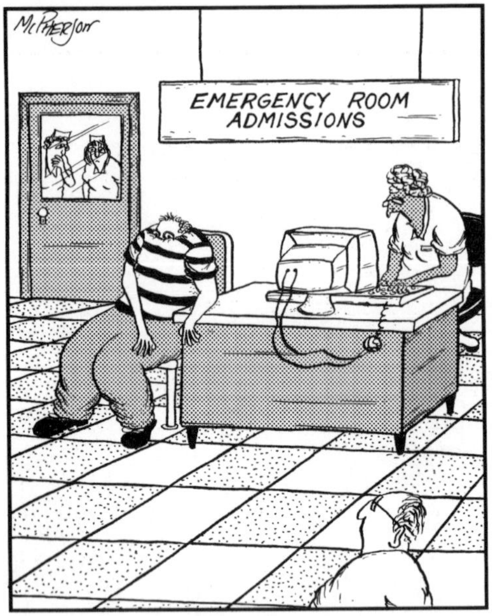
McPHERSON
EMERGENCY ROOM ADMISSIONS

"B-U-N . . . G-E-E . . . J-U-M-P-I-N-G."

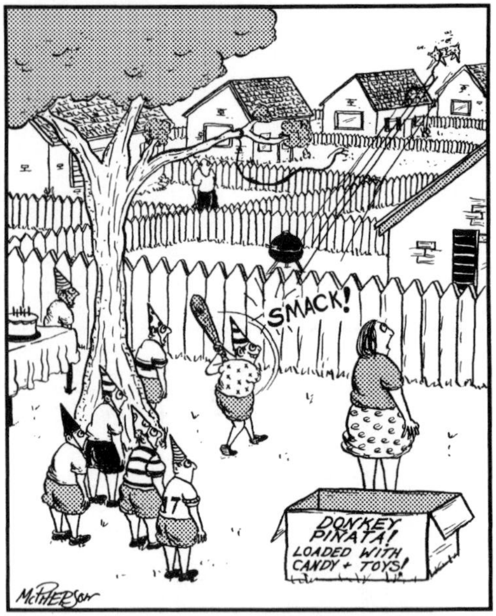
SMACK!
DONKEY PIÑATA! LOADED WITH CANDY + TOYS!
McPHERSON

At Mark McGwire's tenth birthday party

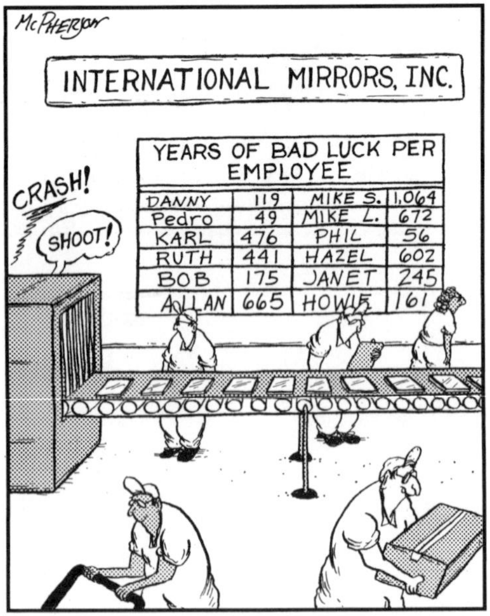
McPHERSON
INTERNATIONAL MIRRORS, INC.
YEARS OF BAD LUCK PER EMPLOYEE
DANNY 119 MIKE S. 1,064
Pedro 49 MIKE L. 672
KARL 476 PHIL 56
RUTH 441 HAZEL 602
BOB 175 JANET 245
ALLAN 665 HOWIE 161
CRASH!
SHOOT!

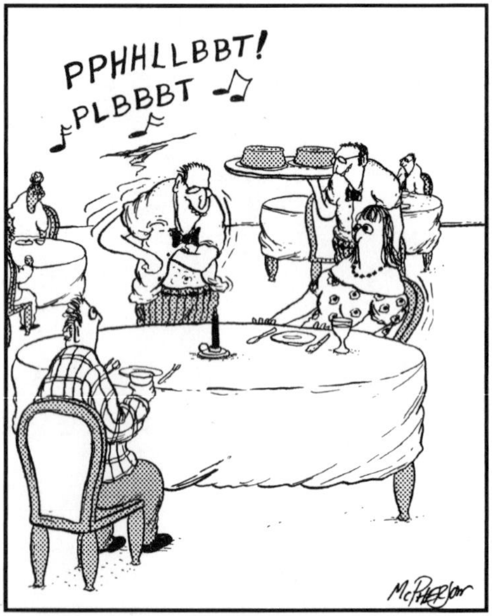
PPHHLLBBT!
PLBBBT
McPHERSON

With the restaurant's violinist out sick, waiter Randy Vorkle filled in with his rendition of "Some Enchanted Evening."

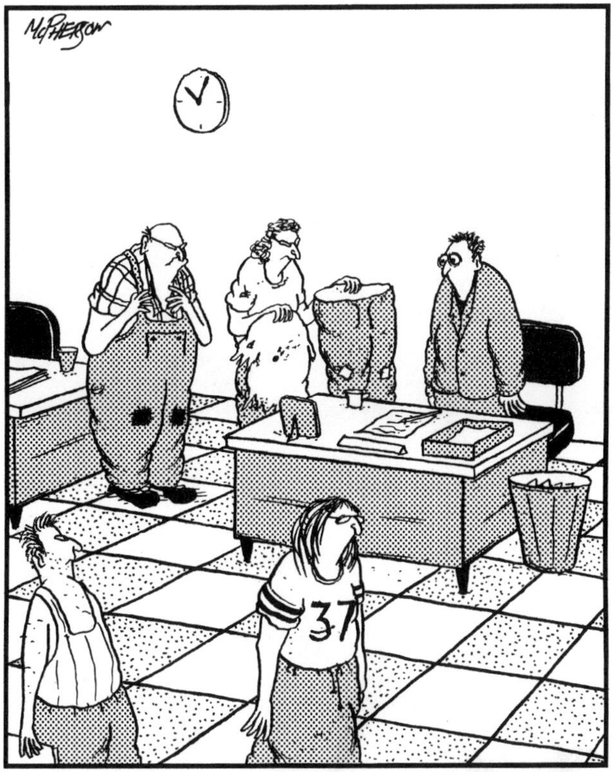
McPHERSON
37

Having forgotten that it was Casual Day, Winslow was forced to change out of his Armani suit and into a ratty T-shirt and sweats.

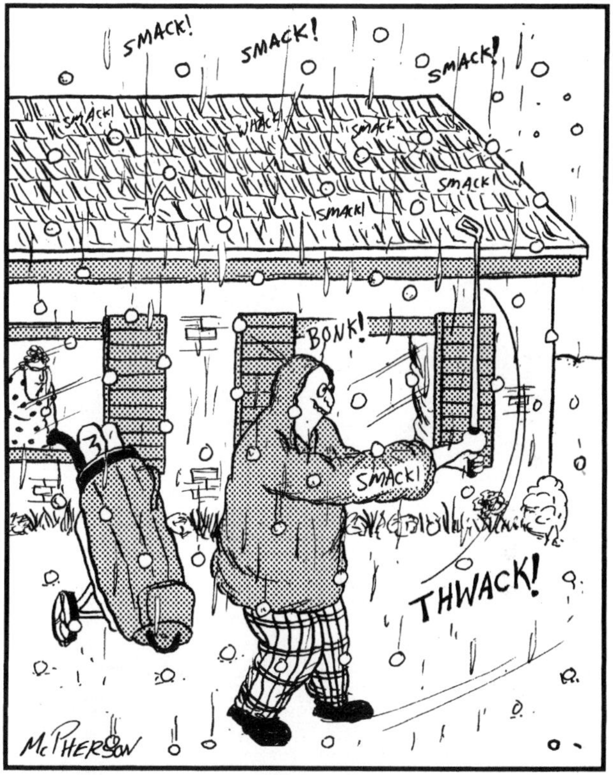
SMACK!
SMACK!
SMACK!
SMACK!
SMACK!
BONK!
SMACK!
THWACK!
McPHERSON

While most people shuddered at the sight of the golf-ball-sized hail, Bruce saw it as an opportunity to hone his wedge-shot skills.

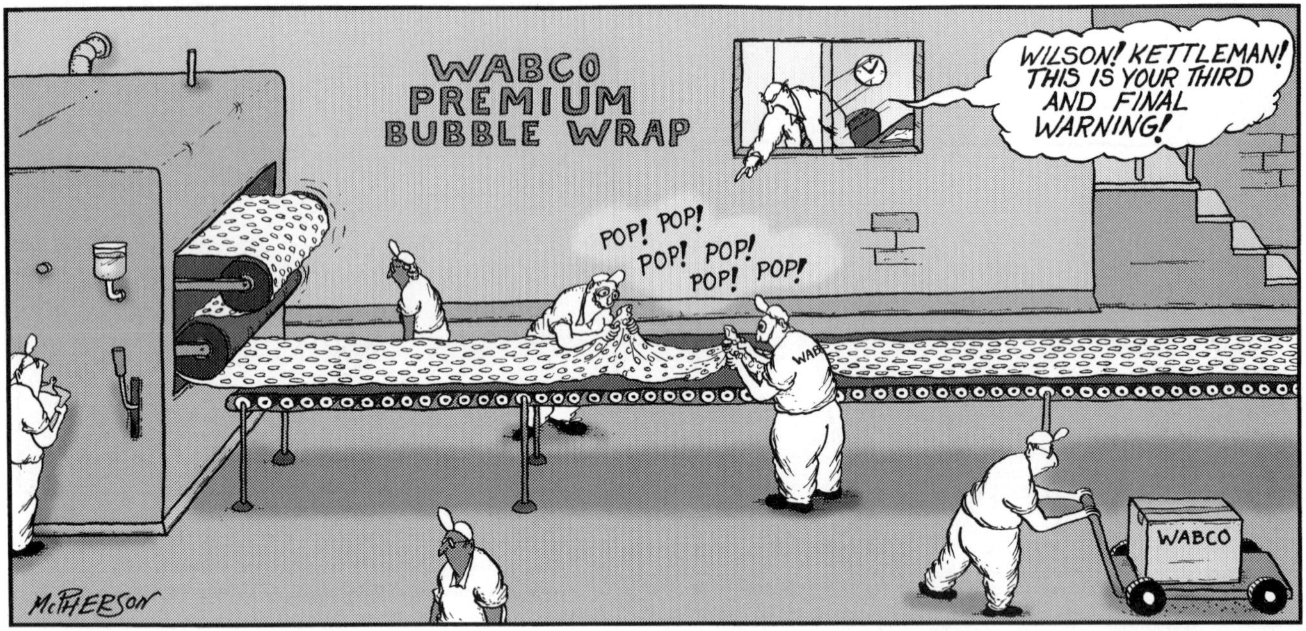
WABCO
PREMIUM
BUBBLE WRAP
WILSON! KETTLEMAN! THIS IS YOUR THIRD AND FINAL WARNING!
POP! POP! POP! POP! POP! POP!
WABCO
McPHERSON

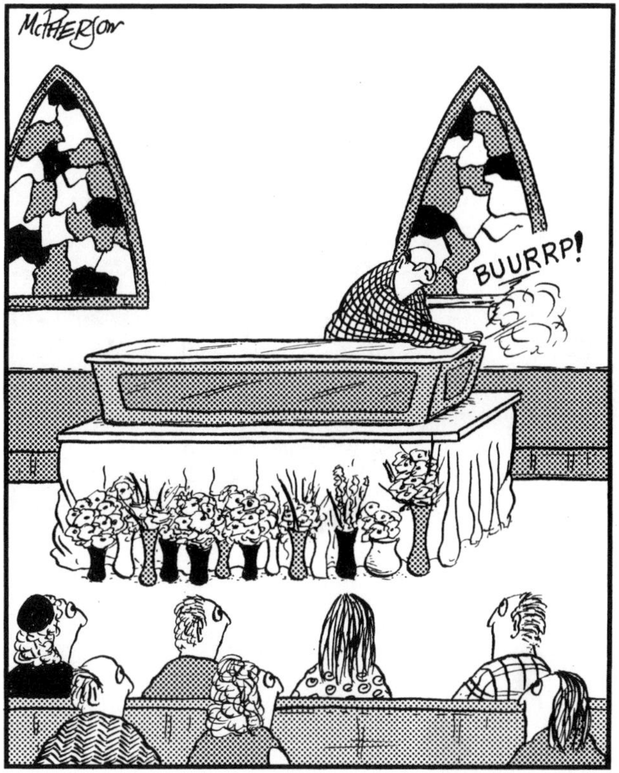
BUURRP!

**At the funeral for the inventor of Tupperware**

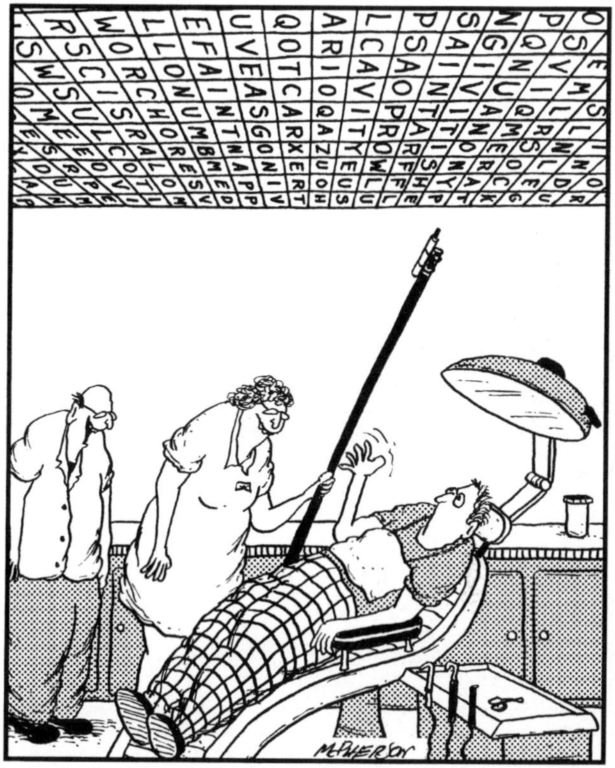

**"To help you pass the time during your root canal, see if you can find twenty-five dental terms in the word-search above your head."**

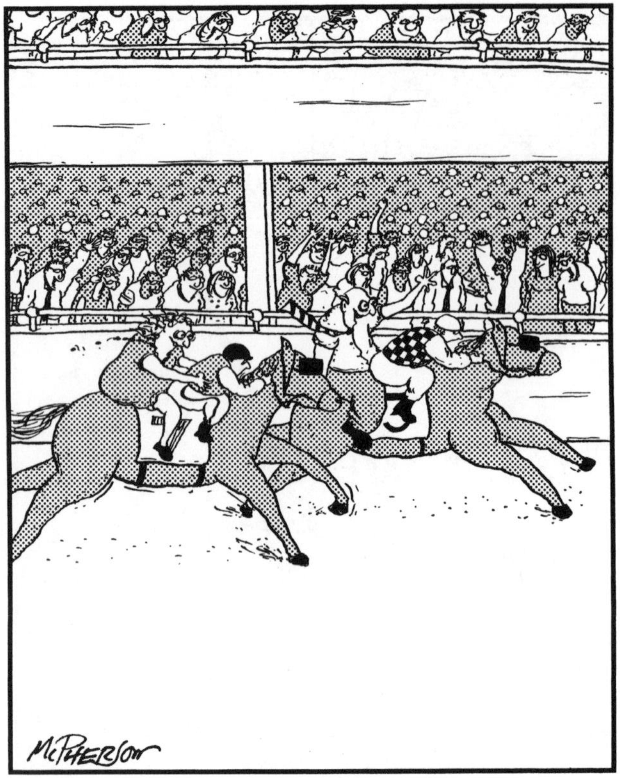

Fan Appreciation Night at Fernmont Raceway

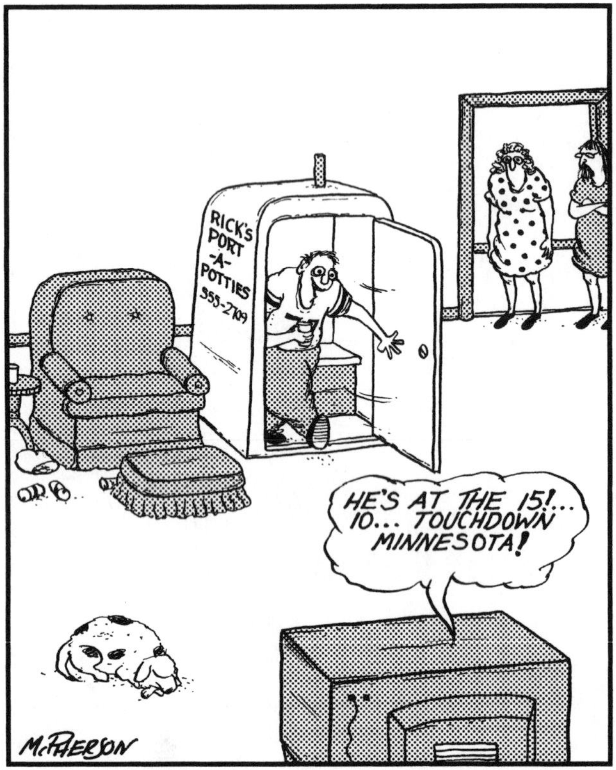
RICK'S PORT -A- POTTIES 555-2709
HE'S AT THE 15!... 10... TOUCHDOWN MINNESOTA!

"Ed rents it for the entire NFL season."

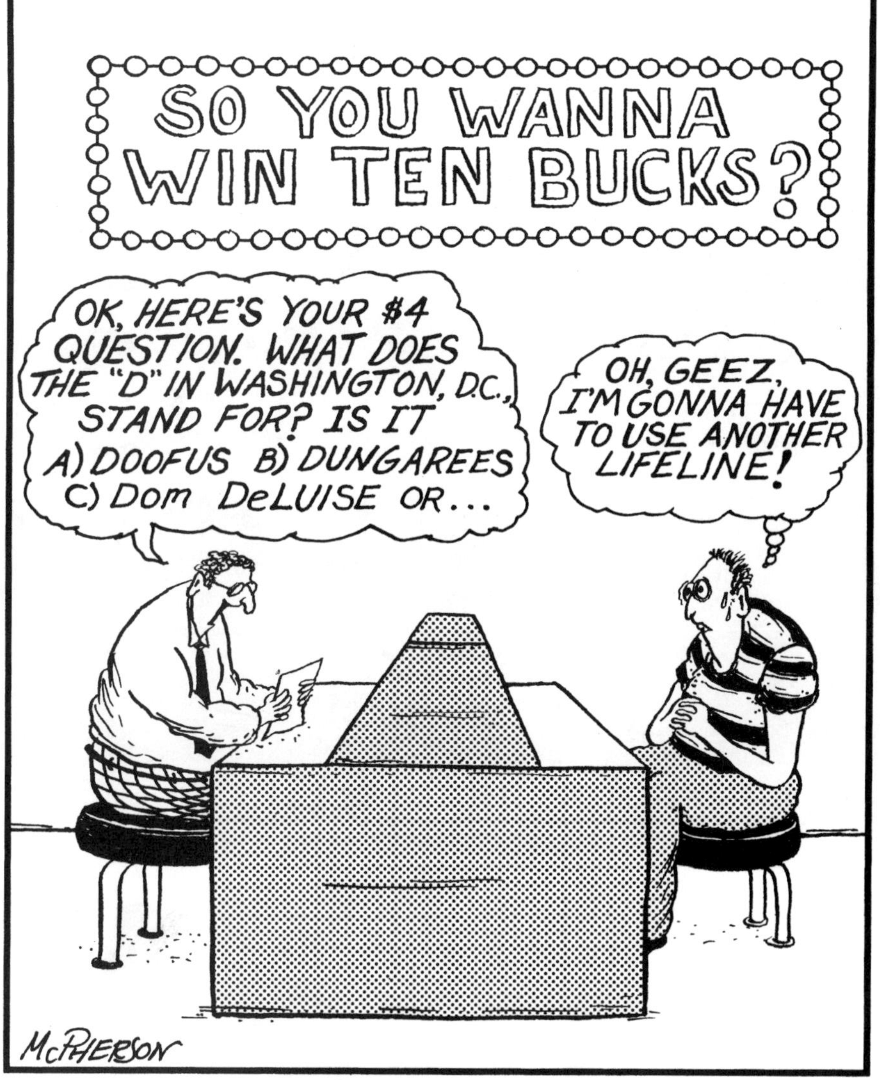
SO YOU WANNA WIN TEN BUCKS?
OK, HERE'S YOUR $4 QUESTION. WHAT DOES THE "D" IN WASHINGTON, D.C., STAND FOR? IS IT A) DOOFUS B) DUNGAREES C) Dom DeLUISE OR...
OH, GEEZ, I'M GONNA HAVE TO USE ANOTHER LIFELINE!
McPHERSON

**Budget game shows**

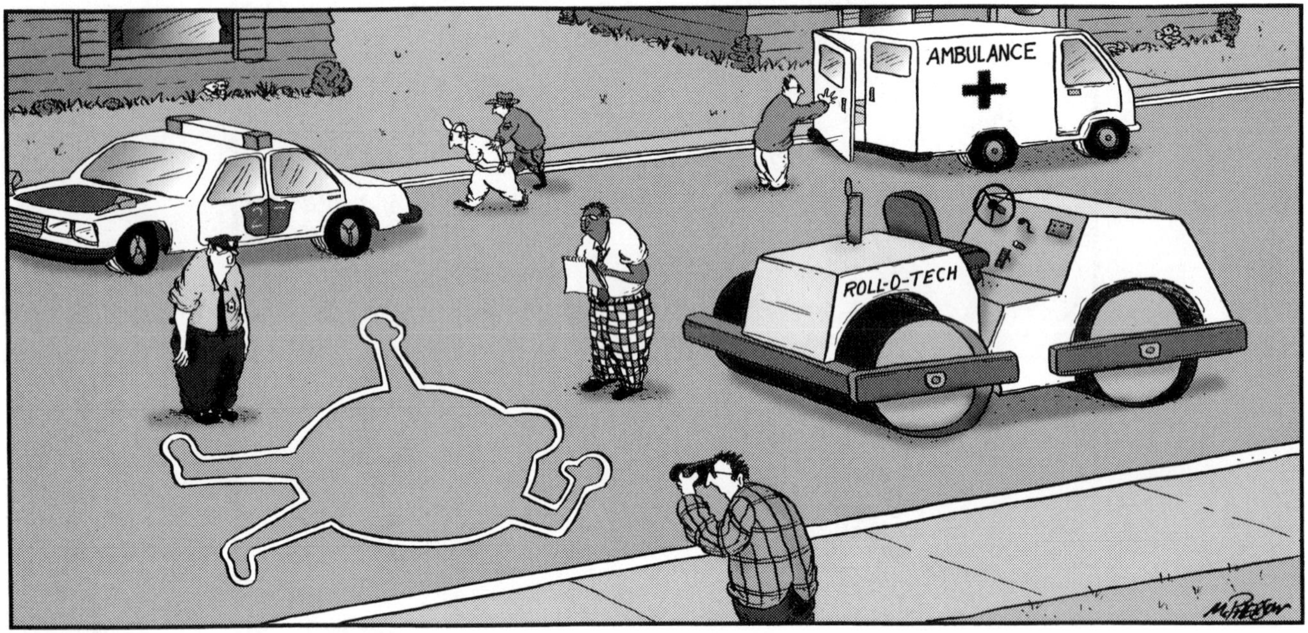
AMBULANCE
ROLL-O-TECH

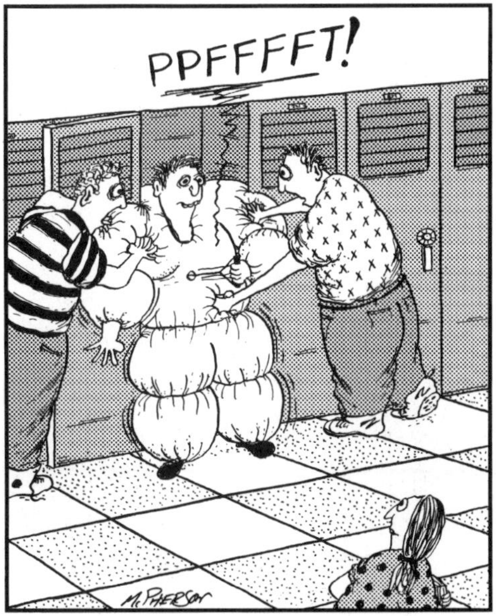
PPFFFFT!
McPHERSON

Just as the upperclassmen were about to close the door, Lenny activated his inflatable Anti-Locker-Stuffing Suit™.

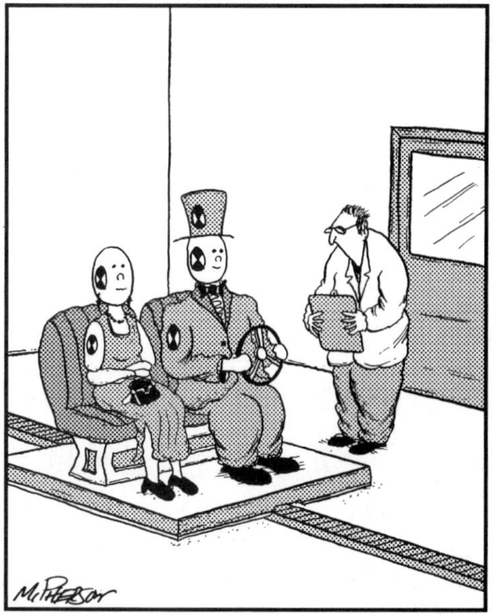
McPHERSON

Crash-test dummies for luxury cars

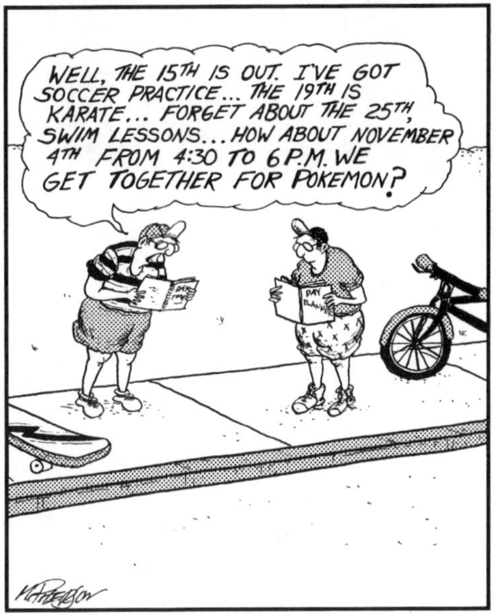
WELL, THE 15TH IS OUT. I'VE GOT SOCCER PRACTICE... THE 19TH IS KARATE... FORGET ABOUT THE 25TH, SWIM LESSONS... HOW ABOUT NOVEMBER 4TH FROM 4:30 TO 6 P.M. WE GET TOGETHER FOR POKEMON?
DAY PLANNER
McPHERSON

Children of the '90s

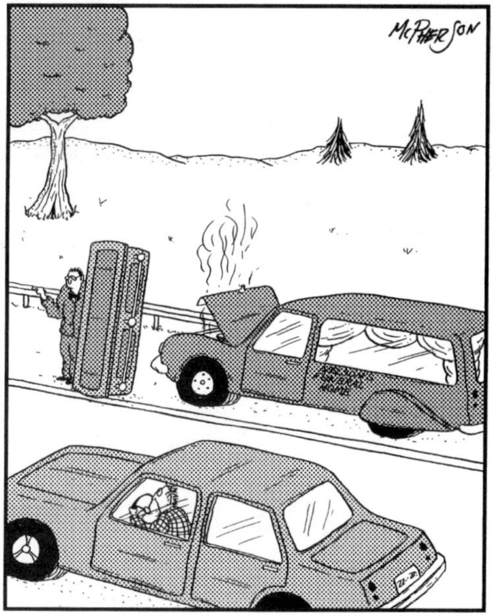
McPHERSON

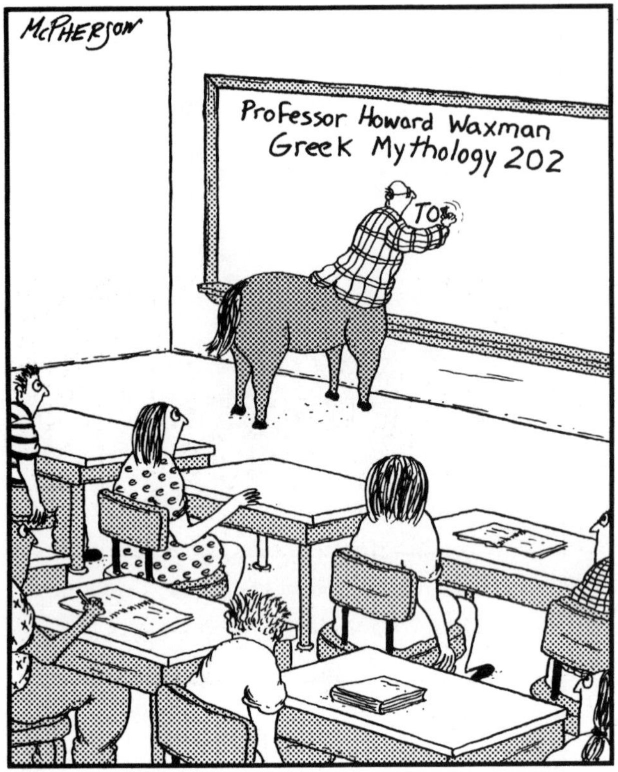
MCPHERSON
Professor Howard Waxman
Greek Mythology 202
TO

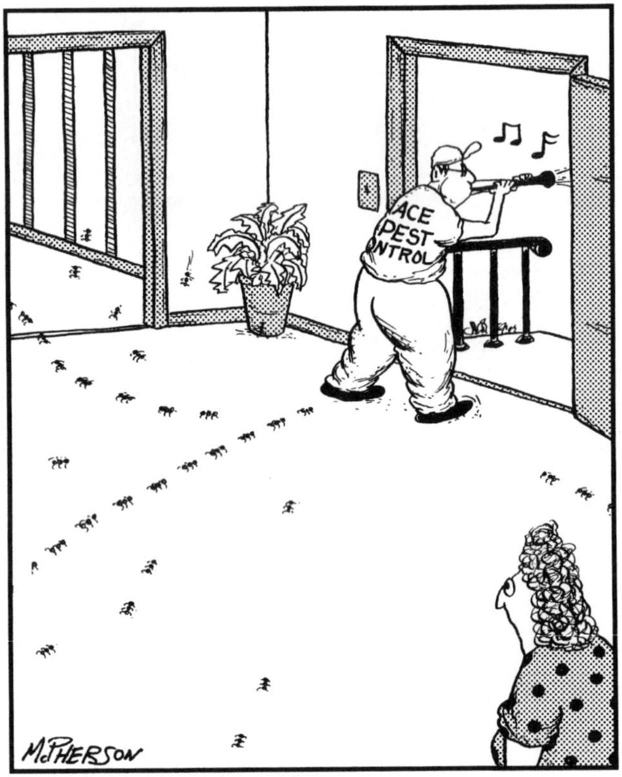
ACE
PEST
NTROL
MCPHERSON

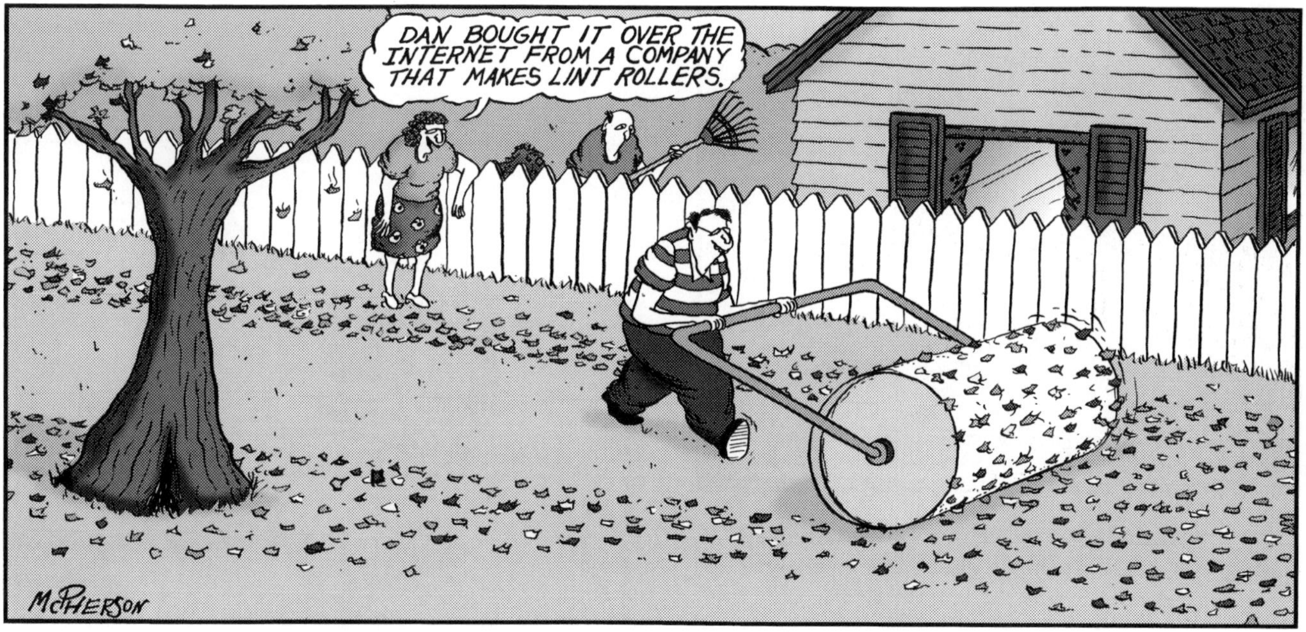
DAN BOUGHT IT OVER THE INTERNET FROM A COMPANY THAT MAKES LINT ROLLERS.
McPHERSON

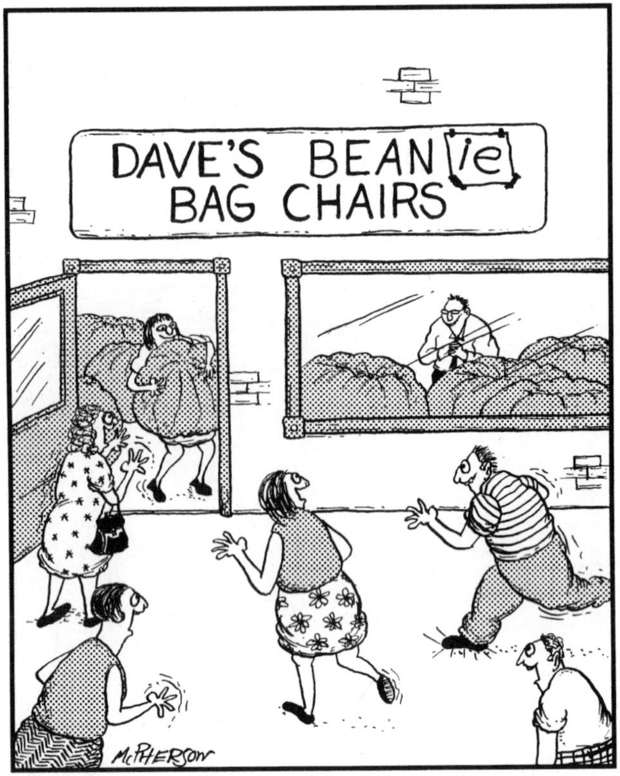
DAVE'S BEANie BAG CHAIRS
McPHERSON

**By simply adding two letters, Dave turned his stagnant business into a gold mine overnight.**

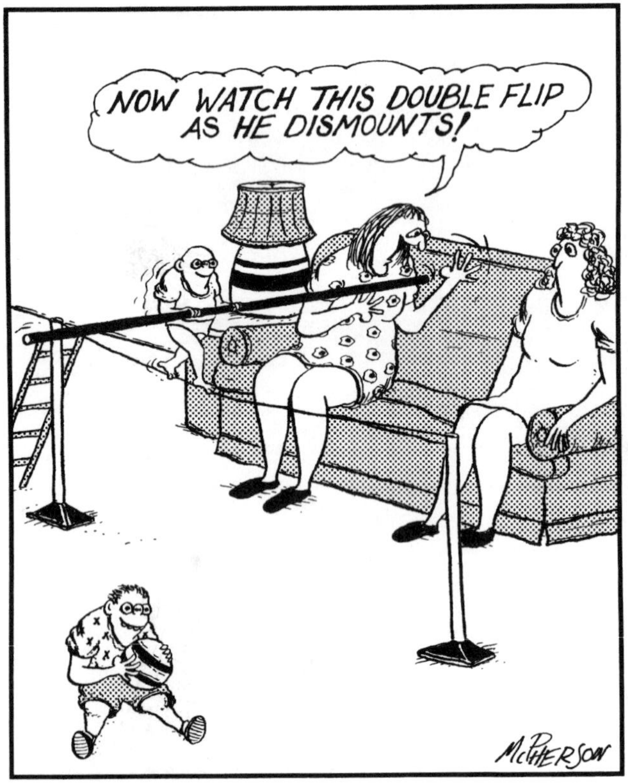
NOW WATCH THIS DOUBLE FLIP AS HE DISMOUNTS!
McPHERSON

**With her fifteen-month-old still not walking, Brenda felt a subtle competition building between her son and the Wilson's nine-month-old.**

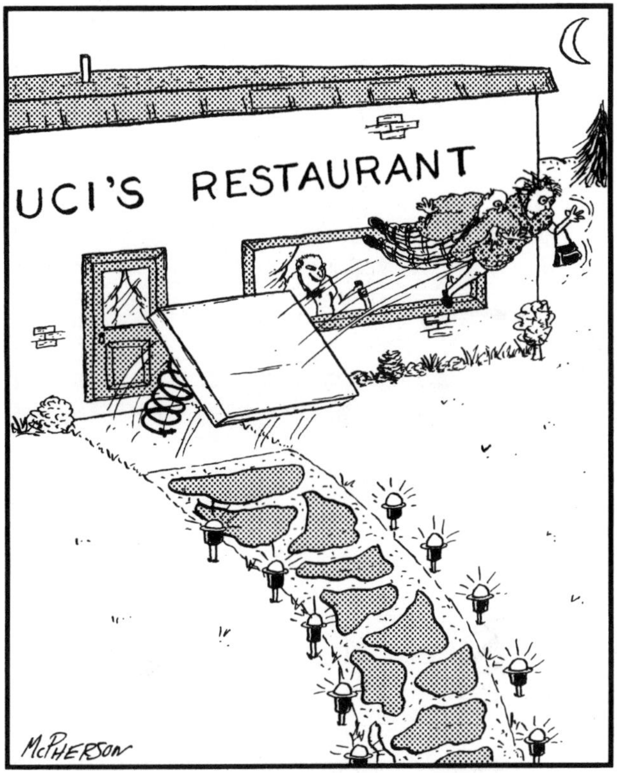
UCI'S RESTAURANT

**As the couple departed, head waiter Alfonse Ludner activated the Lousy Tipper Ejection System.**

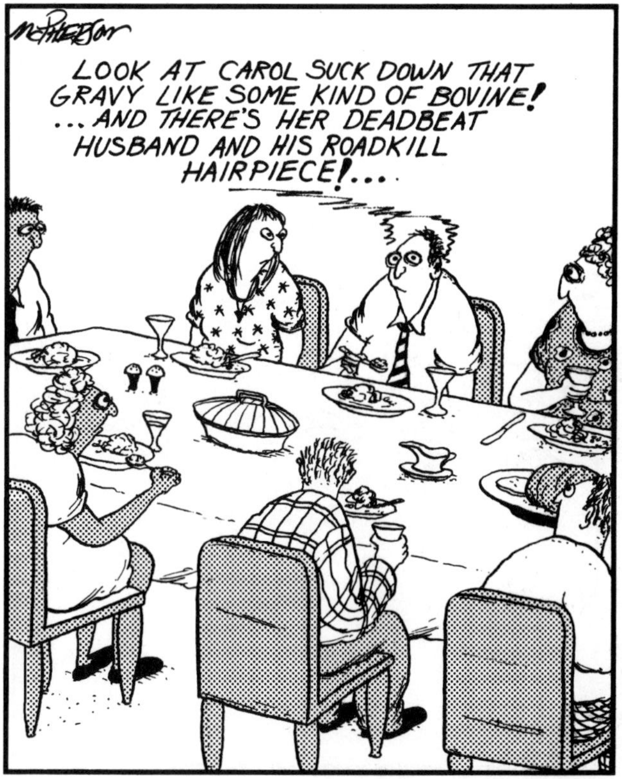
LOOK AT CAROL SUCK DOWN THAT GRAVY LIKE SOME KIND OF BOVINE! ...AND THERE'S HER DEADBEAT HUSBAND AND HIS ROADKILL HAIRPIECE!...

**Through a freak scientific phenomenon, Jim's hearing aid begins to broadcast his inner thoughts.**

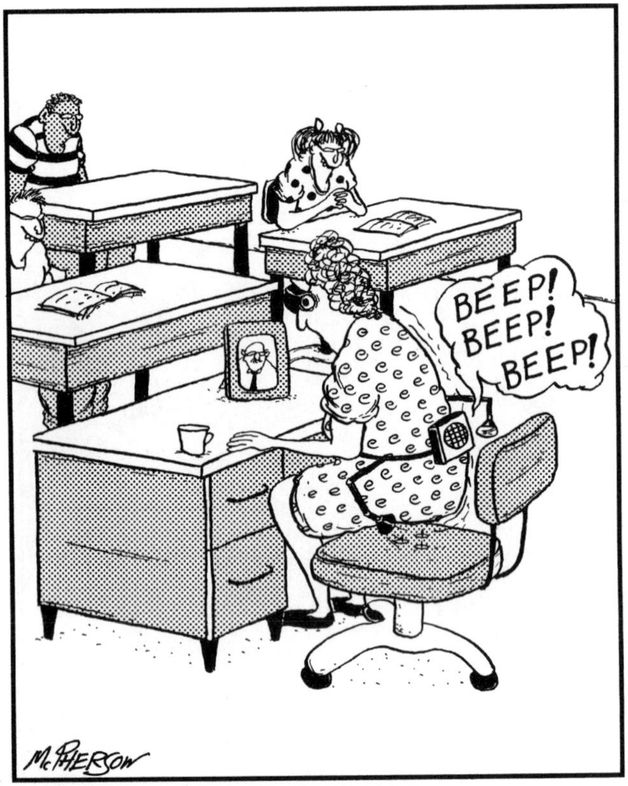
BEEP! BEEP! BEEP!
McPHERSON

Fortunately, Mrs. Gratchman's Thumbtack Detection System spared her a trip to the school nurse.

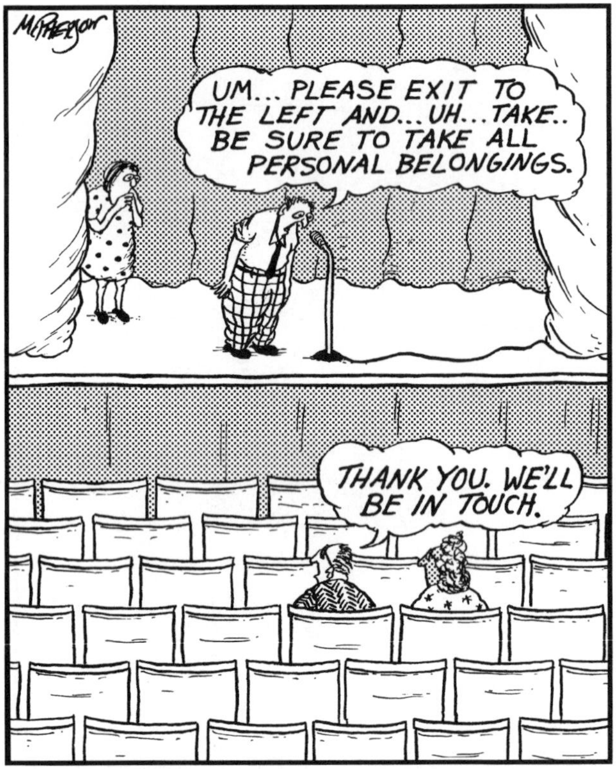
McPHERSON
UM... PLEASE EXIT TO THE LEFT AND... UH... TAKE.. BE SURE TO TAKE ALL PERSONAL BELONGINGS.
THANK YOU. WE'LL BE IN TOUCH.

Prospective employees audition for positions in Disney's transportation department.

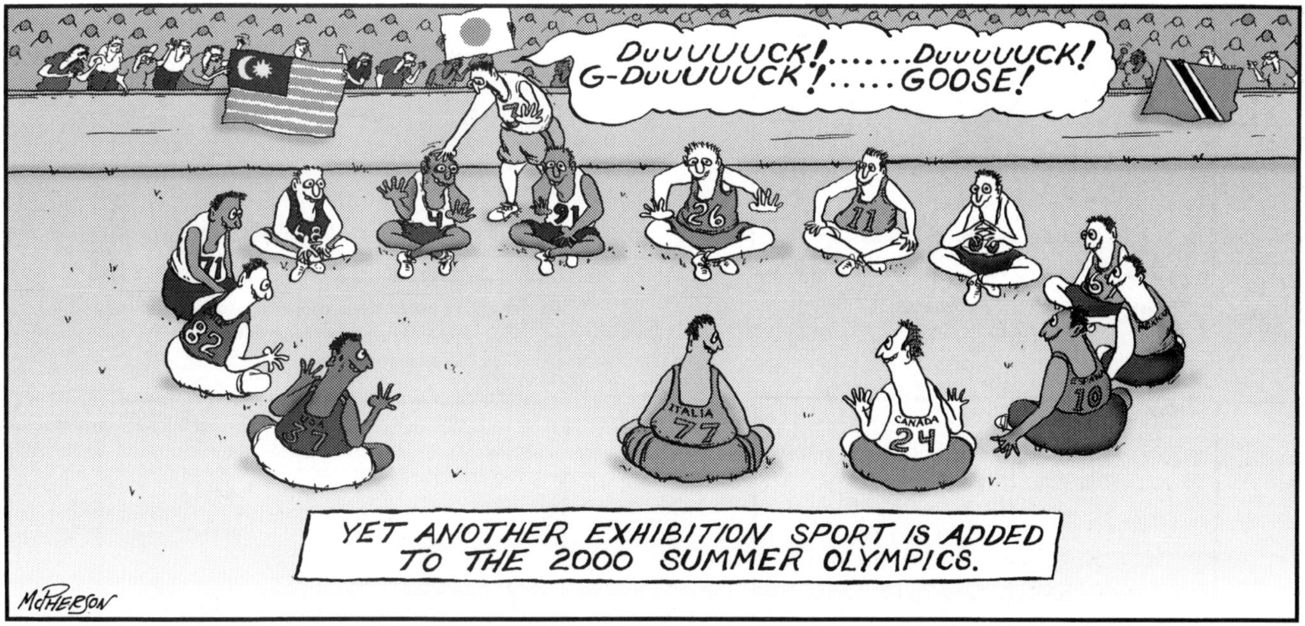
DUUUUUCK!.......DUUUUUCK!
G-DUUUUUUCK!.....GOOSE!
YET ANOTHER EXHIBITION SPORT IS ADDED TO THE 2000 SUMMER OLYMPICS.
McPHERSON

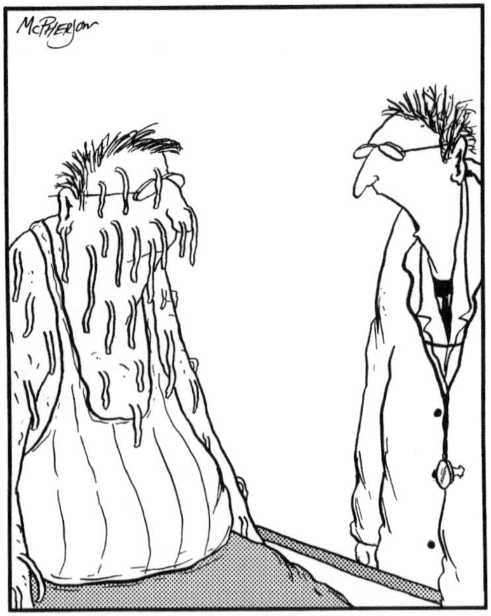

"It's a new strain—chicken noodle pox."

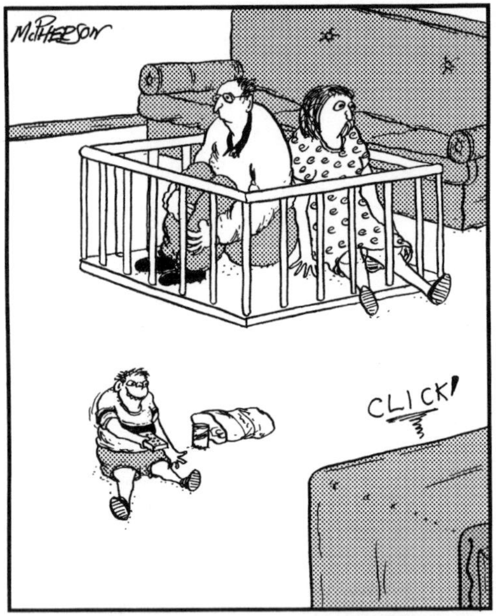
CLICK!

At the age of only fifteen months, Jason was already a master of reverse psychology.

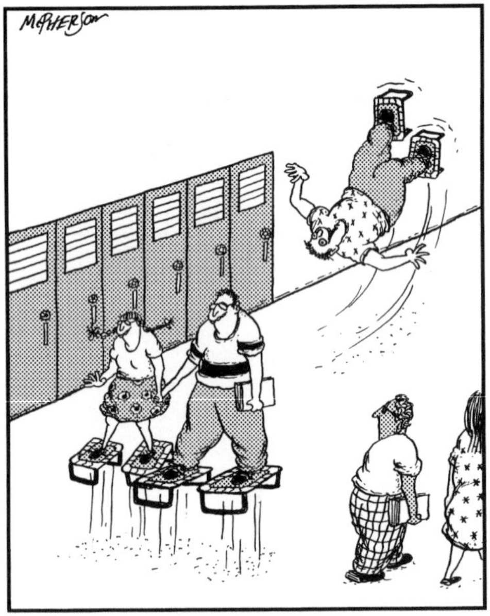

The latest fad to sweep the nation's high schools: trampoline shoes

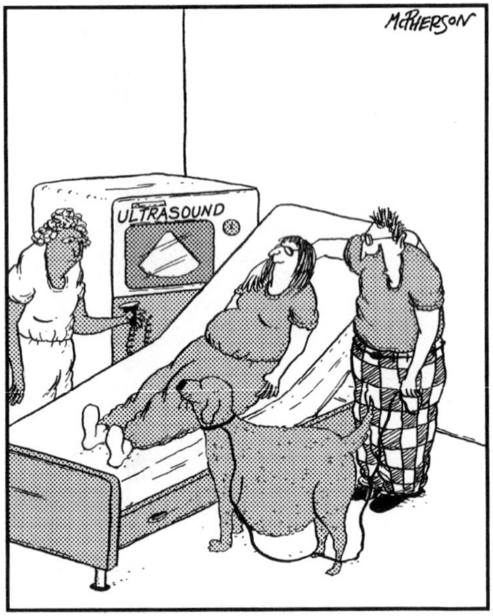
ULTRASOUND

"After you're done with Linda's ultrasound, would you mind doing one on Raven so we can see how many puppies we can expect?"

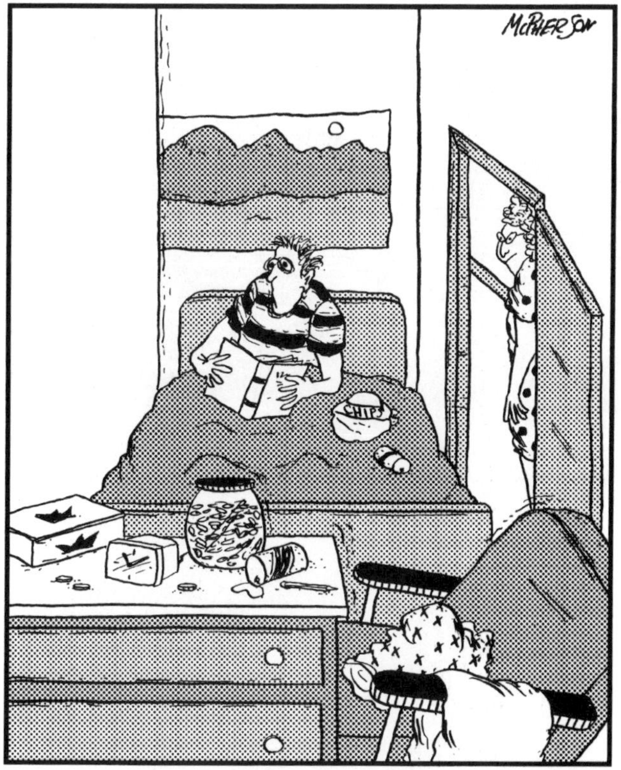
McPHERSON
CHIPS

**Having installed a hydraulically operated wall in their twenty-five-year-old's bedroom, the Fullers hoped to coax him into moving out on his own.**

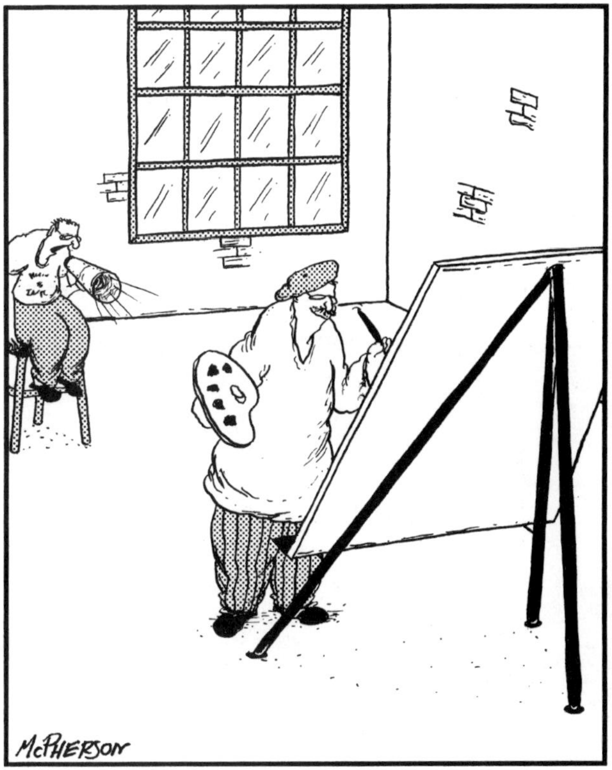
McPHERSON

**"Stroke! Stroke! Stroke! . . ."**

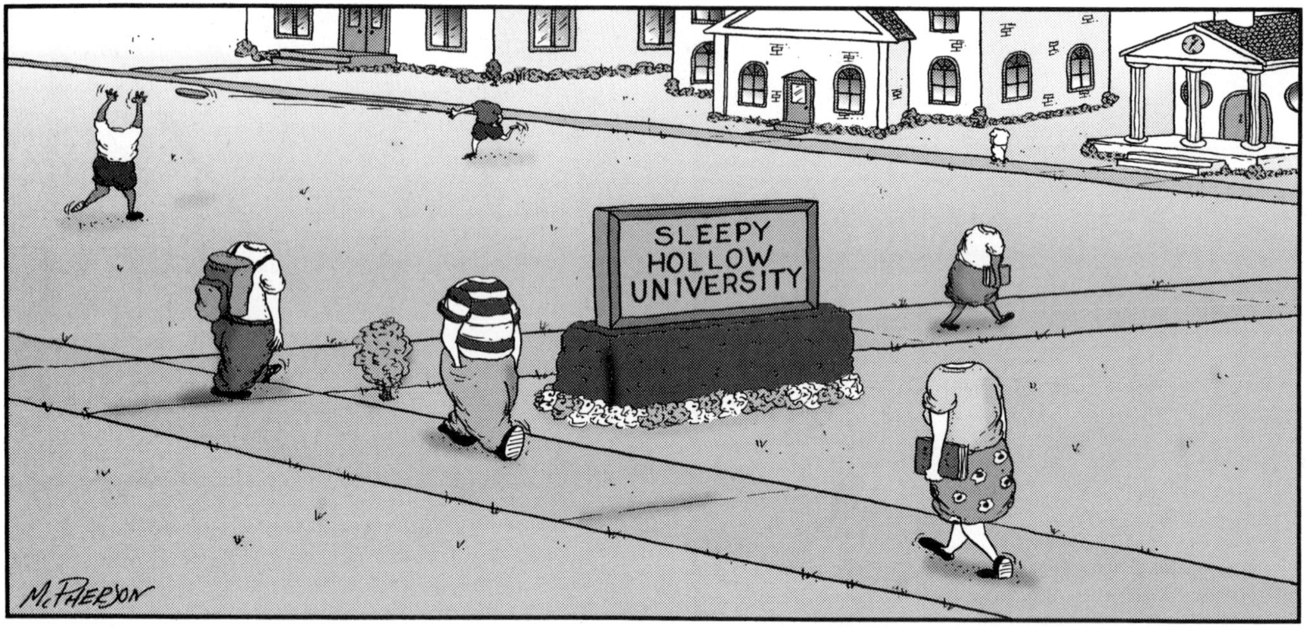
SLEEPY
HOLLOW
UNIVERSITY
McPHERSON

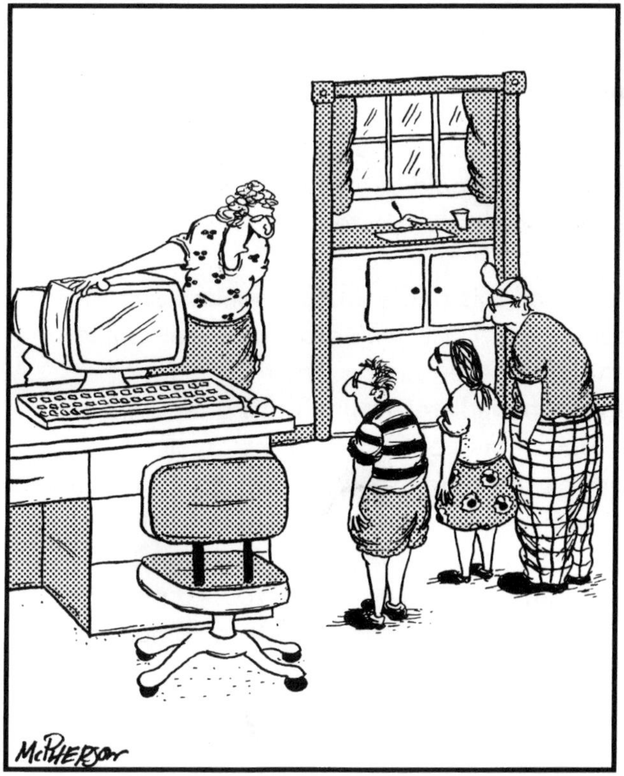
McPHERSON

"So now, when you want to know what's for dinner or when soccer practice is, don't come bug me! Just log on to the family Web site and you'll be all set."

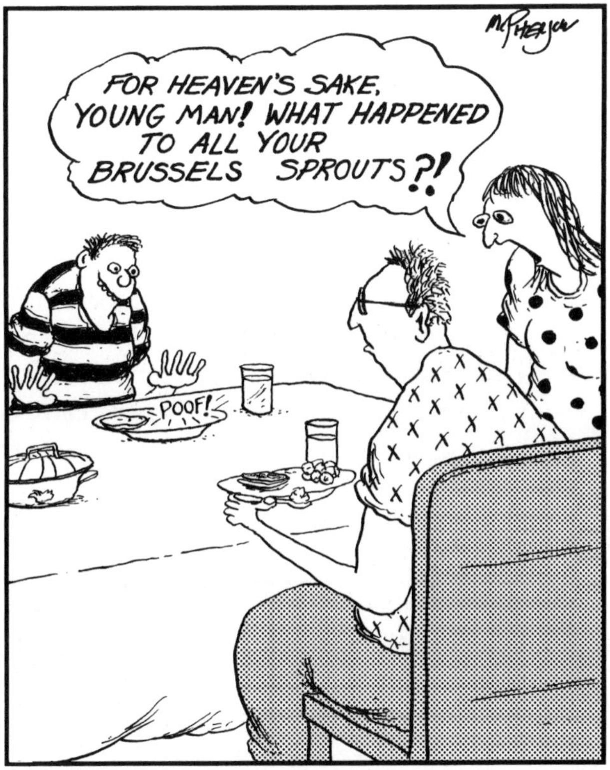
McPHERSON
FOR HEAVEN'S SAKE, YOUNG MAN! WHAT HAPPENED TO ALL YOUR BRUSSELS SPROUTS?!
POOF!

David Copperfield as a child

## Killed by the Editor

It would be nice if every cartoon that I turned in to my editor was met with peals of laughter and snorting, but, alas, this is not the case. (I remember once that happened.) What I typically do is send him maybe ten or fifteen rough sketches of cartoons via fax, and then we go through them to see what works, what doesn't, and what is just downright offensive to anyone who would read it. (My personal favorites.)

He might give feedback like, "Is that a rabbit or a taco that the man is holding?" Sometimes my artwork can be a little vague. Other times he'll feel a cartoon is simply not funny enough to work, or that it's too complex. Some of these issues I can change, but now and then a cartoon comes along that he just says, "No, we can't do that!" to. These are yanked immediately, and after a brief argument with him, I sulk away. The editor is always right. (They made me tattoo that phrase onto my upper arm).

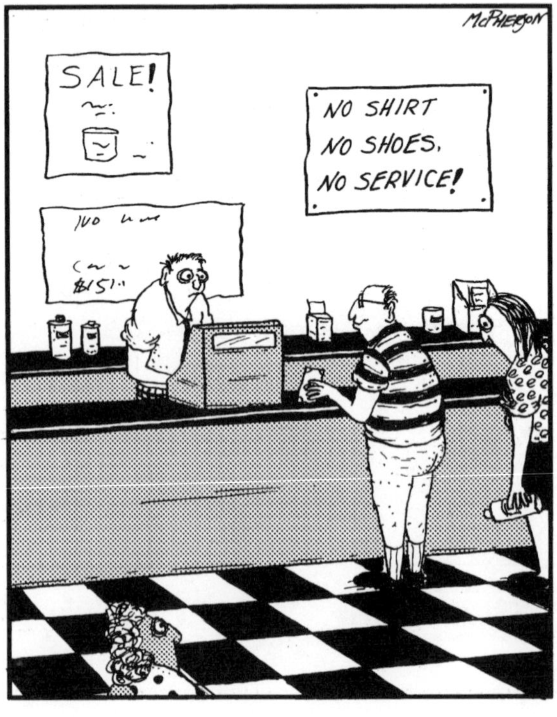
McPHERSON
SALE!
NO SHIRT
NO SHOES.
NO SERVICE!

Here are some samples of cartoons that my editor just felt would be too upsetting for newspaper readers to lay eyes on.

I always liked this one a lot. Captionless cartoons are something that I think most cartoonists like to aim for, but they can be a rare find. However, my editor immediately canned this one, saying no naked butts could be shown in the comics. I argued that Bart Simpson runs around naked on TV all of the time. Didn't work. I think it was the little hairs that really pushed him over the edge. I ultimately did run the cartoon, but with little jockey shorts on the guy, which completely watered down the cartoon.

MY HUSBAND WAS INMATE OF THE MONTH AT HILLCREST PENITENTIARY

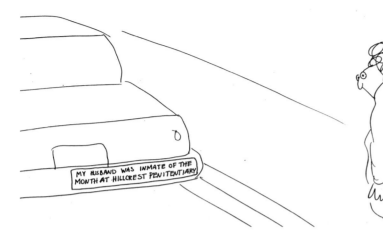

My editor said I just couldn't do this cartoon. Not good to make fun of prisoners; they can get very touchy. So, off it went into the DOA pile.

I tried once again to visit the bare-butt topic, this time being more covert. It didn't work. I was told this would not fly either. I said, "Come on! Those are one-inch drawings of mannequins' butt cracks, which shrunk down in the newspaper will be about one-eighth-inch drawings of manequins' butt cracks. People can walk into Sears right now and see a totally *nude* mannequin up close." Nope, it was canned (so to speak).

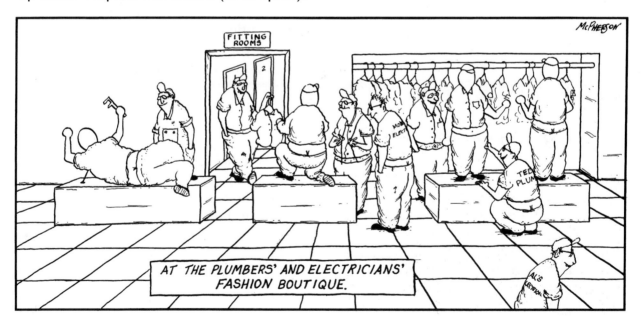

McPHERSON
FITTING ROOMS
AT THE PLUMBERS' AND ELECTRICIANS' FASHION BOUTIQUE.

To this next one, my editor just said, "*No*, you can't have a litterbox flying out of a window spewing cat litter all over a neighborhood!" I told him this family lived in the country, as though we were talking about something that would really happen. He said then the dirty litter would be strewn all over little woodland creatures. I just sighed.

Three years later I sent it in to him again. He had forgotten it and this time, he liked it. Memory lapses can be a good thing.

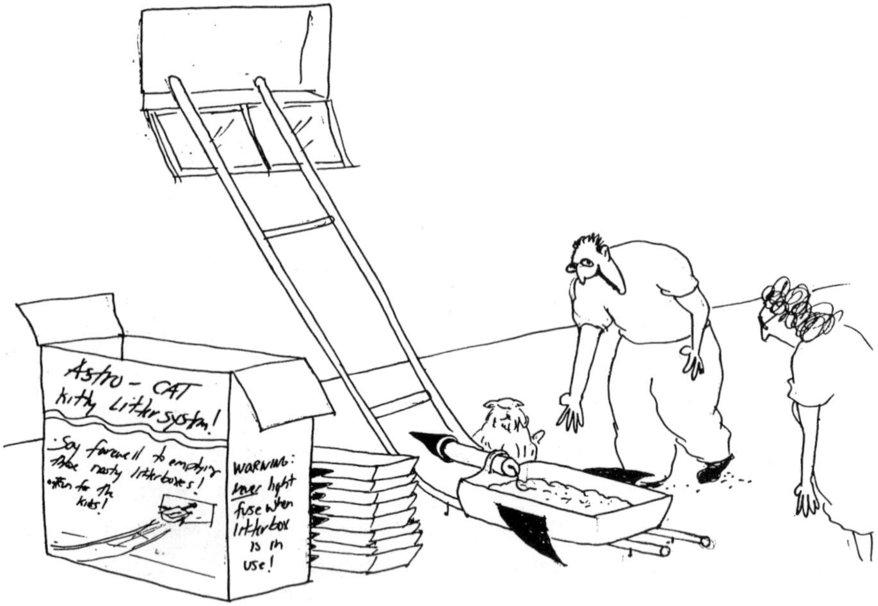
Astro-CAT
kitty Litter system!
WARNING: Never light fuse when litterbox is in use!

**"So when it's full you just light the fuse and . . ."**

About five minutes after I heard Tom Brokaw announce the arrival of this drug on the market, this cartoon idea popped into my head. I immediately drew it up and faxed it into my editor, but was told we couldn't do it because it was just too delicate a topic for the comic pages. Little kids would wonder why the water was swooping up into the air and pose awkward questions at the dinner table. (Sigh.)

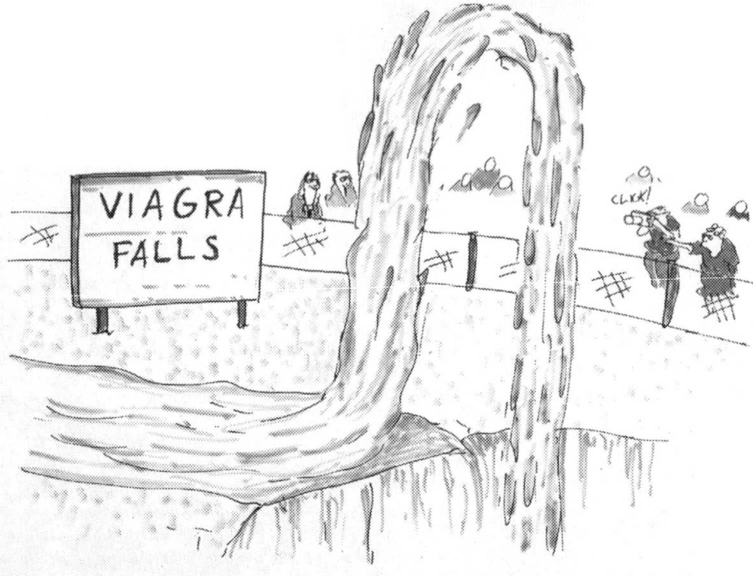
VIAGRA FALLS

"Hi, Hon! How did your mammogram go?"

My editor Greg is a great guy and much of the time tries to rally support from other editors for those of my cartoons that are teetering on the edge of acceptance. But every once in a while I like to mess with his head and send him a cartoon that I *know* they can't run, but is close enough that he'll still try. This cartoon was perfect for the task. He tried on and off throughout a day to get this one in, but of course I knew it would never make it past the "Big Guy." I was told the editorial director canned it before even reading the caption.

A relentless prankster, Carol couldn't resist pulling the old dribble-IV-bag joke on Mr. Sweeney.

With textbook loads ever increasing, many students are finding alternatives to backpacks.

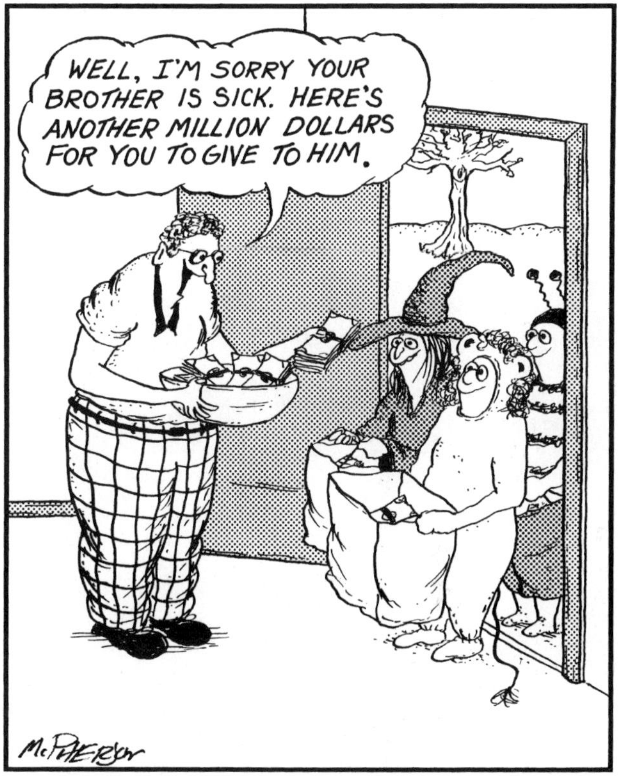
WELL, I'M SORRY YOUR BROTHER IS SICK. HERE'S ANOTHER MILLION DOLLARS FOR YOU TO GIVE TO HIM.
McPHERSON

Trick-or-treating at Bill Gates's house

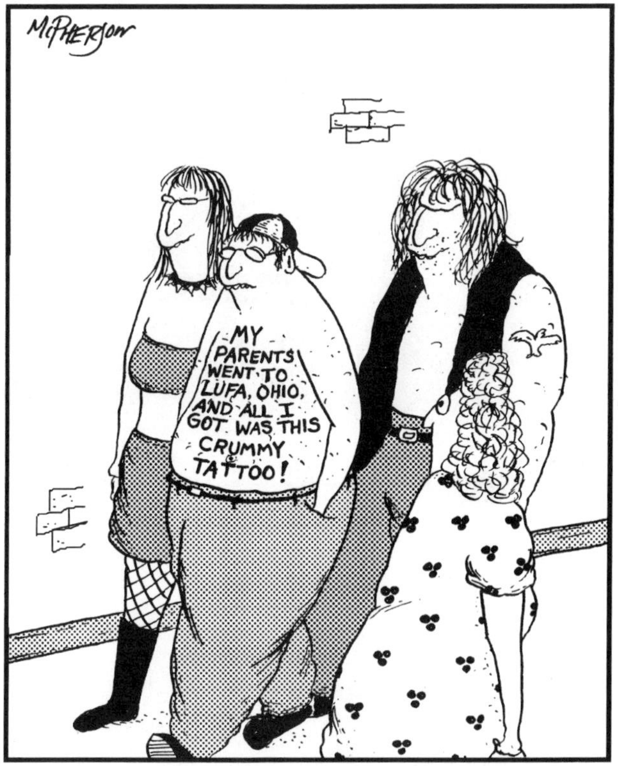
McPHERSON
MY PARENTS WENT TO LUFA, OHIO, AND ALL I GOT WAS THIS CRUMMY TATTOO!

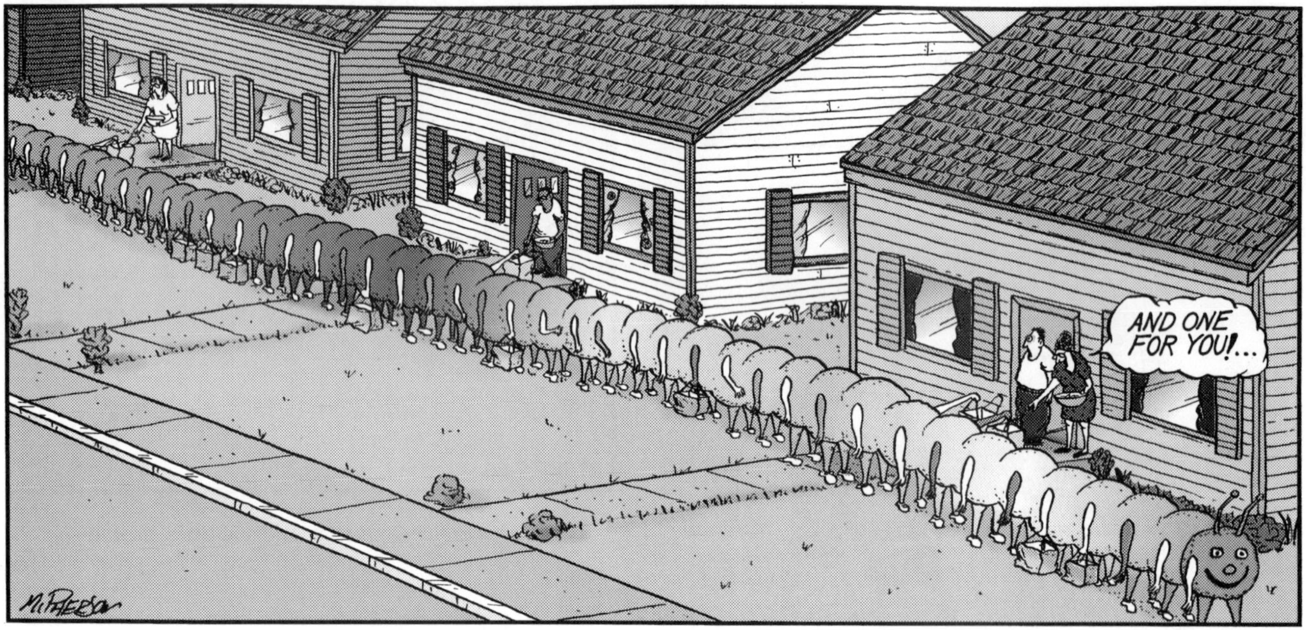
AND ONE FOR YOU!...

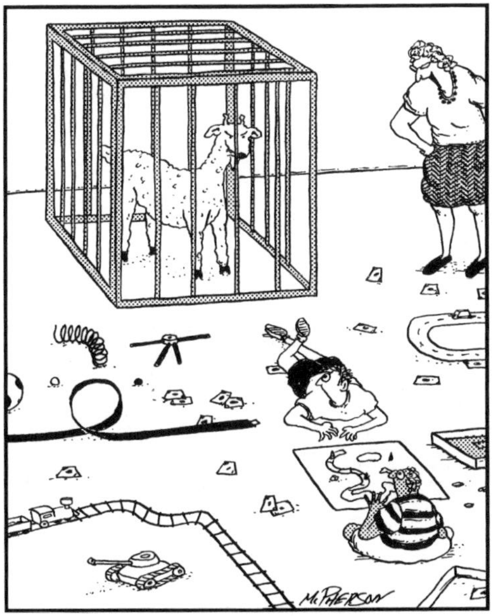

"Okay, you boys have five minutes to clean up this room, or I'll have to let out Chompy the goat. And you know what he'll do to your toys!"

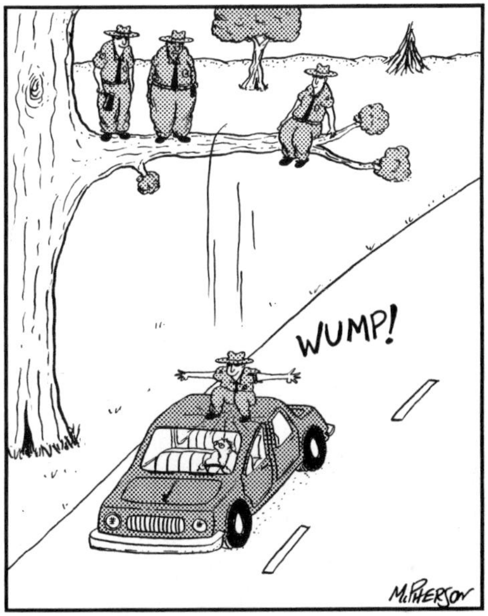
WUMP!

Despite recent budget cuts, the Chemung County Sheriff's Department continued to ticket speeders.

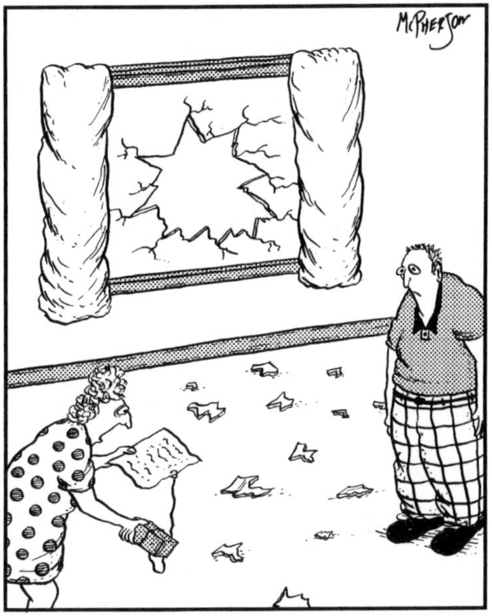

"It's a rejection letter from that masonry company you interviewed with!"

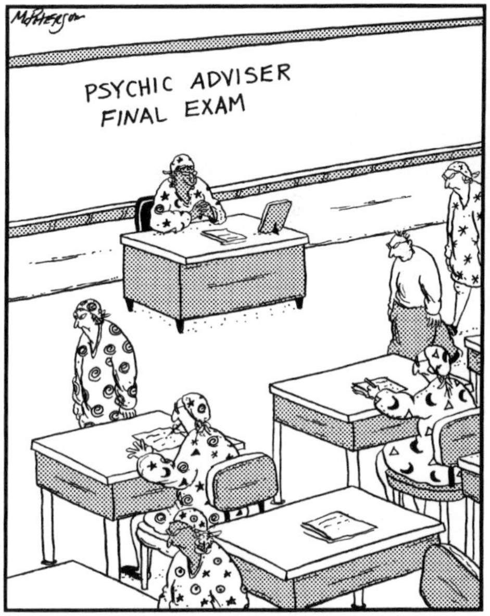
PSYCHIC ADVISER
FINAL EXAM

Having premonitions that they were going to flunk the exam, several students walked out without even lifting a pencil.

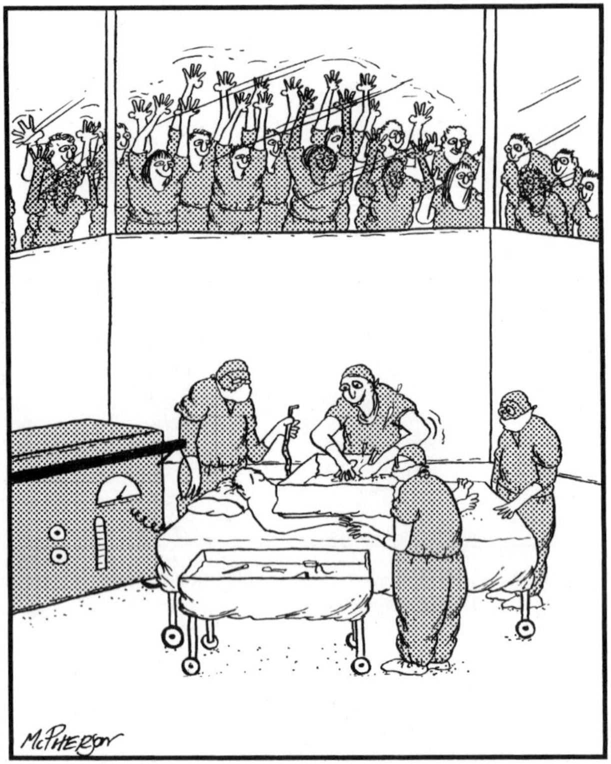
McPHERSON

**Dr. Callahan knew he was on a roll when the observing med students started doing the wave.**

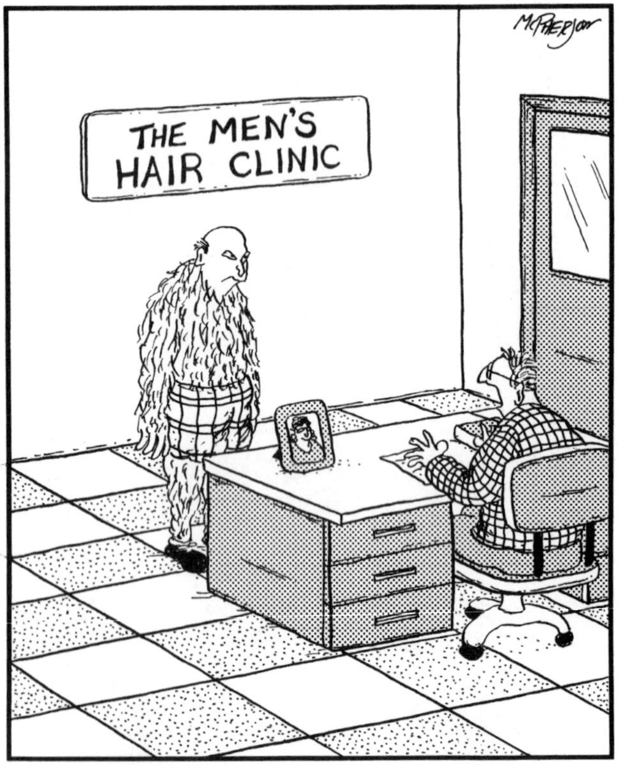
THE MEN'S HAIR CLINIC
McPHERSON

**"Mr. Brown, we warned you that everyone responds differently to the medication. You've got to admit, you have grown lots of new hair."**

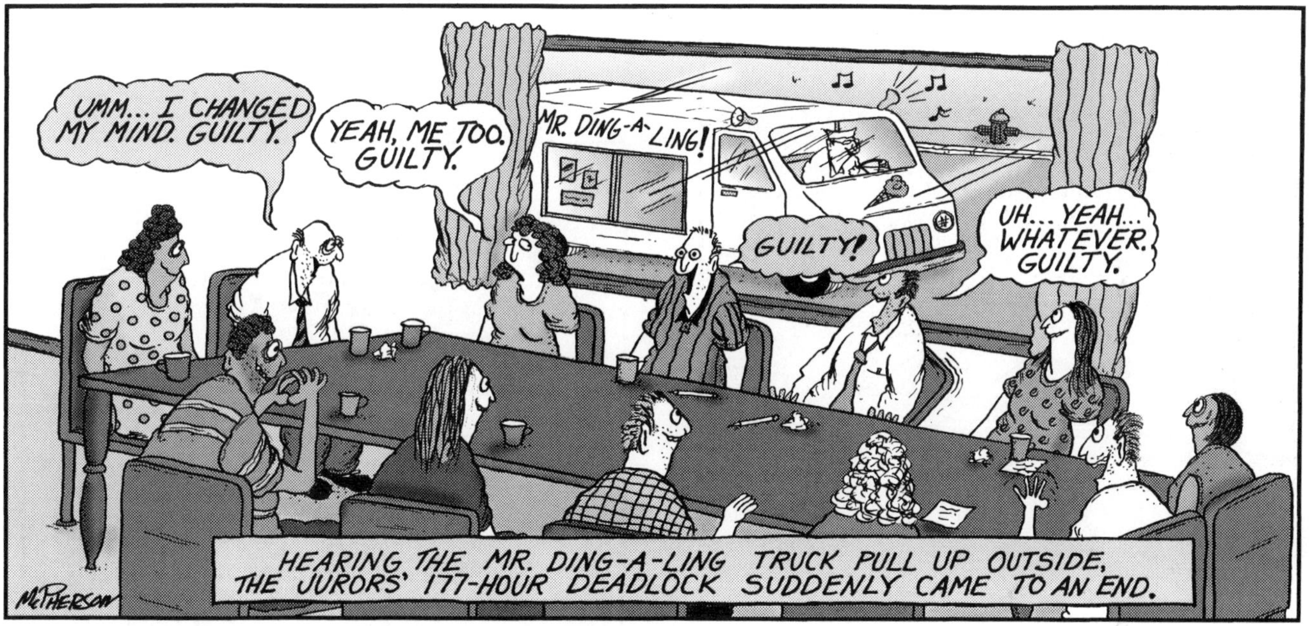
UMM... I CHANGED MY MIND. GUILTY.
YEAH, ME TOO. GUILTY.
MR. DING-A-LING!
GUILTY!
UH... YEAH... WHATEVER. GUILTY.
HEARING THE MR. DING-A-LING TRUCK PULL UP OUTSIDE, THE JURORS' 177-HOUR DEADLOCK SUDDENLY CAME TO AN END.
McPHERSON

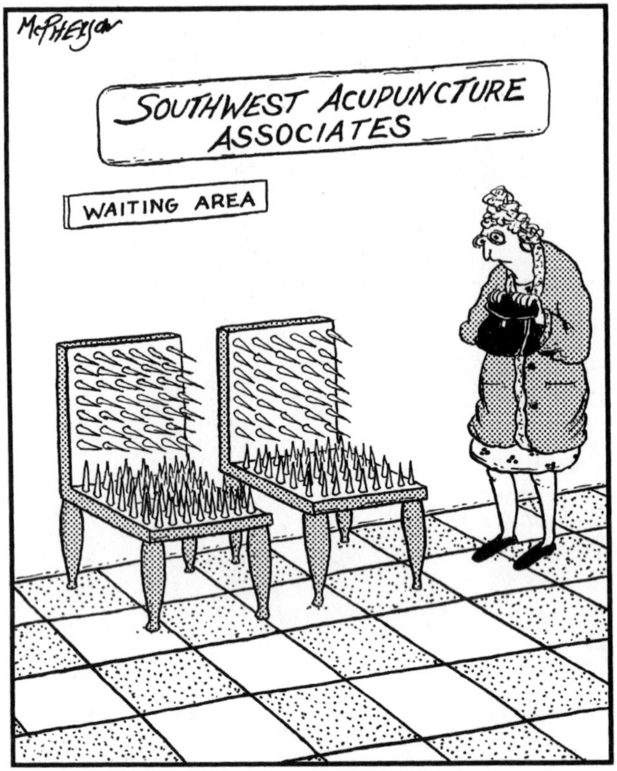
McPHERSON
SOUTHWEST ACUPUNCTURE ASSOCIATES
WAITING AREA

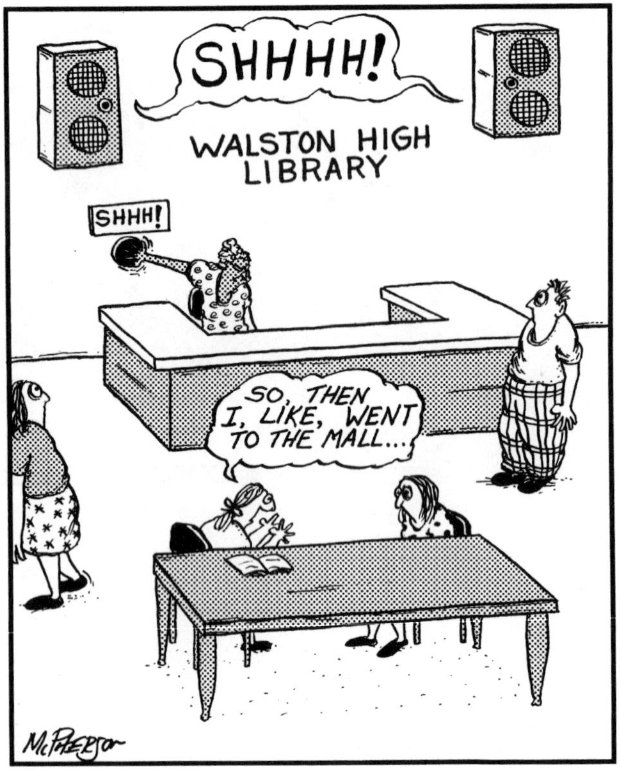
SHHHH!
WALSTON HIGH LIBRARY
SHHH!
SO, THEN I, LIKE, WENT TO THE MALL...
McPHERSON

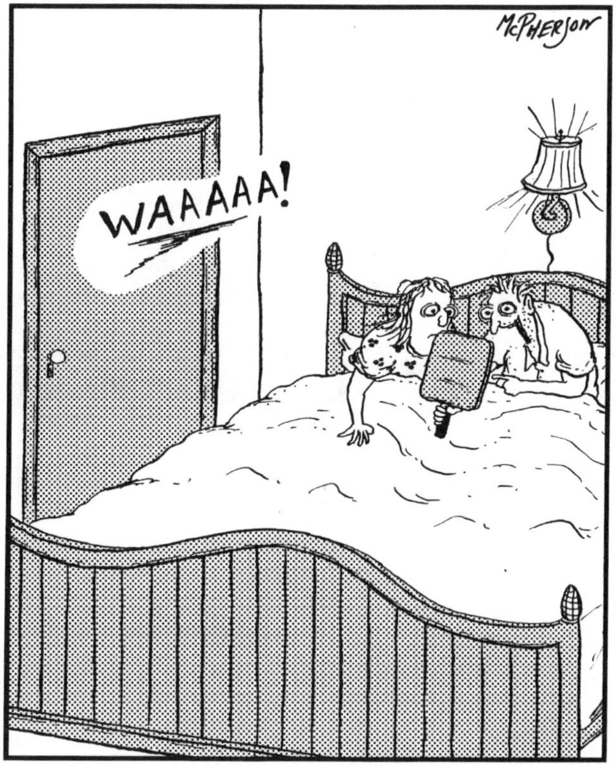
WAAAAA!
McPHERSON

"Ha! There! You see?! My eyes are *twice* as bloodshot as yours! It's *your* turn to get up with the baby!"

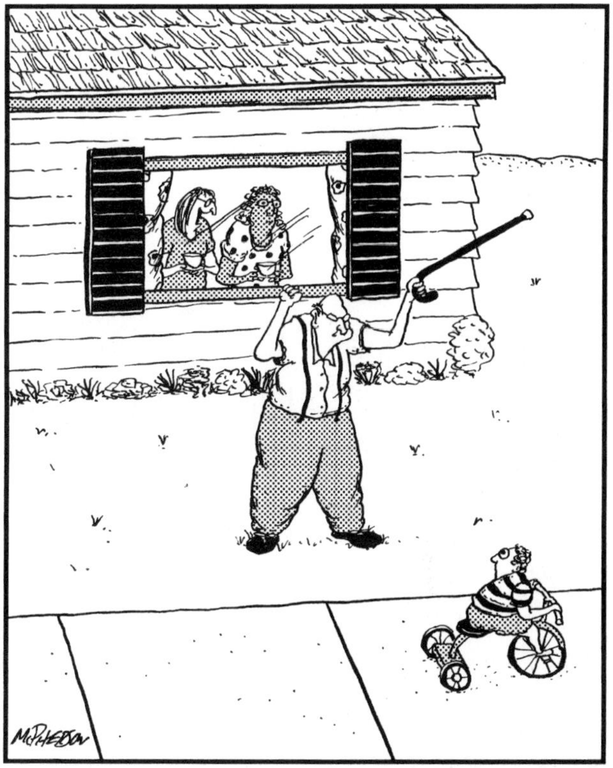
McPHERSON

"He's not *real*, silly! It's just a wax figure we bought to keep neighborhood kids from tromping through our yard."

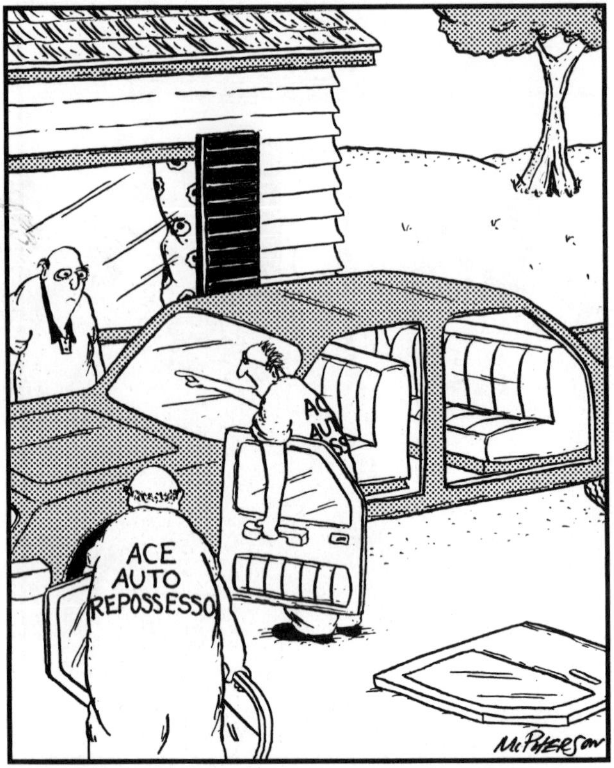
ACE
AUTO
REPOSSESSO
McPHERSON

"We're lettin' you off easy this time! But if the bank doesn't have your payment by next Wednesday, we're comin' back for your seats!"

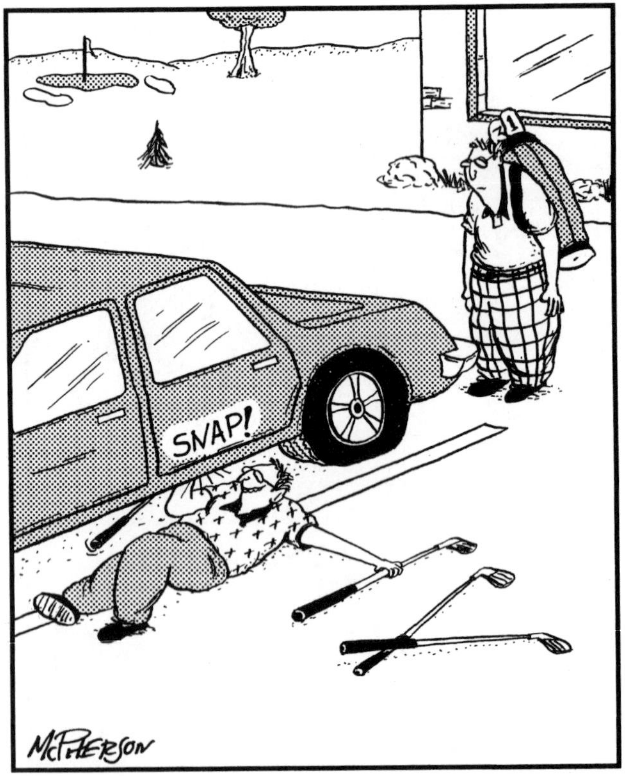
SNAP!
McPHERSON

Bert's undercarriage golf club rack allowed him to sneak off for a round of golf without arousing his wife's suspicion.

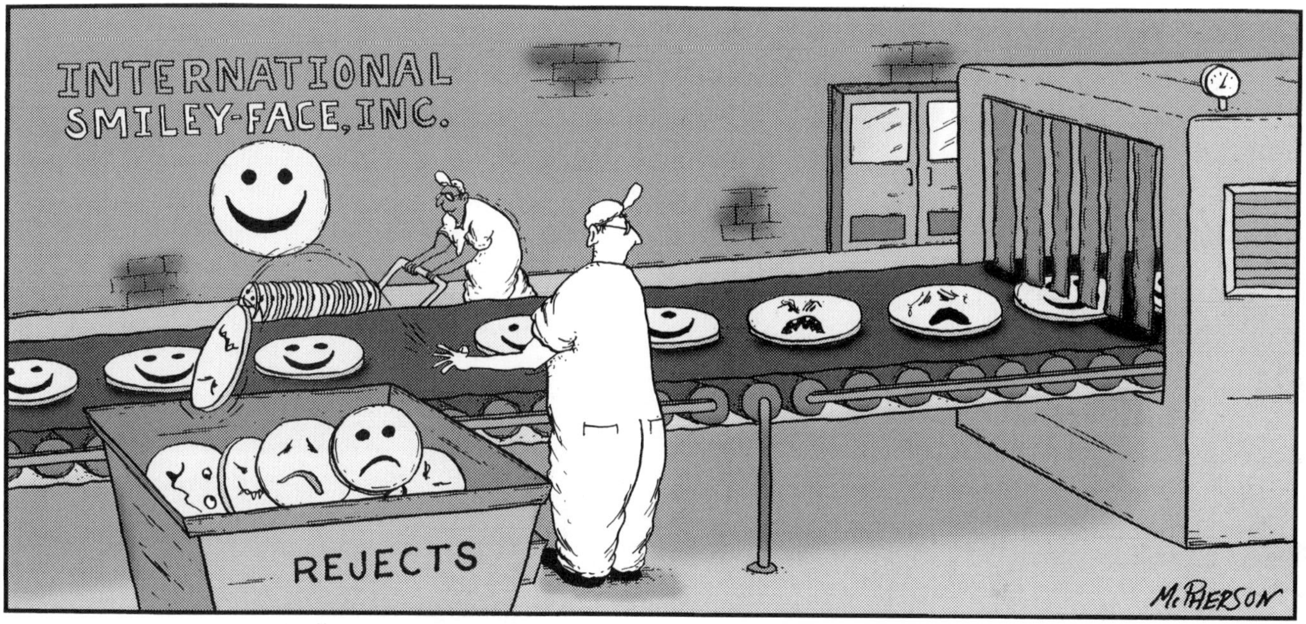
INTERNATIONAL SMILEY-FACE, INC.
REJECTS
McPHERSON

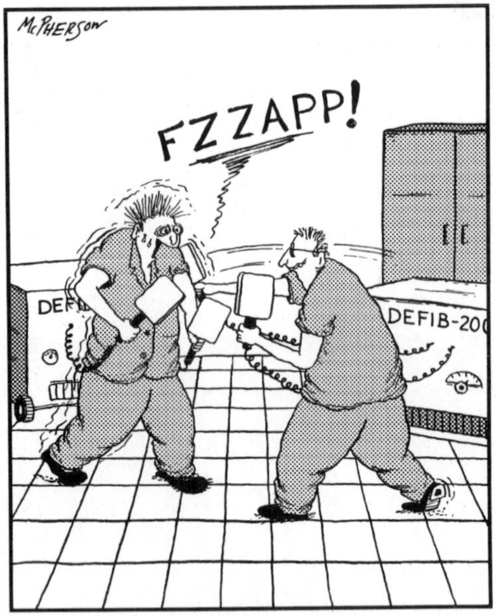
McPHERSON
FZZAPP!
DEFIB-20

How ER physicians unwind

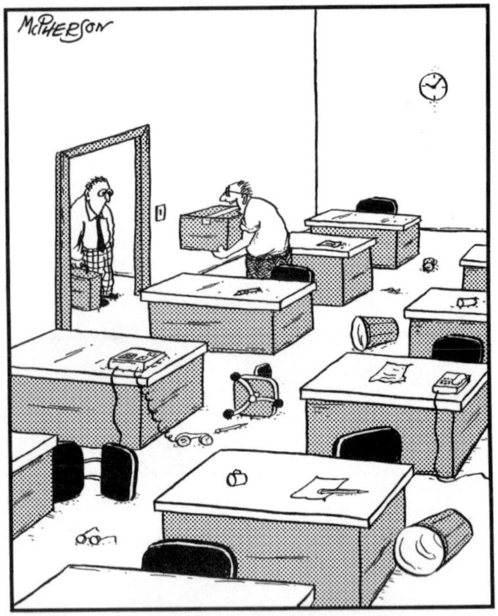
McPHERSON

"Geez, I guess you didn't hear! While you were away, everyone in the office kicked in for some lottery tickets and we hit it for $84 million!"

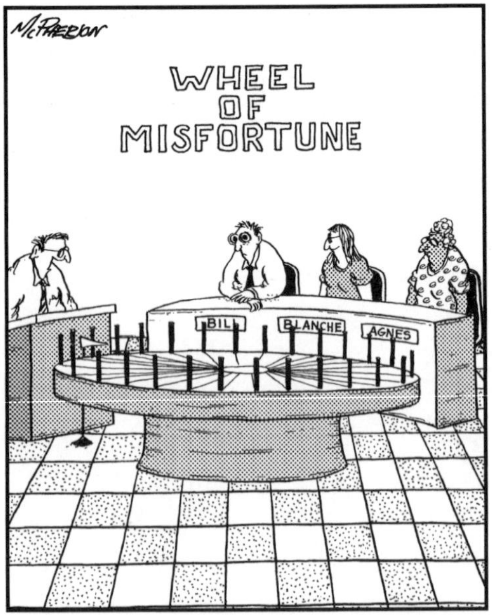
McPHERSON
WHEEL
OF
MISFORTUNE
BILL
BLANCHE
AGNES

"I'm sorry, Mr. Muckler, that's incorrect. As a penalty, your wife has agreed to run off with your best friend! One more wrong answer and we'll wipe out all of your assets!"

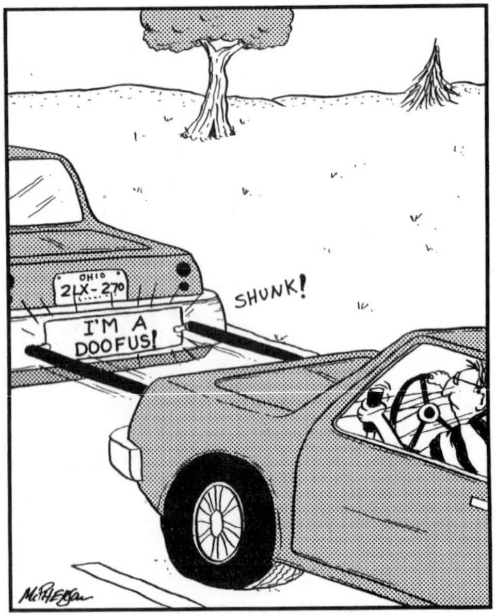
OHIO
21X-270
SHUNK!
I'M A
DOOFUS!
McPHERSON

Angered by yet another slow driver, Andy activates his remote bumper-sticker applicator.

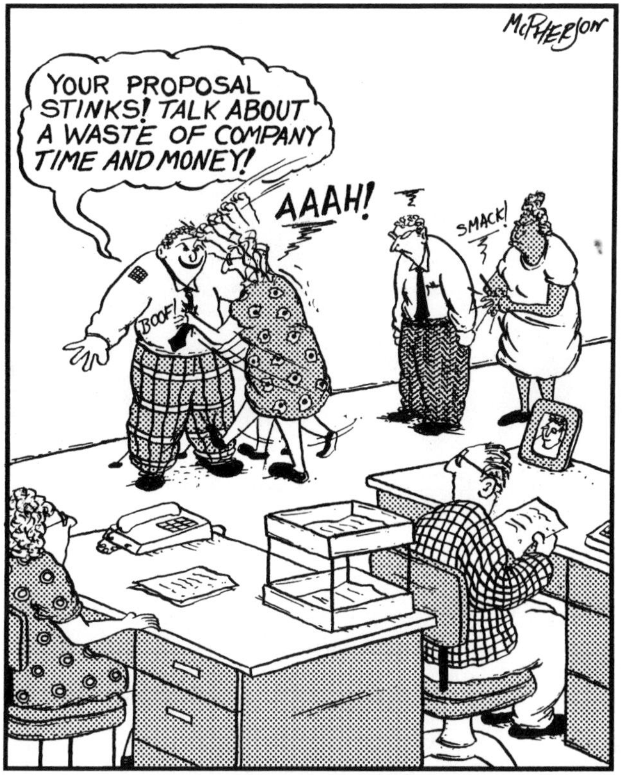
McPHERSON
YOUR PROPOSAL STINKS! TALK ABOUT A WASTE OF COMPANY TIME AND MONEY!
AAAH!
SMACK!
BOOF!

To help employees safely vent their frustrations, many companies have installed life-size Mr. Heckle™ dolls.

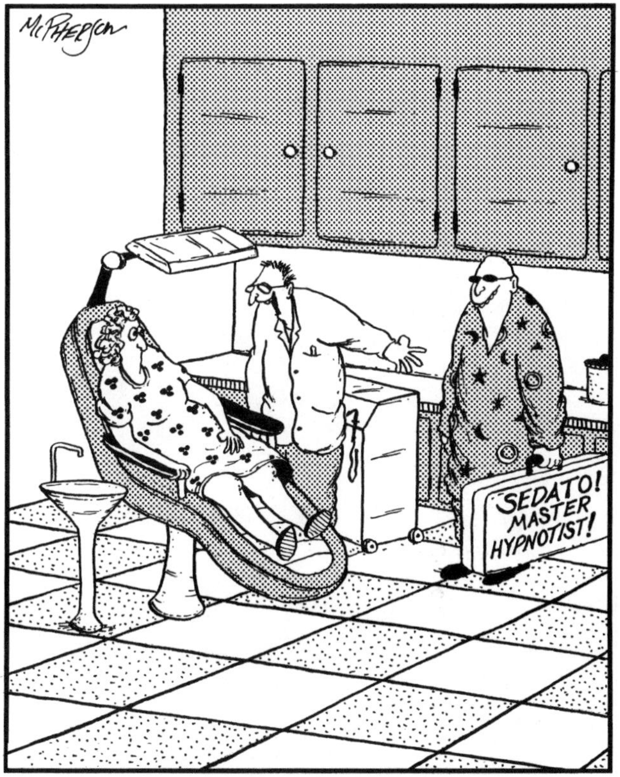
McPHERSON
SEDATO! MASTER HYPNOTIST!

"Unfortunately, Mrs. Kettleman, we're all out of Novocain. However . . ."

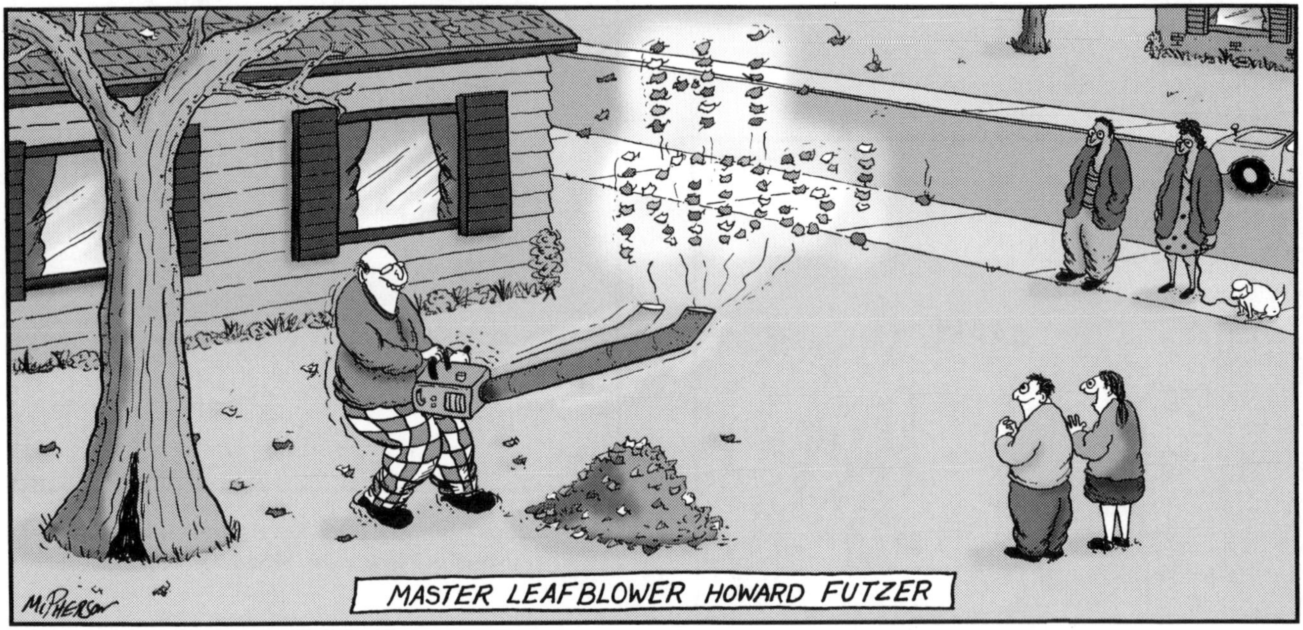
McPHERSON

MASTER LEAFBLOWER HOWARD FUTZER

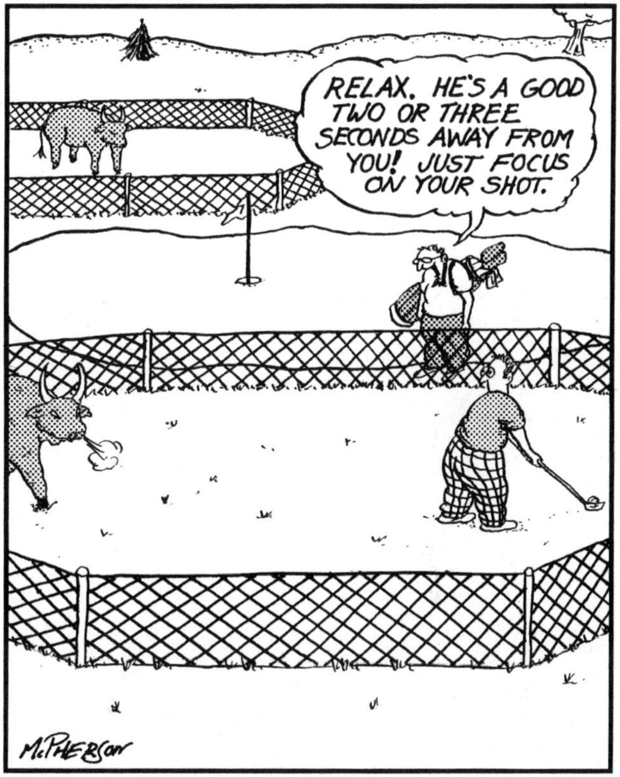
RELAX. HE'S A GOOD TWO OR THREE SECONDS AWAY FROM YOU! JUST FOCUS ON YOUR SHOT.
McPHERSON

Steve's approach shot lands in one of Pine Valley Country Club's notorious bull traps.

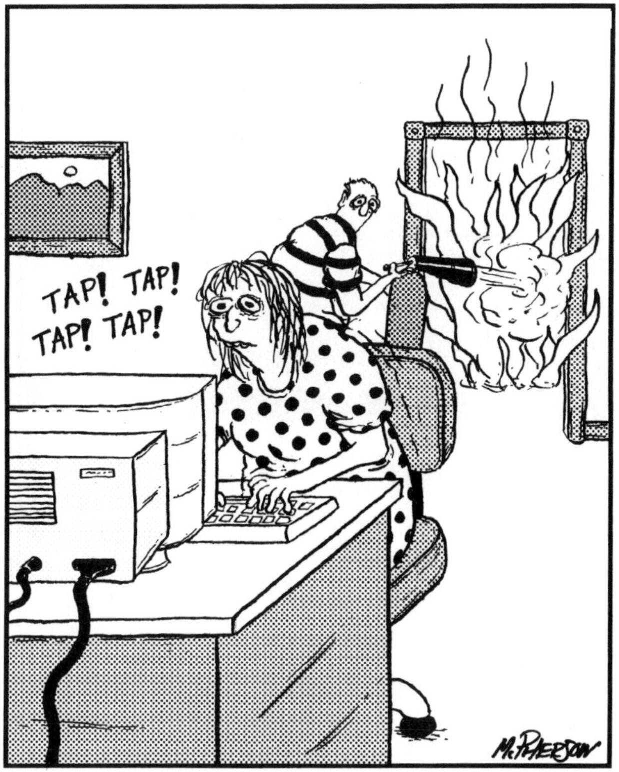
TAP! TAP! TAP! TAP!
McPHERSON

Dave realized the full magnitude of Jamie's e-mail addiction when she e-mailed the fire station instead of calling.

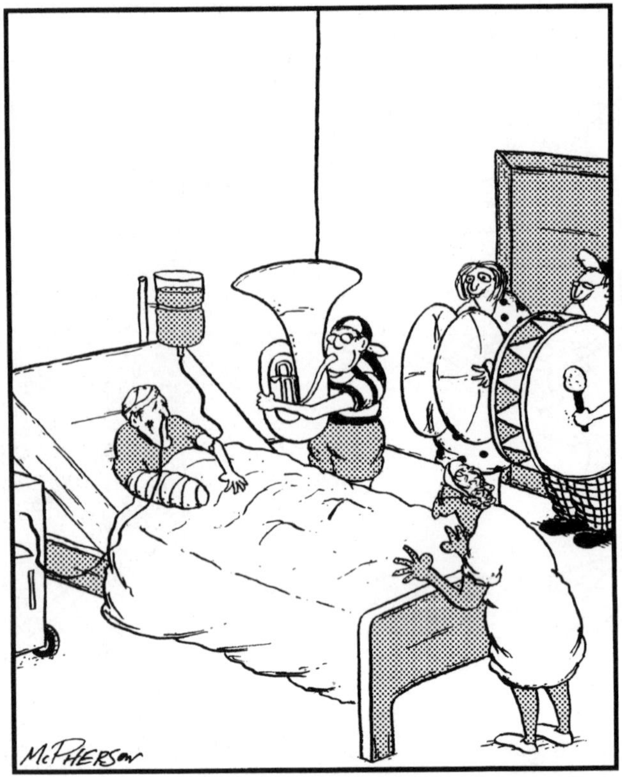
McPHERSON

"Mr. Collins, how would you like to try out our new music therapy program?"

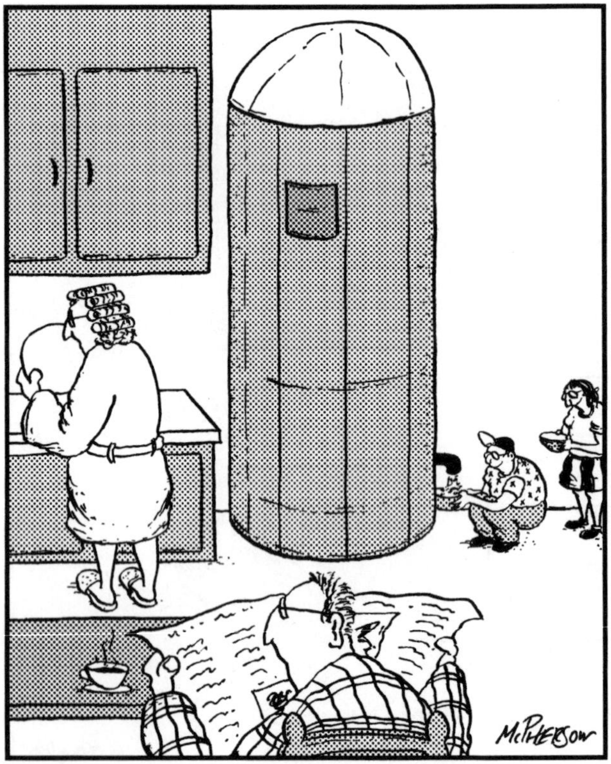
McPHERSON

Striving to make weekday mornings less hectic, the Hollowoods installed a cereal silo.

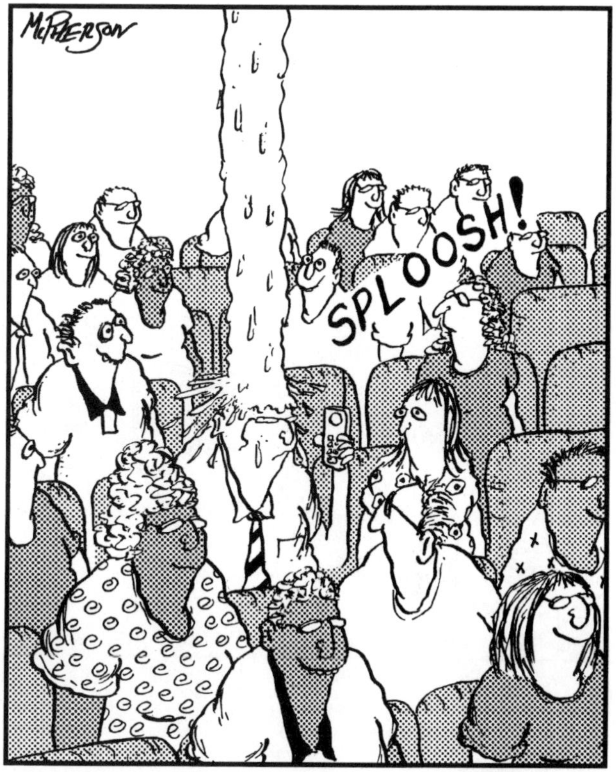
McPHERSON
SPLOOSH!

Having detected the ringing, the theater's automatic cell phone suppression system kicked in.

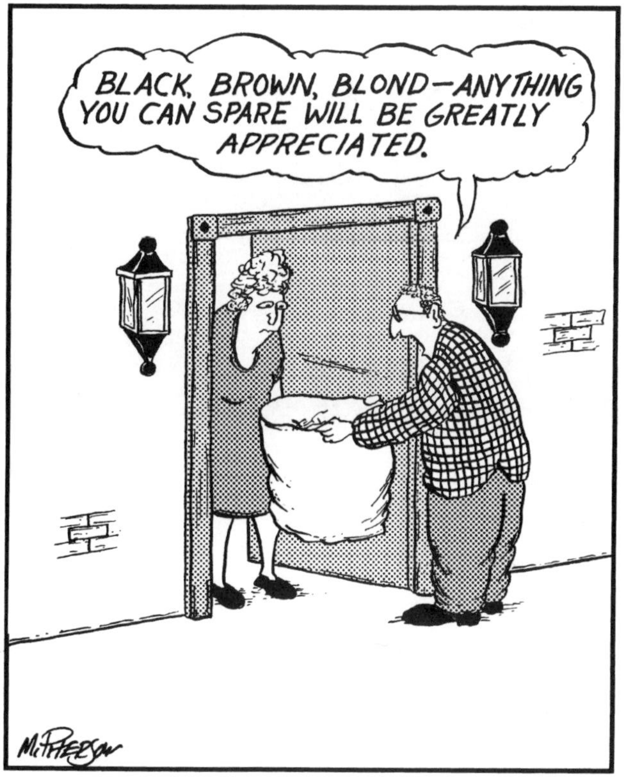
BLACK, BROWN, BLOND—ANYTHING YOU CAN SPARE WILL BE GREATLY APPRECIATED.
McPHERSON

The Hair Center for Men's donor drive

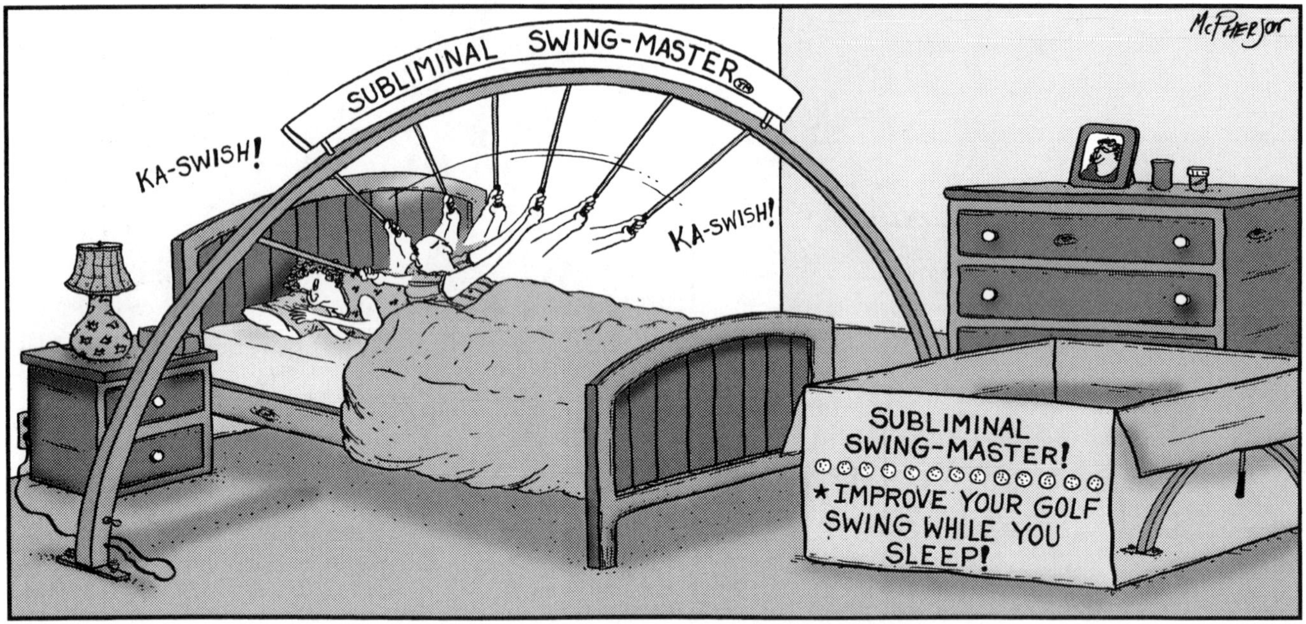
SUBLIMINAL SWING-MASTER
KA-SWISH!
KA-SWISH!
McPherson
SUBLIMINAL
SWING-MASTER!
★IMPROVE YOUR GOLF
SWING WHILE YOU
SLEEP!

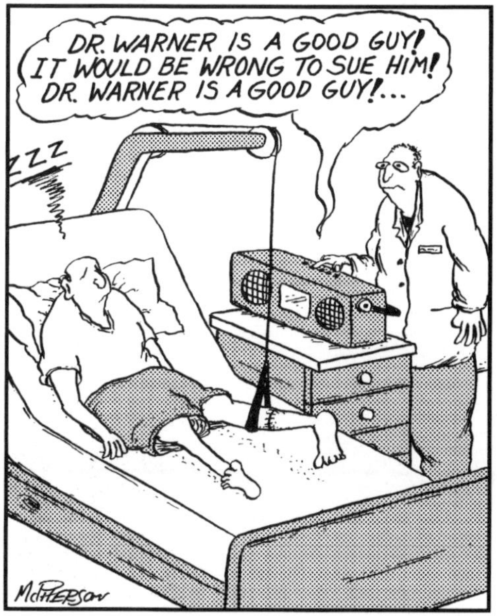
DR. WARNER IS A GOOD GUY!
IT WOULD BE WRONG TO SUE HIM!
DR. WARNER IS A GOOD GUY!...
ZZZ
McPHERSON

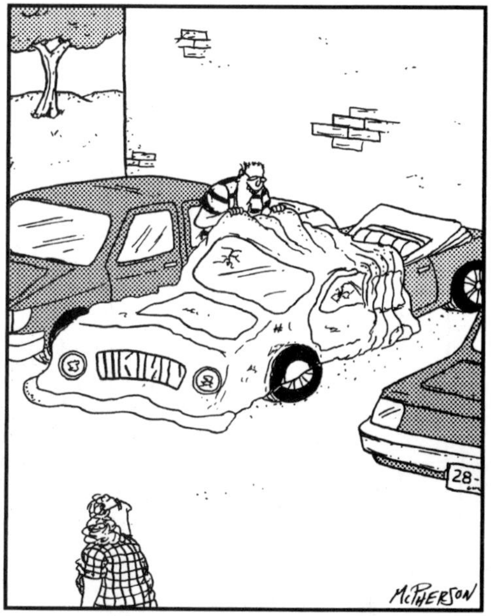
28-
McPHERSON

Dwayne's new Tacky-Tarp Auto Security System kept his car safe from vandalism and theft.

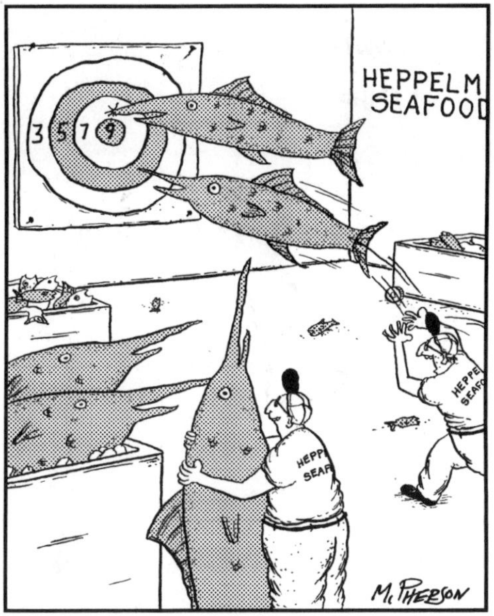
3 5 7 9
HEPPELM
SEAFOOD
McPHERSON

When business is slow at Heppelman's Seafood Company

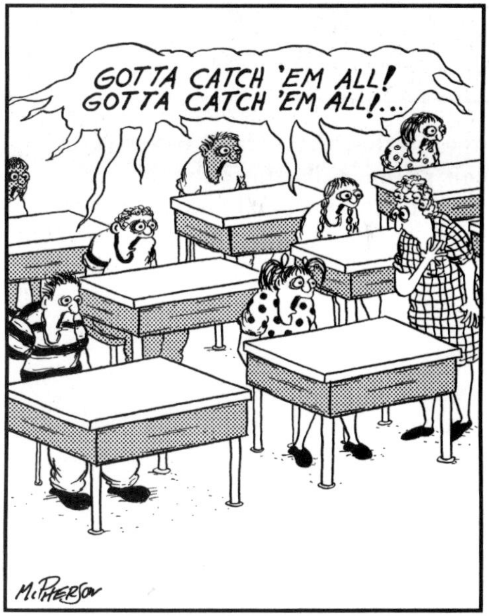
GOTTA CATCH 'EM ALL!
GOTTA CATCH 'EM ALL!...
McPHERSON

Mrs. Wingate's third-grade class succumbs to the dreaded Pokemon virus.

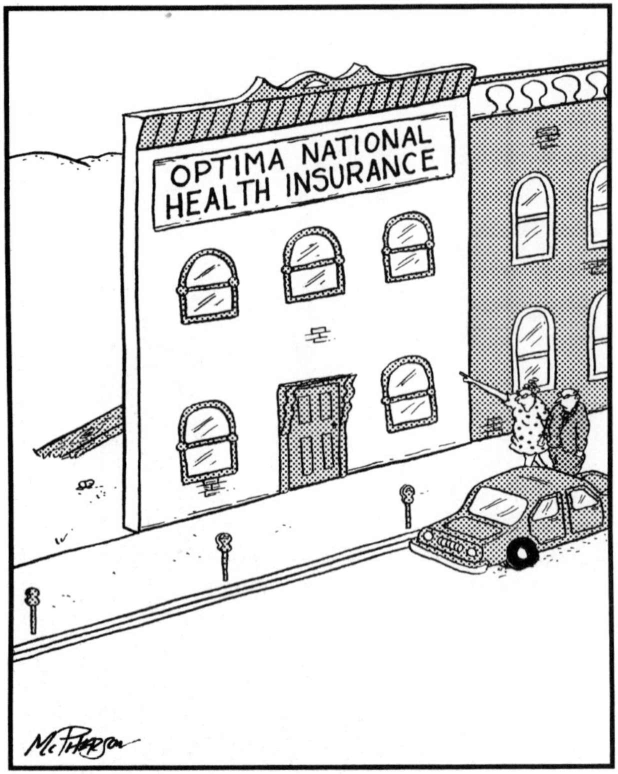
OPTIMA NATIONAL
HEALTH INSURANCE
McPHERSON

**Angered that their HMO never returns their phone calls, the Zabners decided to visit the national headquarters.**

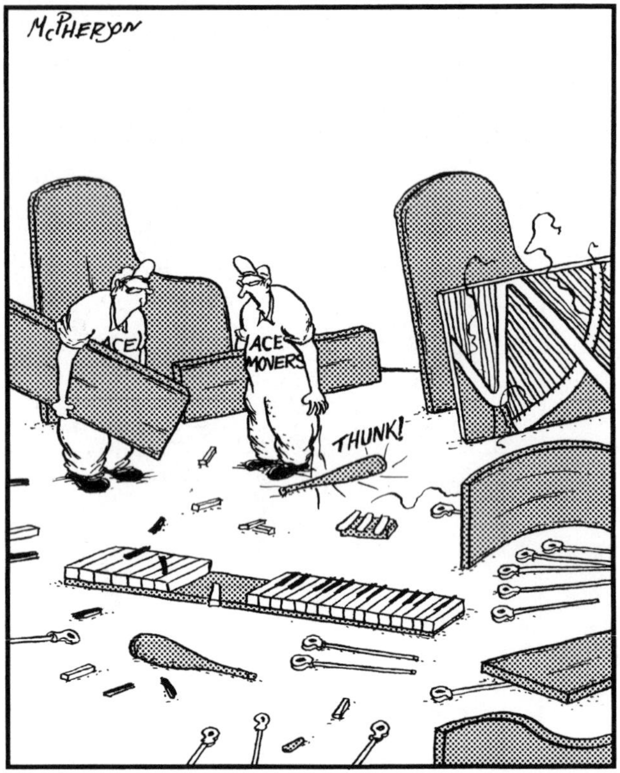
McPHERSON
ACE
ACE MOVERS
THUNK!

**"OK, Liberace! You're the genious who said it would be easier if we disassembled it! Let's see YOU put it back together!"**

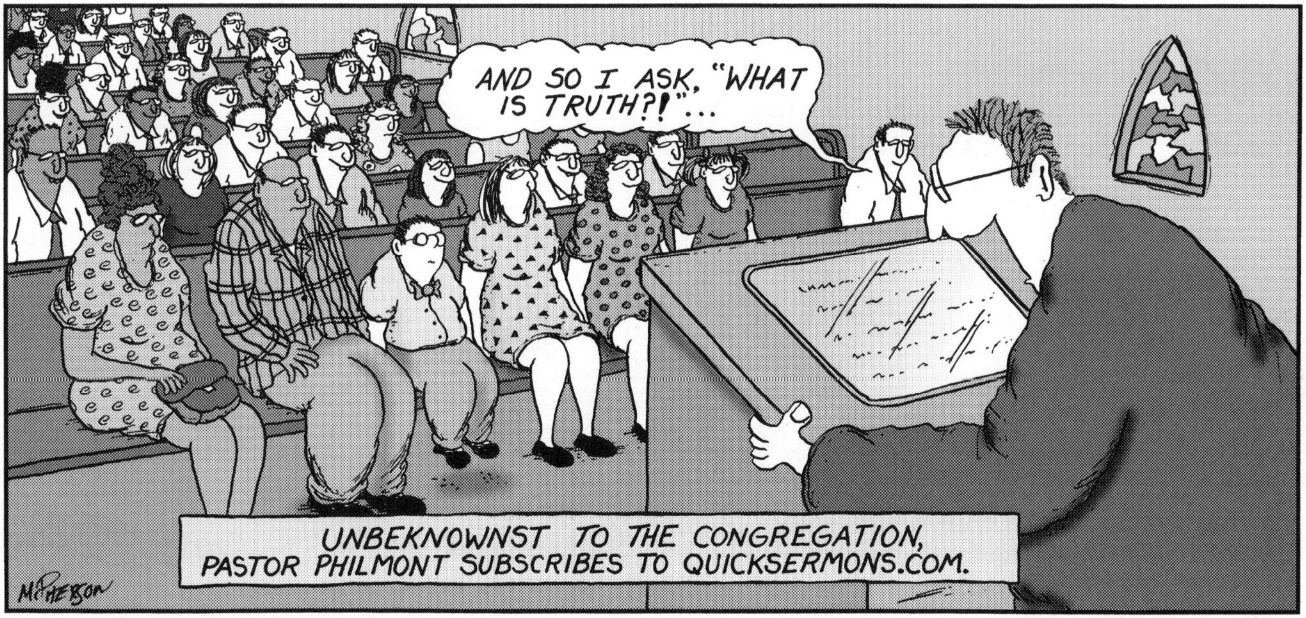
AND SO I ASK, "WHAT IS TRUTH?!"...
UNBEKNOWNST TO THE CONGREGATION, PASTOR PHILMONT SUBSCRIBES TO QUICKSERMONS.COM.

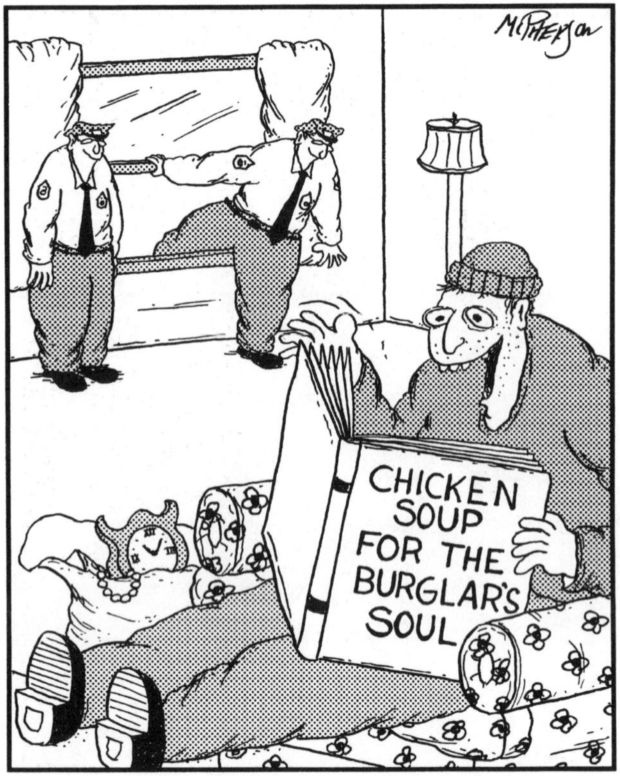
McPherson
CHICKEN SOUP FOR THE BURGLAR'S SOUL

**Having encouraged homeowners to leave a copy of *Chicken Soup for the Burglar's Soul* on their coffee tables, police are able to nail yet another loafing thief.**

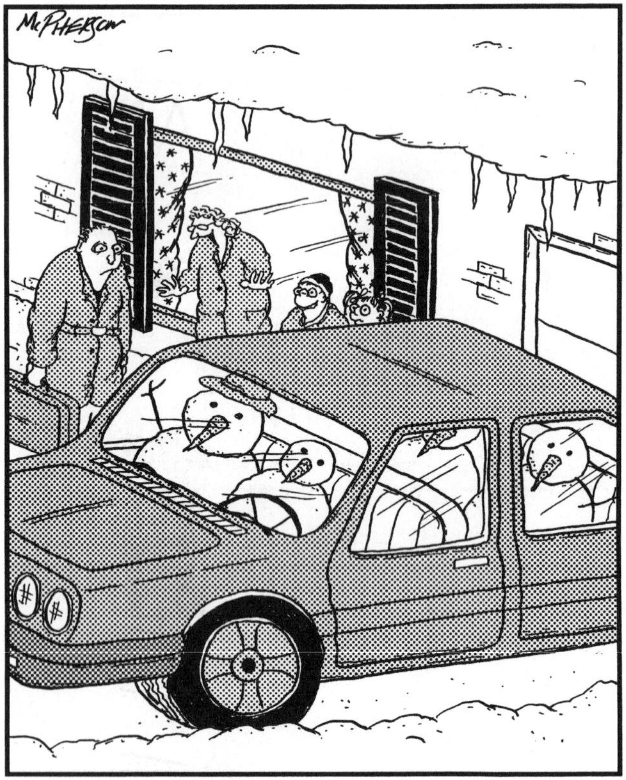
McPherson

**"Now don't be upset with the kids, Ray. They only did it so you'd be able to drive in the carpool lane."**

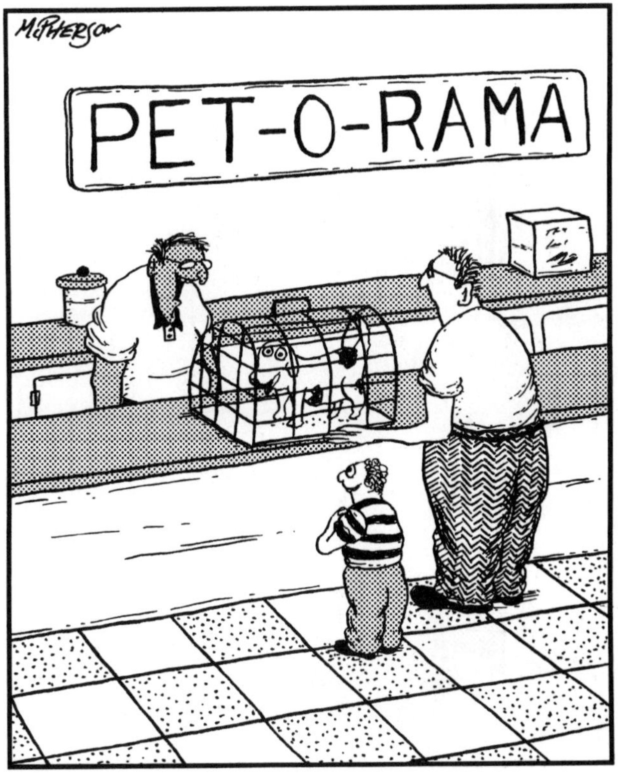
McPHERSON
PET-O-RAMA

"For an additional $50 can I interest you in our one-year stain-removal warranty?"

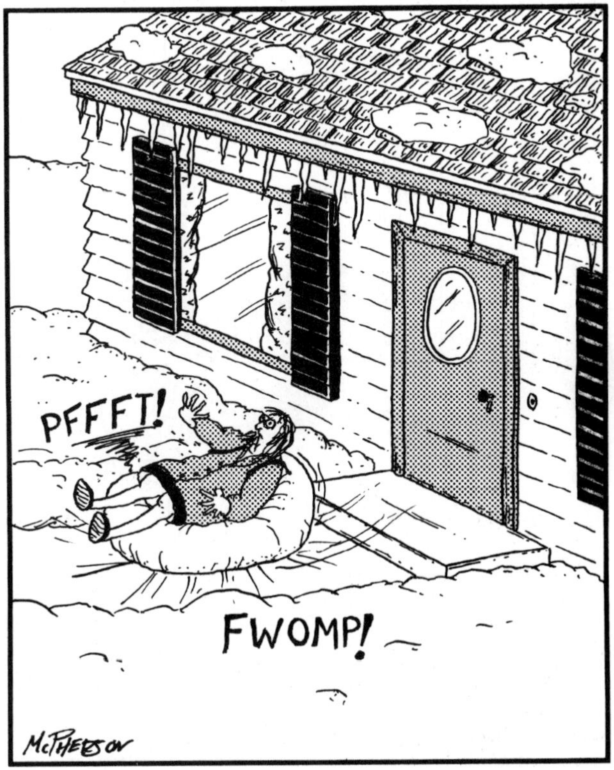
PFFFT!
FWOMP!
McPHERSON

Thanks to her new personal airbag system, Holly was no longer afraid to venture out on icy mornings.

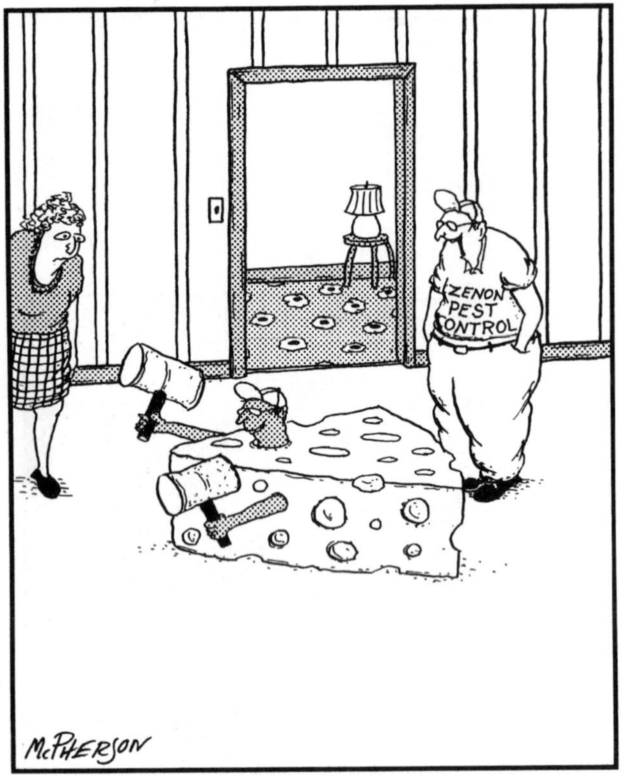
ZENON
PEST
CONTROL
McPHERSON

"Conventional mousetraps are next to useless. Just let us leave Jimmy here overnight and I guarantee your mouse trouble will be over, Mrs. Hoffman."

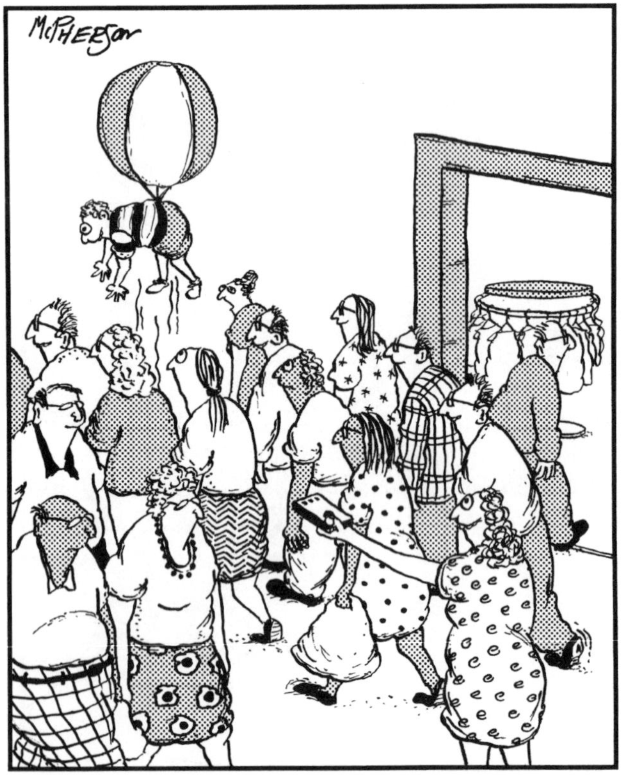
McPHERSON

Momentarily losing her toddler in the crowded mall, Denise calmly activates the Panic-Be-Gone™ helium balloon attached to his diaper.

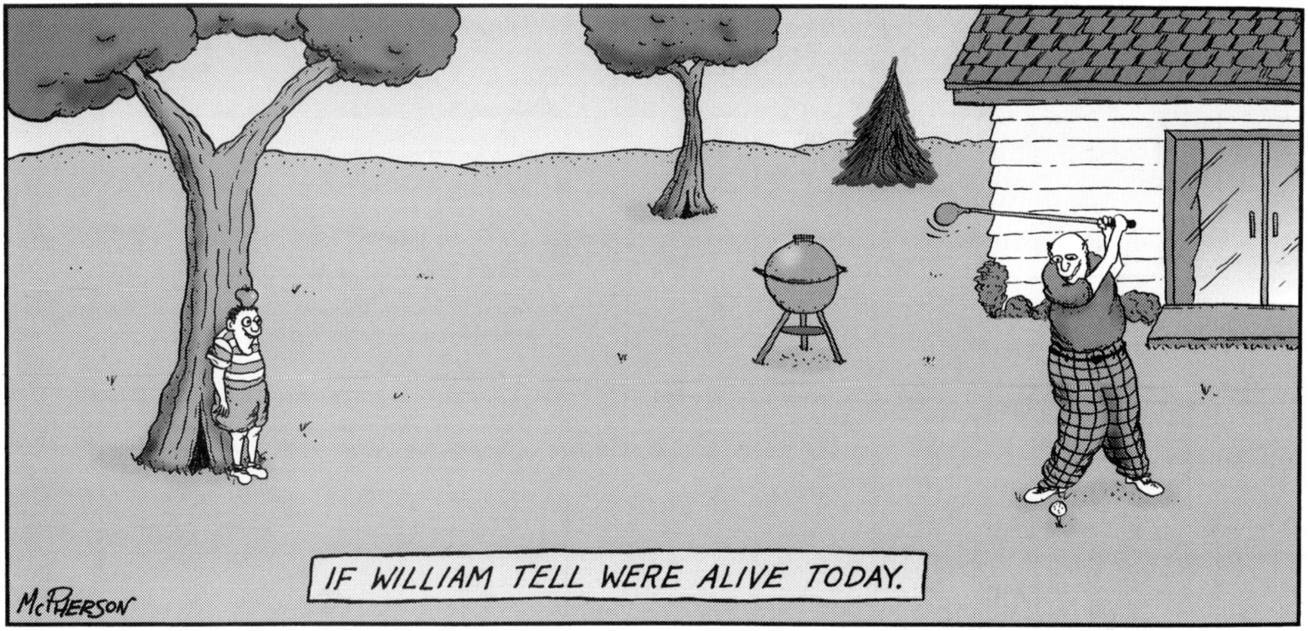
IF WILLIAM TELL WERE ALIVE TODAY.
McPHERSON

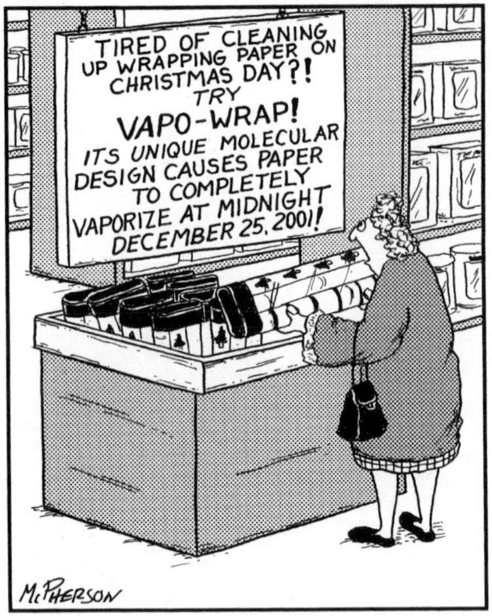
TIRED OF CLEANING UP WRAPPING PAPER ON CHRISTMAS DAY?!
TRY
VAPO-WRAP!
ITS UNIQUE MOLECULAR DESIGN CAUSES PAPER TO COMPLETELY VAPORIZE AT MIDNIGHT DECEMBER 25, 2001!
McPHERSON

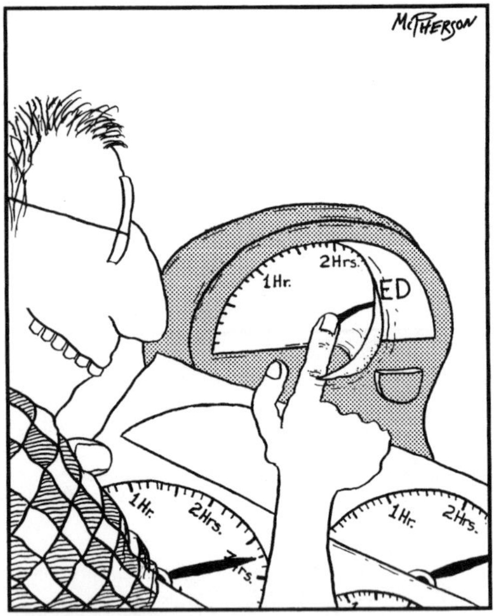
McPHERSON
1Hr.
2Hrs.
1Hr.
2Hrs.
1Hr.
2Hrs.

Armed with his new stickers, Skip was able to save several hundred dollars a year in parking fees.

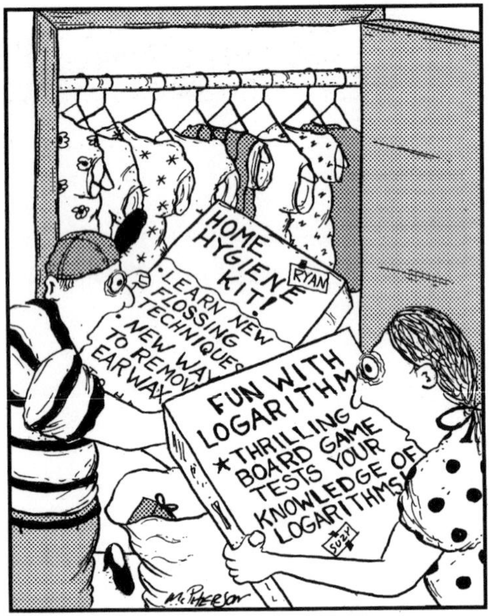
HOME HYGIENE KIT!
RYAN
•LEARN NEW FLOSSING TECHNIQUES
•NEW WAY TO REMOVE EARWAX
FUN WITH LOGARITHMS
★THRILLING BOARD GAME TESTS YOUR KNOWLEDGE OF LOGARITHMS!
SUZY
McPHERSON

Knowing that their kids would inevitably snoop for their Christmas gifts, the Vurtmans planted decoy gifts where they would easily be found.

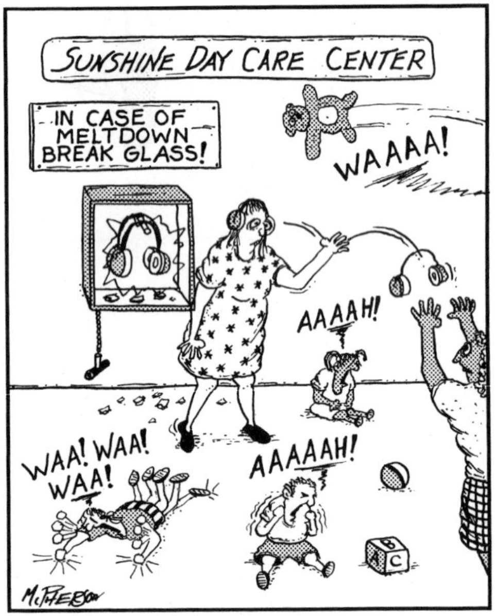
SUNSHINE DAY CARE CENTER
IN CASE OF MELTDOWN BREAK GLASS!
WAAAA!
AAAAH!
WAA! WAA! WAA!
AAAAAH!
McPHERSON

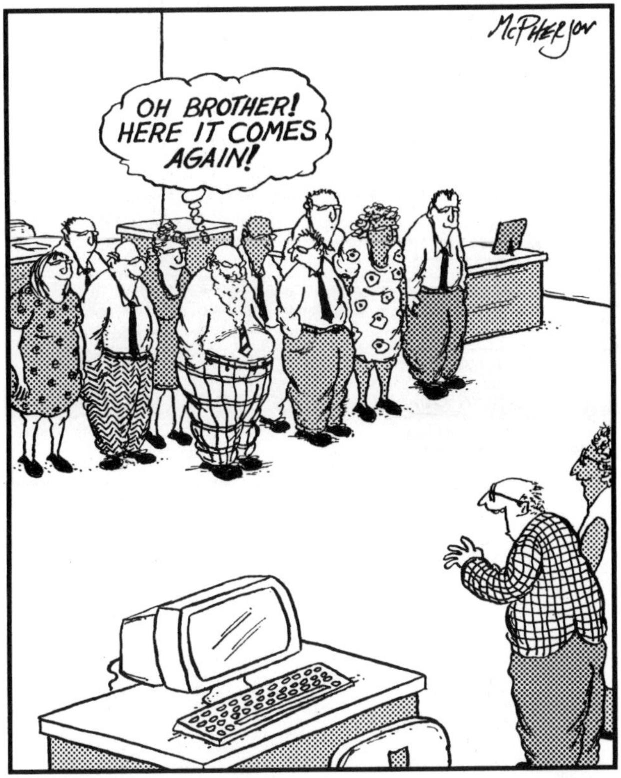
OH BROTHER! HERE IT COMES AGAIN!

**"Well folks, it's time once again for the office Christmas party. As in the past, we need a volunteer to play the part of Santa Claus. . . ."**

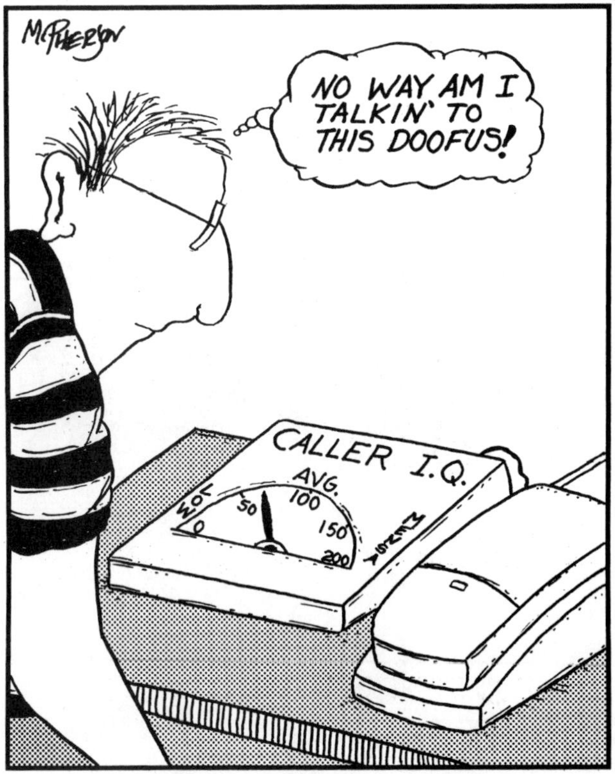
NO WAY AM I TALKIN' TO THIS DOOFUS!
CALLER I.Q.
AVG.
LOW
0
50
100
150
200

**New phone technology we'd all like to see**

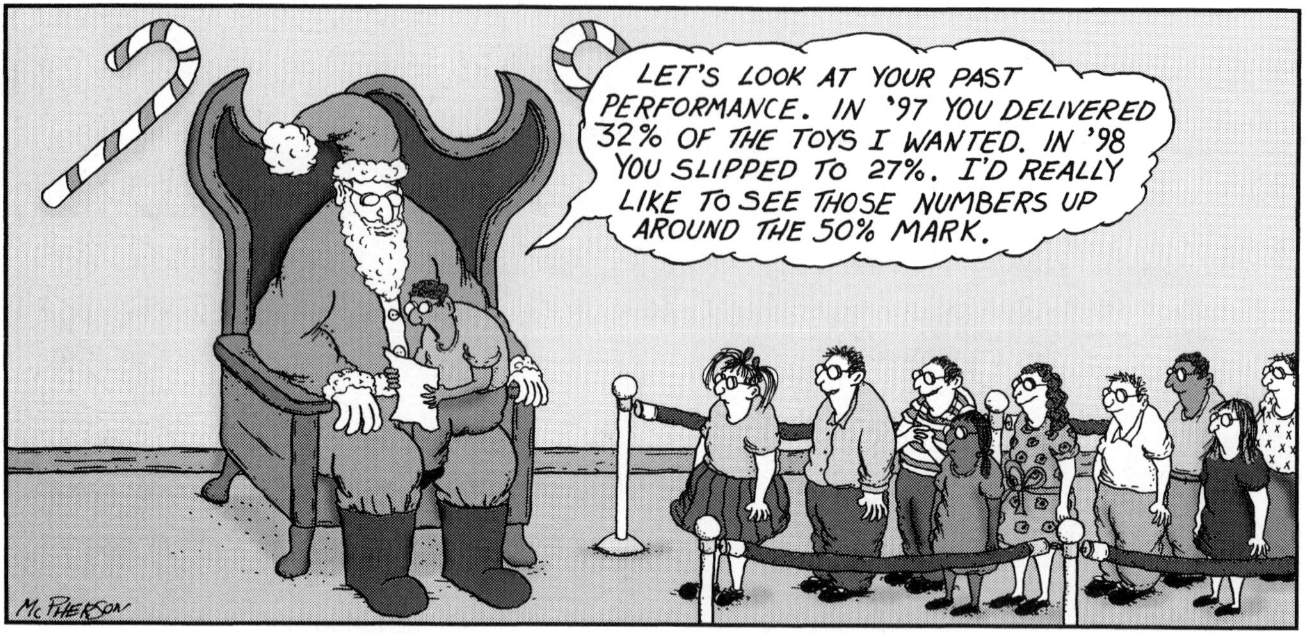
LET'S LOOK AT YOUR PAST PERFORMANCE. IN '97 YOU DELIVERED 32% OF THE TOYS I WANTED. IN '98 YOU SLIPPED TO 27%. I'D REALLY LIKE TO SEE THOSE NUMBERS UP AROUND THE 50% MARK.
McPHERSON

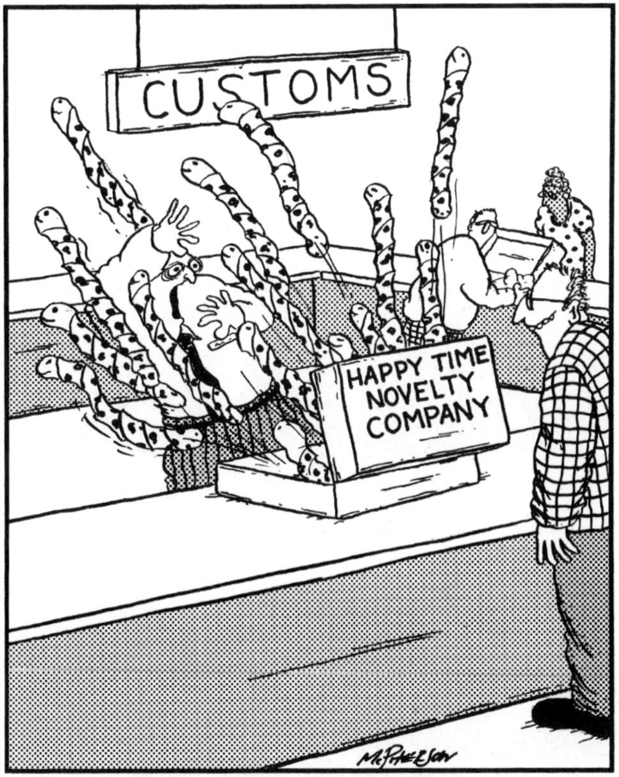
CUSTOMS
HAPPY TIME NOVELTY COMPANY
McPHERSON

Happy Time Novelty sales rep Lenny Yutz
lived for customs searches.

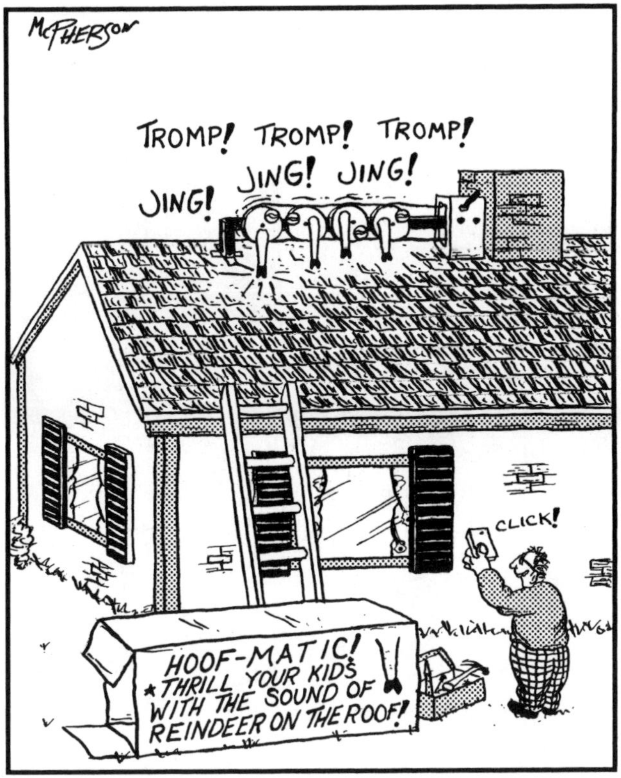
McPHERSON
TROMP! TROMP! TROMP!
JING! JING! JING!
CLICK!
HOOF-MATIC! ★THRILL YOUR KIDS WITH THE SOUND OF REINDEER ON THE ROOF!

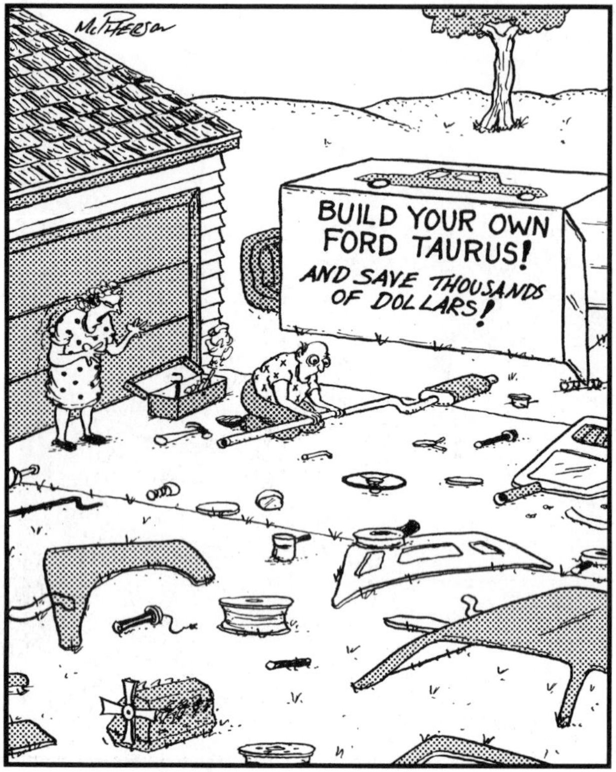
McPHERSON
BUILD YOUR OWN FORD TAURUS!
AND SAVE THOUSANDS OF DOLLARS!

"This?! *This* is the incredible deal that you found on the Internet?!"

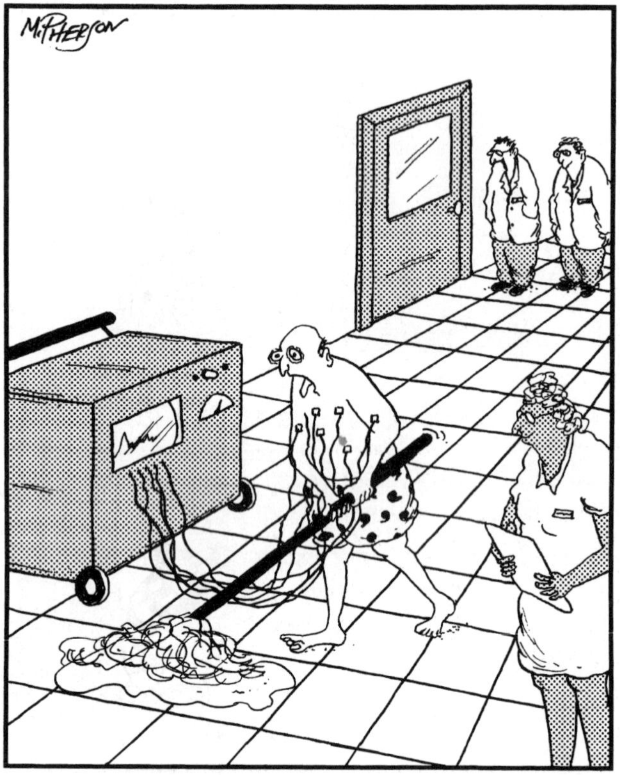
McPHERSON

"We've eliminated the traditional treadmill stress test. Mopping floors raises patients' heart rates just as high, plus we save a bundle on janitorial costs."

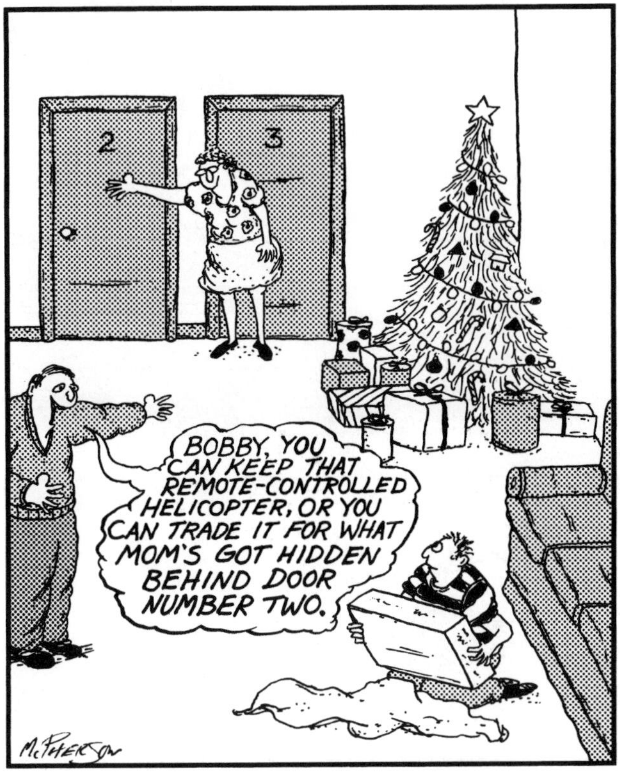
2
3
BOBBY, YOU CAN KEEP THAT REMOTE-CONTROLLED HELICOPTER, OR YOU CAN TRADE IT FOR WHAT MOM'S GOT HIDDEN BEHIND DOOR NUMBER TWO.

**Christmas at Monty Hall's house**

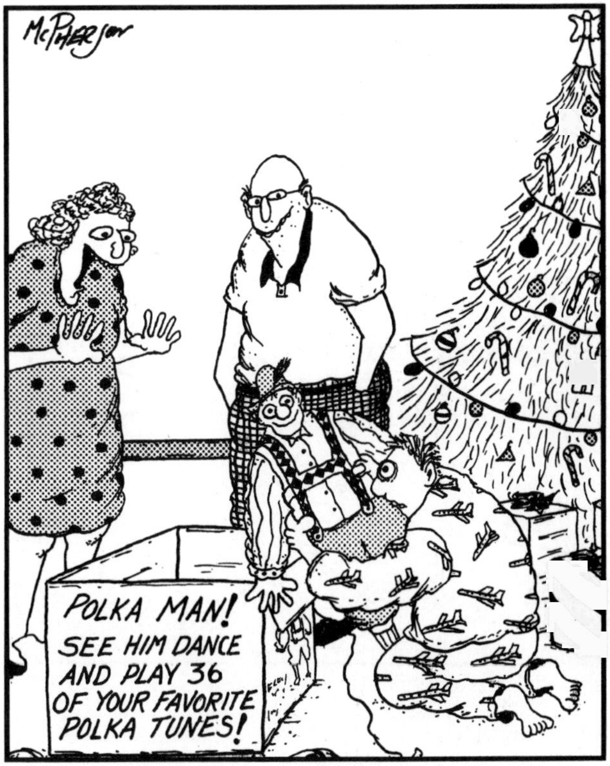
POLKA MAN!
SEE HIM DANCE AND PLAY 36 OF YOUR FAVORITE POLKA TUNES!

**"We looked *everywhere* for the polka man you and your friends are so crazy about! Finally your father found him when he was in Milwaukee on business!"**

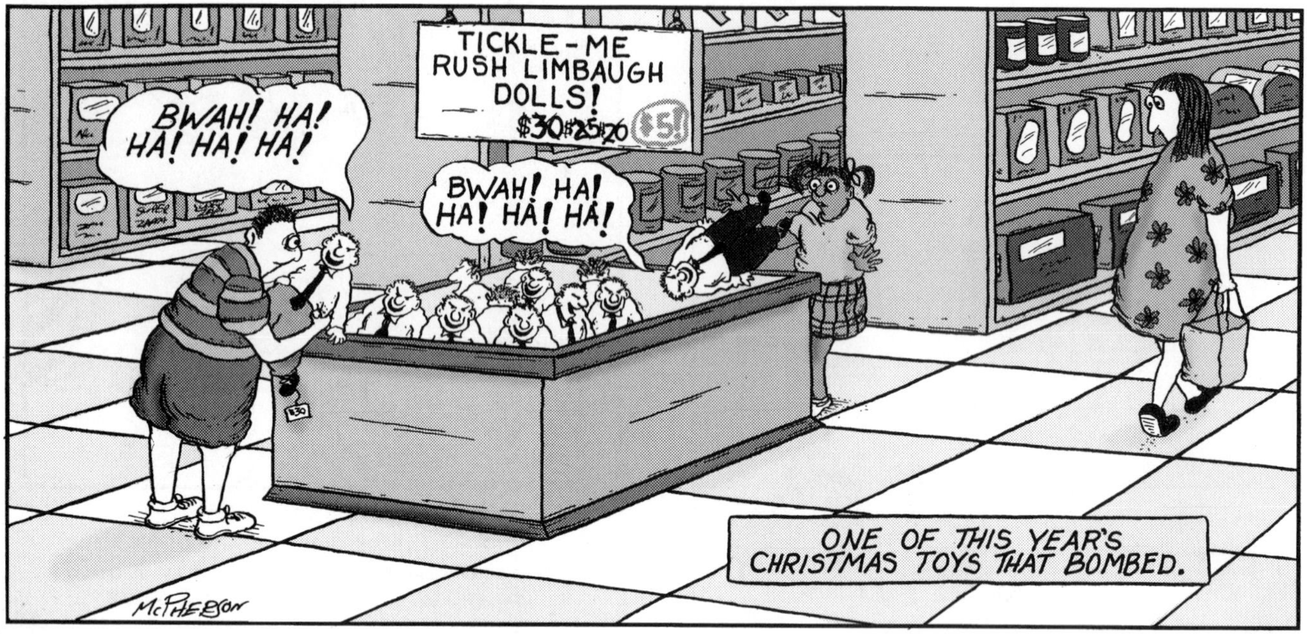
TICKLE-ME RUSH LIMBAUGH DOLLS!
$30 $25 $20 $5!
BWAH! HA! HA! HA! HA!
BWAH! HA! HA! HA! HA!
ONE OF THIS YEAR'S CHRISTMAS TOYS THAT BOMBED.
McPHERSON

0 50837 23616 5

UPC

Tragedy can strike any of us at anytime. But the stupid are especially susceptible to life's catastrophes. It is the author's hope that this book will serve as a healing guide for stupid people everywhere.

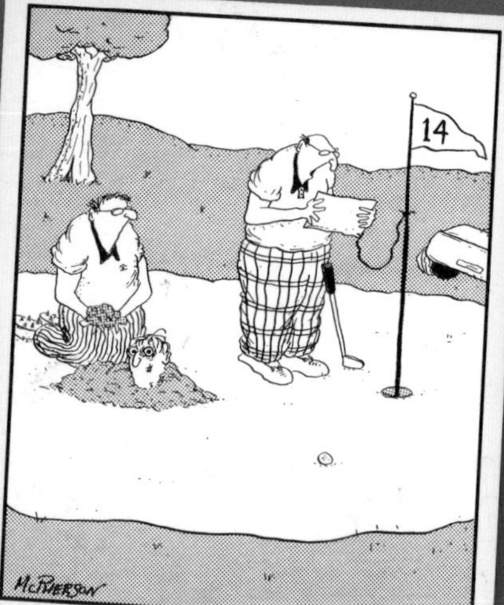

14
McPHERSON


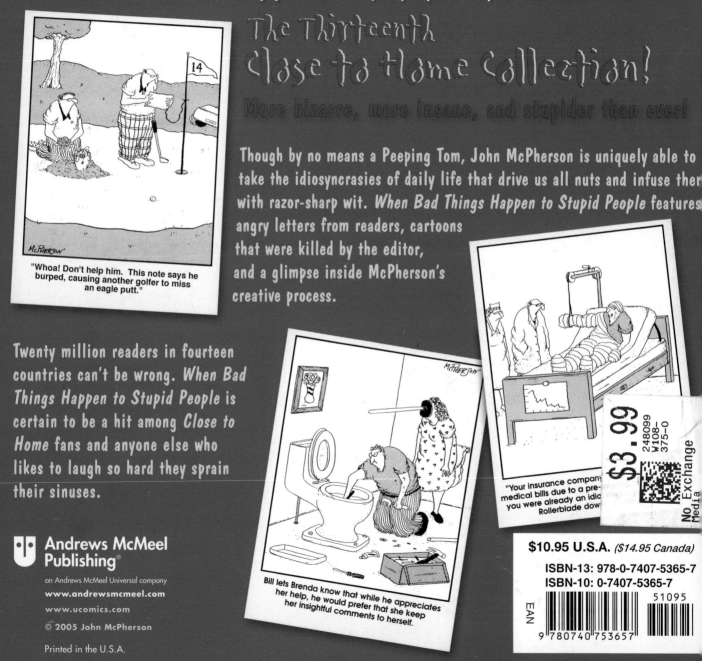

"Whoa! Don't help him. This note says he burped, causing another golfer to miss an eagle putt."

## The Thirteenth Close to Home Collection!

### More bizarre, more insane, and stupider than ever!

Though by no means a Peeping Tom, John McPherson is uniquely able to take the idiosyncrasies of daily life that drive us all nuts and infuse ther[m] with razor-sharp wit. *When Bad Things Happen to Stupid People* features angry letters from readers, cartoons that were killed by the editor, and a glimpse inside McPherson's creative process.

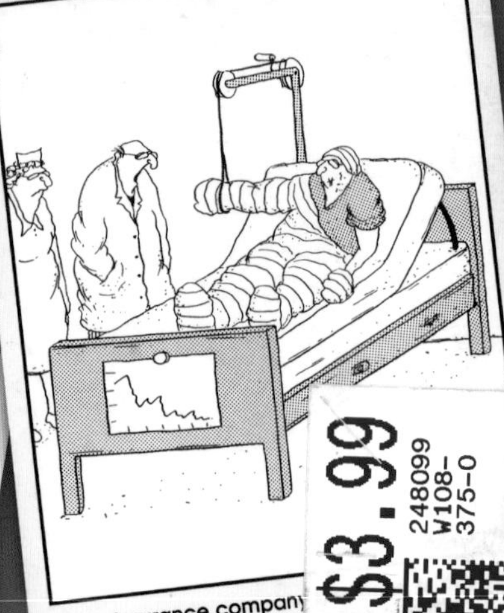

"Your insurance company [...] medical bills due to a pre- [...] you were already an idio[t] [...] Rollerblade dow[n] [...]"

Twenty million readers in fourteen countries can't be wrong. *When Bad Things Happen to Stupid People* is certain to be a hit among *Close to Home* fans and anyone else who likes to laugh so hard they sprain their sinuses.

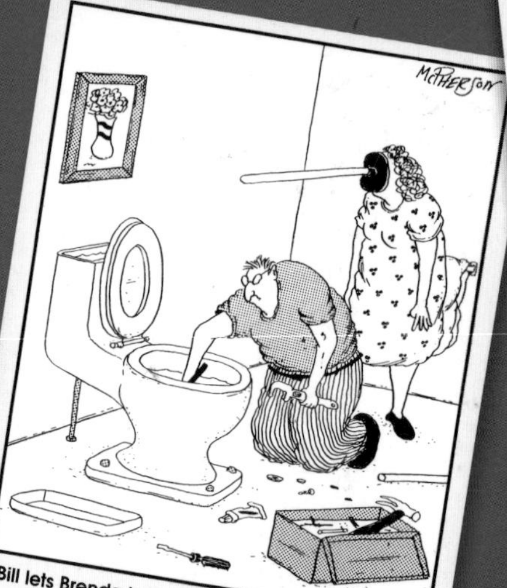

McPHERSON


Bill lets Brenda know that while he appreciates her help, he would prefer that she keep her insightful comments to herself.




**Andrews McMeel Publishing®**

an Andrews McMeel Universal company

**www.andrewsmcmeel.com**

**www.ucomics.com**





Printed in the U.S.A.

**$10.95 U.S.A.** *($14.95 Canada)*

**ISBN-13: 978-0-7407-5365-7**

**ISBN-10: 0-7407-5365-7**

EAN

51095

9 780740 753657